Leon Gouré
Foy D. Kohler
Richard Soll
Annette Stiefbold

# CONVERGENCE
## OF COMMUNISM AND CAPITALISM
# THE SOVIET VIEW

MONOGRAPHS IN INTERNATIONAL AFFAIRS

CENTER FOR ADVANCED INTERNATIONAL STUDIES
UNIVERSITY OF MIAMI
1973

073324

**LEON GOURÉ** is a Professor of International Studies and Director of Soviet Studies at the Center for Advanced International Studies at the University of Miami. A graduate of New York University, Columbia University School of International Affairs and Russian Institute, and Georgetown University, he is the author of *Civil Defense in the Soviet Union, The Siege of Leningrad*, and *Soviet Civil Defense 1969-1970*. He also co-authored *Two Studies in Soviet Controls*, and co-edited Marshal V. D. Sokolovskii, *Soviet Military Strategy* . . . . **FOY D. KOHLER,** career Ambassador of the United States and long associated with Soviet affairs, is Professor of International Studies at the Center for Advanced International Studies at the University of Miami. He is the author of *Understanding the Russians, A Citizen's Primer* and has contributed numerous articles to journals and magazines . . . . **RICHARD SOLL** and **ANNETTE STIEFBOLD** are Research Associates at the Center for Advanced International Studies.

Library of Congress Catalog Number 72-96761
© University of Miami
Center for Advanced International Studies, 1973

# *Contents*

# PREFACE

One of the most intriguing of the speculations now prevalent in the Western world—a speculation that for many has come to have the force of conviction—is that given the workings of the scientific-technological revolution and the industrialization process generally, the differing societies of the United States and the Soviet Union are destined to move closer and closer together until they finally converge at some in-between point, neither capitalist nor socialist but a hybrid of the two.

The idea that differences between the USSR and the United States will at some stage disappear is not new in the West. It is as old as the seizure of power by the Bolsheviks and their first steps toward the establishment of a socialist system. But until quite recently the thought was that movement would be entirely on the Soviet side. Initially, Westerners tended to see a quick reversal of the whole Bolshevik order of things: as soon as Lenin and his revolutionary colleagues encountered the full responsibility of running a great and complex state they would either abandon their experiments or be swept aside by the force of the problems the experiments would generate. When events did not turn out as originally expected, many in the West continued to believe that in one way or another time and the natural order of things would still catch up with and take care of the Soviet enterprise. Successively, the line of thinking was: the regime would not be able to survive a Lenin succession; Stalin's efforts at forced draft industrialization would force a return to capitalist practices; the onslaught of Nazi Germany would either destroy the system or precipitate a basic and lasting modification in its nature; the requirements of post-war reconstruction would lead to fundamental alterations in Soviet internal practices and relationships with the outside world.

None of these hopes, which for some were even expectations, was realized. In February, 1946, while the Soviet Union appeared all but prostrate in the midst of devastation produced by the war, Stalin signaled in a specially contrived "pre-election speech" Soviet renunciation of the wartime alliance and reversion to communist orthodoxy with his thesis of a division of mankind into two irreconcilably hostile camps which were destined to an enduring struggle "to decide the fate of capitalism and communism throughout the world."* Nevertheless, few in the West appeared willing to accept such an outlook. Many clung to the hope that it still would be possible to bring the Soviet Union to a point of reconciliation of its system with that of the capitalist West. And if the Soviet authorities would not move of their own volition,

---

*See Foy D. Kohler, *Understanding the Russians: A Citizen's Primer* (New York: Harper and Row, 1970), pp. 86-94.

they might be pressured into moving by systematically denying to them any fruits from their policies of hostility and struggle. For some, such was the basic concept underlying the policy of "containment." The break might come at any time. Expectations were high that it would come at least with the death of Stalin. Failing this, hopes continued in connection with Khrushchev's innovations and frustrations, and then with the problems of the Khrushchev succession.

Whatever else may be said of the usefulness of the policy of containment,* it demonstrably did not bring about any change of heart, or course, on the part of the Soviet leaders with respect to irreconcilable differences and antagonisms between their system and purposes as against those of the capitalist West. As of the present, the Soviet leadership still proclaims that "communists will never give up their ideas and principles; they have always struggled and in the future will energetically struggle for their worldwide triumph."**

Given all this, many in the West now concede that it is most unlikely that the communists, at least of the USSR, will ever deliberately move from a socialist system back to a capitalist system. But neither do they foresee Western capitalism simply falling prey to communism. Hence the relatively new concept of movement on both sides toward the ultimate convergence of the two systems.

Since the late fifties, a great many economists, sociologists, political scientists, physical scientists, journalists, and so forth in a wide range of Western countries, but most of all in the United States, have espoused the convergence concept in one form or another. Wide differences exist with respect to the theoretical arguments and reasoning underlying varying versions of the concept. But they all end up at essentially the same place, that is, with the disappearance of basic differences between the US and Soviet systems and the convergence of the two at, in the words of John Kenneth Galbraith, "all fundamental points." † What makes the concept especially attractive, is that, as Galbraith says, and a great many echo in one way or another, "In time, and perhaps in less time than may be imagined, it will dispose of the notion of inevitable conflict based on irreconcilable difference." ‡

---

*The authors of this monograph consider this usefulness to have been very great, since, in fact, the prime objective of the activities in which the US and its allies engaged under the so-called containment effort was to restore and preserve viability and security in vulnerable areas of the free world rather than to bring about a breakdown within the USSR and other parts of the communist world.

**Editorial. "The Leninist Course of the Foreign Policy of the USSR," *Kommunist*, No. 9, June 1972, p. 79.

† John Kenneth Galbraith, *The New Industrial State* (Boston: Houghton Miflin Company, 1967), p. 391.
‡ *Ibid.*

As the saying goes, however, it takes two to tango. What of the Russians? How do they view convergence and the various theories Westerners have put forward in its support? It is to this question that this analysis and its supporting documentation are addressed. We have not attempted in this work to describe or discuss the various Western views referred to above, from the standpoint of either attempting to explain them as developed by their authors or passing any sort of judgement on them. In any event, as they represent predictions of future developments, the proof of their soundness or failure must be left to history to record. The only consideration given to these Western views is as they are interpreted and dealt with by Soviet commentators. Often, it should be said, Soviet treatments of the views take a great many liberties, sometimes to the point of outright distortion. But whatever the failings of this treatment by the Soviets, an accurate reflection of what they are saying is, we feel, important to an understanding of the Soviet position on the convergence issue as a whole.

It will come as no surprise to anyone who is aware of the implications for the basic tenets of Marxism-Leninism that to the Soviet leadership the very thought of any possible convergence of the socialist and capitalist systems is simply and strictly anathema. Every theory and argument put forward in the West that lends itself to the direct or indirect support of any such idea is denounced from the highest to the lowest levels of the vast theoretical and propaganda apparatus of the Soviet Union. The very development of the convergence concept, within which a wide variety of highly divergent and even conflicting theories is arbitrarily lumped by the Soviet authorities, is treated as a new but highly virulent manifestation of "anti-communism" which has as its purpose undermining the Soviet system, sowing discord between the USSR and other socialist countries, stifling the "liberation" movement of the Third World, and dulling class consciousness of the masses in advanced Western countries.

For those in the West who believe in convergence all of this may well be taken as beside the point. The line of argumentation is that convergence will be brought about by the force of circumstances, and irrespective of the wishes or will of any who might favor or oppose it. Neither Marx nor Lenin, to paraphrase Galbraith, foresaw convergence and hence it is understandable that the Marxist-Leninists of the Soviet Union will not soon agree to its inevitability.

The question, however, of whether convergence may or may not come about is not the issue in this study. The issue is that the Soviet leaders are conducting a campaign of extraordinary force, intensity, and scope not only against the underlying theories but also against any and all practices and activities which might in one way or another promote convergence or in any way bring about a weakening of the ideological and political competition between the systems. How effective these efforts of the Soviet leaders may be over the long period must be a matter of conjecture. One should acknowledge, however, that for almost six decades the Kremlin has had considerable success in controlling impacts on the Soviet political and social structure of developments both within and outside the USSR.

But leaving this matter of long-term effects aside, it would seem almost certain that the nature of the Soviet campaign against convergence has important implications for prospects of any near term improvements in US-Soviet relations along the lines that are currently so widely hoped for, and even assumed, on the Western side.

For one thing, the Soviet authorities have used the campaign to place definite limits on the implications of "peaceful coexistence." They have made central to their efforts the categorical admonition that the mutual acceptance of the principles of peaceful coexistence by the US and the USSR does not in any way affect basic antagonisms and the inevitability of continuing struggle between the two countries and their systems. The line as repeated over and over is that: "Peaceful coexistence does not extinguish or cancel out class struggle—it is a new form of class struggle employed by the working class and the socialist countries in the world arena. It 'cancels' only one type of struggle—war as a means of settling international issues."*

For another thing, the Soviet leaders are exploiting Western convergence theories to justify a general tightening of controls at home and as a basis for a massive vigilance and ideological indoctrination campaign. Of particular importance from the standpoint of Western expectations incident to recent US agreements and understandings with the USSR is that the Soviet leaders have encompassed within this campaign a wide range of new dictums and measures designed to immunize the Soviet people, particularly the intelligentsia and the youths, from any possible ideological contamination or softening in consequence of contacts and exchanges with Americans, as well as Westerners generally. Warnings are sounded at all levels of US intentions to exploit increasing contacts and relations with the Soviet Union for nefarious purposes. The leaders make clear that the Soviet Union needs and expects to receive important benefits from the new relations, but even as they are entering into the agreements and providing for follow-up they are inaugurating restrictions and creating a climate designed to minimize the resulting impact on the Soviet system and society. In other words they evidence every intention to crush the hope, which appears to have become so strong in the West,

---

*Leninism Today (Moscow: Novosti Press Agency Publishing House, 1970), pp. 123-133.

that a new era of "bridge-building" between the US and the Soviet Union is now at hand.

This study is in two parts: first, an analysis of Soviet views on convergence; second, supporting documentation from Soviet sources. The documentary materials, it should be noted, are presented in chronological order rather than by topical content. Such an arrangement is due to the fact that the documents frequently deal with a variety of different topical elements encompassed in the Soviet treatment of convergence and consequently do not lend themselves to logical divisions according to subject matter.

# CONVERGENCE
## OF COMMUNISM AND CAPITALISM
# THE SOVIET VIEW


## PART ONE: ANALYSIS

# CONVERGENCE OF COMMUNISM AND CAPITALISM
# THE SOVIET VIEW

The Soviet leaders constantly maintain that regardless of any turn formal relations between capitalist and socialist states may take, ideological peace between the two world systems is unthinkable. They insist that not only can there be no reconciliation by way of agreements or understandings; there can be no reconciliation through a progressive mitigation of differences in consequence of the workings of any social, economic, or technological forces, be they new or old. Because in the Soviet view all social-political relations are determined by their class nature and the laws of class conflict, the Soviet leaders perceive the conflicts and contradictions between the two systems as inherent in the systems themselves and hence immutable, short of the eradication of one system or the other. "Marxist-Leninists do not entertain any illusions in relation to the anti-people's essence of imperialism and its aggressive aspirations," General Secretary of the Soviet Party Leonid Brezhnev asserted in June, 1972 following President Richard Nixon's journey to Moscow. He added that successes with respect to the doctrine of peaceful coexistence "in no way signify the possibility of weakening the ideological struggle"; instead, it is necessary "to be prepared that this struggle will intensify, will become a still sharper form of the antagonism between the two social systems."[1]

# I
# THE BASIC SOVIET VIEW OF CONVERGENCE

In keeping with this thinking, the Soviet leaders have taken strong issue with Western speculation and theories which predict the "convergence" and ultimate commonality of the capitalist and socialist systems on the ground that modern industrial practices require and dictate the emergence of common cultures and values and similar forms of political, economic and social organization. As the Soviet leaders interpret them, the proponents of "convergence"

---

[1]Speech in Moscow at dinner for Fidel Castro, *Pravda*, June 28, 1972. [85—This number and succeeding bracketed numbers refer to corresponding documentation as numbered in Part II.] It is important to note that President Nixon also placed strong emphasis on the limited nature of the results achieved in Moscow. "We must remember," he said in his report to Congress after his return from Moscow, "that Soviet ideology still proclaims hostility to some of America's most basic values. The Soviet leaders remain committed to that ideology." For a more detailed analysis of these points and other results of the Moscow Summit see Foy D. Kohler, "Peaceful Coexistence? It's Hard to Define," in *The Miami Herald*, September 10, 1972, p. 3G.

3

foresee not only the "death of ideology" and the emergence of a "universal man," but a fundamental transformation of the Soviet system into a pluralistic, essentially "open" and consumer-oriented society which, like its Western counterparts, would be run by an apolitical technocratic and managerial elite.

> The basic and sole sense of these theories, despite their great number and outward variety (the "convergence," "stages of economic growth," "deideologization," the "technetronic" age, and other such theories) boils down to the fact that in the process of industrial development socialism and capitalism assume common features and in the final analysis meet halfway and form some form of "hybrid society," in which ideology, having lost its former significance, "will disappear."[2]

The "convergence" theory, therefore, is seen as implying not only the futility of East-West competition but the desirability and ultimate inevitability of an entente between the Soviet Union and the United States.

The Soviet response has been to characterize "convergence" as an insidious form of Western ideological subversion and as an effort to extend peaceful coexistence to the spheres of class relations and ideology. Brezhnev told the 1969 World Conference of Communist and Workers' Parties, for example, that, "the hired ideologists of the imperialists have created a special pseudo-culture designed to befuddle the masses, to blunt their social consciousness."[3] The Soviets claim to see in these theories a scheme to camouflage and make more palatable the true nature of capitalism and as attempts to update and make more plausible US postwar policies of "containment," "rolling back communism," and dealing with the communists "from positions of strength."[4]

In 1970 an authoritative anthology of writings on the subject of convergence was published by the USSR Academy of Sciences.[5] The essays included in the volume characterize the theories of convergence as a new, "positive" form of anticommunism:

> Adapting to new conditions, the bourgeois ideologists in a new fashion are formulating a slogan of struggle: "to know not only that *against* which we fight, but also that *for* which it is necessary to fight." Along with "negative" anticommunism, so-called "positive" anticommunism is receiving increasingly wider dissemination, the objective of which is to fill the "vacuum of ideas" in the capitalist countries, the basis of "a positive program of mass action," which maintains the "positive" bourgeois ideas and ideals.[6]

---

[2]Iu. Kashlev, "Tactics of the Doomed: How the West Tries to Modernize the Old Doctrines of Ideological Subversion," *Izvestiia*, August 19, 1969. [14]

[3]*Pravda*, June 8, 1969. [13]

[4]Kashlev, *op. cit.* [14]

[5]M.B. Mitin, *et al.*, *Sovremennye Burzhuaznye Teorii o Sliianii Kapitalizma i Sotsializma (Kriticheskiy Analiz)* (Contemporary Bourgeois Theories on the Convergence of Capitalism and Socialism [Critical Analysis]), (Moscow: Nauka, 1970) [48]. See also the review of the book in *Kommunist*, No. 13, September 1971, pp. 125-128. [64].

[6]*Ibid.*

Soviet leaders consider the dissemination of such ideas by the West as "elevated to the level of governmental policy"[7] and as a direct challenge to communist ideals, accomplishments and prospects.

In more specific terms, the overall case which the Soviets make against convergence centers on two main points.

One is that proponents of the theories aim at "rejuvenating decrepit capitalism."[8]

> The bourgeois ideologists and theoreticians strive to describe capitalism not in terms of its social traits, nor in terms of the production relations that exist, but in terms of its technical and economic indices. They deliberately depart from a social description of capitalist and socialist societies, gloss over the fundamental contradiction between them, detach the productive forces from production relations, and ignore the latter. . . . From the standpoint of domestic problems, the class and political purpose of the bourgeois ideological conceptions, particularly the official doctrines, is to defend capitalism, to embellish it, to prove its viability and progressiveness.[9]

> Bourgeois apologists try hard to show that capitalist society is now renovated, just and flourishing in all respects. . . . The "old" capitalism—which had thoroughly compromised itself—is referred to by bourgeois politicians and ideologists as a kind of inevitable historical evil which is gone forever. New names are suggested for the present social system in the Western countries, such as "the postindustrial society," "people's capitalism," "collective capitalism" and "neo-capitalism."[10]

The second main point relates to an alleged Western purpose of portraying a softening or weakening of communism. "The contemporary slander of imperialist propaganda against socialism," *Pravda* asserted in January 1972, "differs in form from the previous anticommunist roars of the dinosaurs of 'the cold war,' but it is the same in content and in direction." To this *Pravda* added: "The Jesuits of bourgeois propaganda frequently appear in our days under the mask of 'concern' about the fate of socialism, declaim about its 'democratization,' 'liberalization,' and 'modernization.' "[11]

> Never before have we seen such a flood of books, articles, motion pictures and radio broadcasts in which the bourgeois theoreticians and propagandists are trying to "interpret" in their own fashion the trends governing the development of the economic, political and spiritual life of the socialist countries. This entire propagandist

---

[7]Brezhnev, *Pravda*, June 8, 1969. [13]

[8]V.I. Gromeka and V.S. Vasilyev, "Bourgeois Theorists on the Scientific and Technical Revolution," *S.Sh.A.: Ekonomika, Politika, Ideologiia*, No. 1, January 1971. [52]

[9]V.S. Semenov, "Certain Traits of Apologetic Conceptions of Capitalism," *S.Sh.A.: Ekonomika, Politika, Ideologiia*, No. 4, April 1971. [58]

[10]A. Pokrovsky, "Some Sociological Aspects of the Scientific-Technological Revolution in the Capitalist World," *International Affairs* (Moscow), No. 2, February 1971, p. 24. [53]

[11]V. Bol'shakov, "The Subversive Strategy of the War of the Minds," *Pravda*, January 13, 1972. [77]

wave is aimed at weakening socialism, eroding its foundations and breaking the unity of our society.[12]

Thus, the Soviets argue, the promotion of the convergence theory as conducted by the West is two-pronged in its objectives. They see it as simultaneously defensive, with the aim of shoring up declining capitalism, and offensive, with the aim of subverting rising communism. According to Brezhnev, "all those instruments influencing minds which are in the hands of the bourgeoisie—the press, films, radio—are mobilized to deceive people, to suggest to them the concept of almost heavenly life under capitalism [on the one hand], to slander socialism [on the other]."[13]

The Soviets in their attacks on the convergence theory are in their turn clearly both defensive and offensive minded. They openly avow an intent to put a limit on peaceful coexistence and its implications—to insure that the doctrine shall in no way lead to a relaxation on the communist side: The methods and aims of the continuing class enemy must be constantly exposed and guarded against. At the same time, the fact that convergence theories have evolved in the West and are being so strongly put forward is being publicly interpreted as a sign of weakness and hence as an added reason for communist confidence in ultimate victory.

The Soviet leaders have made a special effort to insure that nothing in the way of a relaxation of ideological militancy be read into agreements reached with the US at the summit meetings with President Nixon in May 1972. Instead, they argue, as indicated in the above cited Brezhnev statement following Nixon's departure from Moscow, that as the US is prevented by the changing balance of power from attempting to solve East-West competition by violent means and consequently is forced to accept the Soviet principles of peaceful coexistence, ideological struggle between the camps will increase, and the more insidious will be Western efforts at subverting the communist system.

Even before President Nixon had departed Moscow, a commentator of the Soviet domestic radio service was asserting with respect to the agreements being reached at the meeting:

> The times have gone, never to return, when the imperialist circles could dictate their conditions to the rest of the world or direct the development of events in a direction favorable to them. A decisive factor which has basically altered the balance of power in the international arena is the emergence of a world socialist system, the strengthening of the might of the Soviet Union and the fraternal states. . . . Naturally, we cannot forget the fact that the historic

---

[12]P.N. Demichev, "The Development of Topical Problems of the Building of Communism in the Resolutions of the 24th CPSU Congress," *Kommunist*, No. 15, October 1971, p. 35. [71]

[13]"Accountability Report," at the 24th Party Congress, *Pravda*, March 31, 1971. [55]

antagonism between socialism and imperialism has not under any circumstances been erased from the agenda, nor has the necessity to be prepared for every kind of recidivism of aggressive policy on the part of the more adventurist circles in the imperialist camp.[14]

Subsequently the Kremlin organized a mass campaign throughout the country to impress its interpretation of the summit talks on all Soviet citizens—and to warn them against "misinterpretations." The campaign is, of course, managed by the Communist Party apparatus, which has a quarter million full-time officials and over fourteen million members; and by such associated organizations as the Znaniye (Knowledge) Society which has two and a half million "ideological workers—propagandists, political information workers, agitators and lecturers."[15] Illustrative of the line adopted was the claim of *Komsomol'-skaia Pravda* on the morrow of the summit that "the strategic course of US policy is now changing before our very eyes from 'pax Americana' . . . to a definite form of necessity for peaceful coexistence." But, "We must clearly understand that this change is a forced one and it is precisely the power—the social, economic and, ultimately, the military power of the Soviet Union and the socialist countries—that is compelling American ruling circles to engage in an agonizing reappraisal of values."[16] Moreover, as Politburo member and CPSU Central Committee Secretary M.A. Suslov explained at the Sixth Congress of the All-Union Znaniye Society:

> It should be stressed . . . that . . . since the futility of attempts at military, political and economic pressure on the Soviet Union and the socialist community as a whole is becoming increasingly obvious as the situation in the world arena changes in socialism's favor, it is precisely the struggle in the ideological sphere—the sphere where peaceful coexistence between capitalism and socialism does not and cannot exist—that is assuming particular urgency. . . . The class enemy is attempting to counter the great truth of Marxism-Leninism with a whole conglomeration of pseudoscientific doctrines and concepts combining a direct apology for capitalism, reformist views and revisionist formulas for "improving" socialism.[17]

Further, according to the authoritative CPSU journal *Kommunist*, this

> . . . ideological struggle retains all of its sharpness and acquires even greater significance. Furthermore, under conditions of the wider acceptance of the principles of peaceful coexistence, imperialism deploys the most refined activities with the aim of ideological penetration into the socialist countries. In the West they have not given up, for example, attempts to prove that international detente is impossible supposedly without the "convergence" of the two systems. It is impossible not to see the ill intents and lies of this assertion, which is being portrayed as "a sign of the times" and

---

[14]Radio Moscow, May 27, 1972.
[15]See *Pravda*, June 20, 1972; June 21, 1972.
[16]*Komsomolskaia Pravda*, June 4, 1972.
[17]*Pravda*, June 21, 1972.

obviously aimed at naive, politically unsophisticated people. No, communists will never give up their ideas and principles, they have always struggled and in the future will energetically struggle for their worldwide triumph.[18]

The *Kommunist* editorial went on to exhort the reader not to fall into complacency and "ideological demobilization" and reminded him of Lenin's words, "The form of the struggle may change according to various, relatively special and temporary causes, but the essence of the struggle, its class content as such cannot change, while classes exist."[19]

Warnings have also been sounded regarding added Western efforts to promote "cosmopolitanism," whose "essence" is the "demand for 'broader contacts,' for 'fusion' with Western culture and morality, and a frank aspiration to replace the class concept of internationalism with abstract schemes about 'a citizen of the world.' "[20] In response to such bourgeois contrivances:

> Marxist-Leninists have consistently associated peaceful coexistence with the prospect of further deepening and extending the inevitable development of the world revolutionary process. The documents collectively formulated by the communist and workers' parties have repeatedly stressed that the communists regard peaceful coexistence as a form of confrontation between the two social systems.[21]

## II
## SOVIET TREATMENT OF SPECIFIC
## THEORIES OF CONVERGENCE

For the most part, Soviet spokesmen tend to lump all Western theories of convergence together as different aspects of essentially the same thing. As explained by one commentator, "over the last two decades or more the imperialist bourgeoisie has formulated a large number of conceptions whose purpose is to defend the capitalist system and to falsify Marxism-Leninism and has put them to practical propaganda purposes."[22] These views are said to have gone through a definite evolutionary process, moving from an original concentration on an apology for capitalism "to a set of bourgeois views concerning the processes of the interaction, interrelationship, and prospects for development of capitalism and socialism" which have collectively "come to

---

[18]"The Leninist Course of the Foreign Policy of the CPSU," editorial article, *Kommunist*, No. 9, June 1972, p. 79. [86]

[19]*Ibid.*

[20]Colonel D. Volkogonov, "A Patriot, An Internationalist," *Krasnaia Zvezda* (Red Star), July 4, 1972. [87]

[21]A. Sovetov, "Peaceful Coexistence—A Real Factor in International Relations," *International Affairs* (Moscow), No. 9, September 1972, p. 13.

[22]Semenov, *op. cit.*, pp. 63-64. [58]

be called the theory of 'convergence.' "[23] This theory, according to the Soviets, sees capitalism and socialism as "irreversibly progressing toward each other in order to meet at a certain point and converge, i.e., merge once and for all and form a mixed society, a hybrid society, a compromise society, neither socialism nor capitalism but something else bearing certain elements of both."[24] However, while concentrating their major effort on denouncing the total of the convergence theories Soviet spokesmen single out particular ones for special attention. It is important to note also that the Soviets mix in with convergence theories Western, and particularly US, policies that look toward greater contacts between East and West, policies which they characterize as "bridge-building" or "ditch filling."

Soviet reaction is especially focused on convergence theories that tie in with the workings of the scientific-technological revolution. "Scientific-technological progress," according to a *Pravda* editorial, "has now become the main arena of the competition between socialism and capitalism,"[25] that is, a crucial component of the continuing class struggle. Western theories of convergence which foresee growing similarities between the socialist and capitalist systems in consequence of scientific-technological advances are therefore viewed by Soviet leaders as falsifying and negating fundamental principles of Marxist doctrine. Soviet opposition to such theories is based upon claims that the scientific-technological revolution is not a cause but an effect, determined by the nature of the particular system in which it occurs.

Thus the Soviets focus on Western theories related to the concept of "the industrial society" and the more recent concept of "the post industrial society," both of which are said to center on the view that technological progress is an "independent process that automatically entails social changes" and hence "paint illusory pictures of the unlimited progress of capitalism and do not take account of the acute social problems and contradictions of today and tomorrow."[26]

Birthplace of theories relative to the "industrial society," as distinct from the "postindustrial society," is said to have been France, and its original authors French economists and sociologists such as Jean Fourastie, Raymond Aron, and Jacques Ellul. "Having migrated from France to the United States, the theory of the 'industrial society' seems to have fallen upon fertile soil and received an American interpretation in such books as *The New Industrial State* of John Galbraith, *Problems of Industrial Society* by William Founce,

---

[23]*Ibid.*

[24]*Kommunist*, No. 13, September 1971. [64]

[25]*Pravda*, March 31, 1970.

[26]N.D. Gauzner, "The Postindustrial Society and Tendencies in the Socioeconomic Development of the United States," *S.Sh.A.: Ekonomika, Politika, Ideologiia*, No. 12, December 1970. [47]

and *One Dimensional Man: Essays on the Ideology of Advanced Industrial Society* by Herbert Marcuse."[27] Basic to the theories, in the Soviet view, "is a kind of distorted reflection of the scientific and technical revolution" which would have it that "engineering determines everything: the scale of production, the form of its organization, the management system, the make-up of managers, and even the form of administration of the entire production of society."[28] The theories are said to ignore "the difference between social and political structures, taking into consideration only the level of industrialization (the principle of technological determinism)."[29] Moreover, whereas the net effect of scientific-technological progress under socialism is progressive and constructive, under capitalism—so claim the Soviets—it is exploitative and degenerative:

> Under the conditions of socialism the progress of science and technology accelerates the progressive movement of society. . . . Under the conditions of capitalism, scientific and technical progress aggravates the contradictions and deepens the general crisis of this system; the achievements of science and technology, through the fault of imperialism, are directed not toward the good of mankind, but are used for barbaric reactionary purposes.[30]

In fact, according to the Soviet view, the scientific-technological revolution under socialism is used to create "the material and technical foundation for the transition to communism,"[31] i.e., the ultimate stage of the development of the Marxist society which will mark its total victory over capitalism. While science and technology aid capitalism to achieve some temporary advances in productivity, they cannot solve the inherent contradictions in the capitalist system, but on the contrary aggravate them.

The Soviets object particularly to the theories attributed to John Kenneth Galbraith which, they claim, reach a conclusion that convergence will occur in the form of a "new industrial state" by proceeding from the "erroneous" assumption that the organization and planning and the use of technology of a modern economy will become the same under both systems. The Soviets contend that supporters of this theory falsely "try to prove that the tempestuous technological progress today has an identical impact on capitalism and socialism," thus deliberately ignoring the fact that "scientific and technological progress under capitalism, in a society of private ownership and exploitation, serves as a means of enrichment, as a tool of militarism, but under

[27]S.A. Dalin, "The 'Industrial Society' and the Working Class," *S.Sh.A.: Ekonomika, Politika, Ideologiia*, No. 9, September 1970, p. 38. [43]

[28]*Ibid.*

[29]Pokrovsky, *op. cit.*, p. 25. [53]

[30]Colonel V. Serebriannikov, "The 'Convergence' Theory in Military Uniform," *Krasnaia Zvezda* (Red Star), July 8, 1971. [60]

[31]Dalin, *op. cit.* [43]

socialism it serves the workingman."[32] The contention of Galbraith and others that power in the "new industrial state" will be wielded by a managerial elite, "professional specialists and scientists standing above classes and ideologies,"[33] runs counter, in their view, to the most fundamental of communist precepts: the struggle between the proletarian and bourgeois classes will become increasingly acute, until the proletariat achieves total victory. "Galbraith," it is asserted, "has his own approaches but they are fundamentally no different from other technocratic utopias. . . . These attitudes on the part of Galbraith politically disorientate the progressive circles in capitalist countries and replace class struggle with the counter-position of education and ignorance."[34] The theory of the "industrial state"

> . . . also contradicts current social practices which . . . confirm the fact that the working class as a whole, regardless of the changes in its structure, remains the leading revolutionary force of our time. . . .[35]
> In actuality the socioeconomic consequences of the scientific and technical revolution are diametrically opposed under capitalism and socialism. Such consequences as "technological unemployment" or the destruction of the mass of farmers, which is now taking place [in capitalist countries], are altogether impossible in the socialist system. Under capitalism the scientific and technical revolution is demonstrating more and more the incompatibility between present-day productive forces and the production relations that exist there. Under socialism, though, they create the material and technical foundation for the transition to communism. Consequently, "technology" is bringing about completely different socioeconomic consequences for capitalism and socialism.[36]

The Soviets are even more vehement in their denunciation of theories which they bring together under the rubric of "postindustrial society." Attributing initiation of the theories to Colin Clark, Soviet commentators include among principal authors of variants Daniel Bell, Leslie White, Zbigniew Brzezinski, Jacques Ellul, Herman Kahn, Anthony Wiener, Walt Rostow, and, on occasion, a number of others. While noting that different authors give different names to their societies of the future (e.g., Bell "Postindustrial Society," Brzezinski "Technetronic Society"), the Soviets claim that they are all "shot through with subjectivism, arbitrariness, and idealism." They "are very far from science . . . run directly counter to it." The fundamental distinction between them and Marxism-Leninism is said to be that the latter "derives

---

[32] M. Sidorov, "Lenin on Irreconcilability of Socialist and Bourgeois Ideologies," in *Leninism Today (A Collection of Articles)* (Moscow: Novosti Press Agency Publishing House, 1970), p. 127. [49]
[33] G. Khromushin, "Imperialist Reaction Drops Its Mask," *Kommunist*, No. 14, September 1971, pp. 107-116. [68]
[34] I. Yu. Fomin, "On the 'Technocratic' Utopia and 'Managerial Revolution,'" *S.Sh.A.: Ekonomika, Politika, Ideologiia*, No. 2, February 1971. [54]
[35] Khromushin, *op. cit.* [68]
[36] Dalin, *op. cit.* [43]

the new society not from desires, not from subjective conjectures, but from the objective tendency in the development of the previous social organism."[37] "The dialectics of the interaction between the productive forces and production relations, discovered by the founders of Marxism and confirmed by the entire course of history, is completely ignored in the theories of the 'postindustrial society.' "[38] According to one Soviet spokesman, proponents of the theories have given a rebirth to the "old technocratic theories" which have long since been refuted. "They speak of the birth of an omnipotent elite of 'egg-heads,' or an electronic-cybernetic elite, which has taken power over society. In the opinion of Z. Brzezinski, the United States is even now ceasing to be a plutocratic-oligarchic society and is becoming a 'meritocratic democracy.' "[39]

Brzezinski, Bell and Rostow serve as main targets of the Soviets in their campaign against the concept of the postindustrial society. Characterizing the "theory of evolution which has been elaborated in greatest detail by Brzezinski" as the "capstone" of all the theories of convergence, Soviet commentators assert that the special object of this theory is to "try to prove that the socialist countries are evolving towards capitalism and that radical changes are imminent in their sociopolitical system, changes which are presented as a return to capitalism and are welcomed as steps towards 'true democracy.' "[40] While acknowledging that Brzezinski insists he is "diametrically opposed" to the concept of the postindustrial society, the Soviets charge that "in reality his theory [re the technetronic era] is a coarse eclectic compilation of various views expressed by Bell, Galbraith and other 'postindustrialism' theoreticians."[41]

The Soviets insist that Daniel Bell and others who share his view that the present industrialized societies of the advanced countries will be replaced by postindustrial societies with "new . . . people produced by the scientific-technological revolution at the helm. . . ."

> . . . ignore the content of the process of transformation of one social organism into another because they are not interested in the actual replacement of the present society in the United States and the other capitalist countries by a society that is really new. The shaping of a new society encompasses an entire set of phenomena: technical, economic, social, political, ideological, intellectual, and psychological. The entire social organism is changing from top to bottom. Its socioeconomic content, its mode of production, its property relations, and the technical-economic and social structure of society

[37]Semenov, op. cit. [58]
[38]Gauzner, op. cit. [47]
[39]Ibid.
[40]E. Modrzhinskaya, "Anticommunism Disguised as Evolutionism," International Affairs (Moscow), No. 1, January 1969. [10]
[41]Khromushin, op. cit. [68]

are changing above all. This is what is happening in connection with the replacement of capitalist society by socialist society, which is actually being accomplished in history.[42]

W. W. Rostow is relatively old hat in the Soviet campaign against convergence since his *Stages of Economic Growth* appeared almost a decade and a half ago and has been subject to scathing criticism over the years. Nevertheless, ire is still voiced over his audacity in subtitling his study "A Noncommunist Manifesto,"[43] and he is sharply rebuked for his view that there can be a non-Marxian explanation of historico-economic phenomena, and that capitalism is presently in a higher stage of development than socialism—thus implying that capitalism is a superior system. In putting the US at such a higher stage, Rostow is said to paint

> a pretty picture of American capitalism concentrating on the all-round satisfaction of popular needs. As indices of society's development he uses the degree of technical modernization in industry and the level of scientific-technological progress, but ignores the most important, to wit the system of production relations dependent on the nature of the ownership of the means of production.[44]

Rostow's aim, like that of all "postindustrialists," is said to be to "take American capitalism as a prototype treating it as a model for the whole world, thus essentially extrapolating it into the future of all mankind." Such an approach, the Soviet critics aver, attempts

> to suppress the fact that socialism is an immeasurably higher level of social development compared with capitalism, [and to] eliminate the question of communism as the future of all mankind and replace communism with the chimera of the "single industrial society." . . .[45]

Especially anathema to the Soviets are elements of the various convergence theories that suggest the "end of ideology." They see Western contentions as exemplified by Daniel Bell's thesis on the diminishing role of ideology as another instance of the "so-called 'liberal' or 'intellectual' anticommunism"[46] in the West. This approach, they say, which focuses on "so-called universal human interests," is both theoretically unsound and politically harmful, because, regardless of the motives of its proponents, it postulates that "socialism is most probably doomed almost to social stagnation, whereas before capitalism, especially American capitalism, the rosy prospects of the

---

[42]Semenov, *op. cit.* [58]

[43]Colonel V. Bondarenko, "Scientific and Technical Progress and the Ideological Struggle," *Krasnaia Zvezda*, October 3, 1969. [16]

[44]Pokrovsky, *op. cit.* [53]

[45]Review of Mitin, *et al.*, *Kommunist*, No. 13, September 1971. [64]

[46]Colonel K. Paiusov, "What Is Hidden Behind Preaching of a 'Universal' Ideology?" *Krasnaia Zvezda*, September 24, 1971. [63]

'postindustrial society' are allegedly opening up."[47] Soviet commentators also criticize Wolfgang Leonhard for his doctrine of "evolutionary transformation" of the Soviet system which allegedly will "free" the Soviet people from Marxist-Leninist ideology and lead to the development of a "pluralistic society" in the Soviet Union. This doctrine, they say, aims in reality at the "softening up" of Marxist-Leninist ideological principles, the breaking up of the unity of the socialist camp and the restoration of capitalism.[48] Furthermore, Soviet commentators insist, Western expectations of the "dissolution of the socialist into a bourgeois ideology" as a consequence of an emerging predominance of "universal human interests," ignores the fact that there can be no "objective" or "above class" view of such interests, but only "common interests" which are inseparably tied to "the interests of a specific class, nation, etc."[49] In the Soviet view, of course, ideology and class struggle go hand in hand and, with the latter inevitably intensifying as the capitalist system progressively declines, the former must automatically play a greater rather than a lesser role. In a speech on December 21, 1971, Politburo member Suslov asserted that "in our era of the antagonism between the two world systems—socialism and capitalism—the ideological struggle, which extends into all fields of social life, including science, is inevitably exacerbated."[50]

Finally, the Soviets condemn the bourgeois "aspiration to adapt the 'convergence' theory to an explanation of the changes in the armed forces of states with opposed systems . . . [that is] to prove that nuclear weapons, the uniformity of combat equipment and the levels of its development make the military system of the USSR and the United States allegedly similar not only on the technical plane but also on the social plane."[51] Such aspirations, the Soviets contend, are without any "scientific" justification. "It has long been proved that the nature and purpose of armies are determined by the nature of the social system and the policy and the ideology of the dominant classes."[52] They charge that by proclaiming the triumph of technology over ideology, advocates of a "technical approach" to all social questions, such as Bell, are trying to transform the military into "simple executors of established technical norms," thereby distorting the "essence of the changes that are taking place under the influence of the scientific and technical revolution in

---

[47]Iu. Ia. Ol'sevich, "Methodology of Criticism of Anti-Marxist Concepts of Socialism," *Vestnik Akademii Nauk SSSR*, No. 8, August 1971. [62]

[48]G. V. Platonov, *Kartina Mira, Mirovozzrenie i Ideologiia* (The World Image, World Outlook and Ideology) (Moscow: Znaniye, 1972), p. 40.

[49]Paiusov, *op. cit.* [63]

[50]M. A. Suslov, "The Social Sciences Are the Party's Combat Weapon in the Building of Communism," *Kommunist*, No. 1, January 1972, p. 26. [78]

[51]Serebriannikov, *op. cit.* [60]

[52]*Ibid.*

the personnel . . . and in the nature of military activity."[53] The Soviets further argue that for the United States "not peaceful but military production . . . becomes . . . the most important sphere of development and application of science."

> Thus, when we speak about the social meaning of utilizing science and technology and are convinced of the dangers to mankind of their application in capitalist society, we make the only possible conclusion that together with the liquidation of capitalism will be liquidated the danger of turning the achievements of man against himself.[54]

In the Soviet view, such Western theoreticians as Bell, M. Feld, N. Galay, B. Ambramsson, R. Kolkowicz and others, fail to recognize that

> the social consequences of the scientific and technical revolution . . . have different directions and natures under the conditions of contrary systems. . . . Consequently, the outwardly similar processes in the development of armaments do not change and cannot change the class-political nature, the essence and the purpose of armies.[55]

By their theories, "the bourgeois ideologists are fanning the adventurism and aggressiveness of imperialism," corrupting its soldiers, and preparing its armies for "destructive war." "And this," say the Soviets, "is why the task of exposing the apologists of reaction and aggression is so urgent."[56]

### III
### THE TARGETS OF MAIN SOVIET CONCERN
### IN THE CAMPAIGN AGAINST CONVERGENCE

The overall context in which Soviet commentators attack convergence and the various theories they associate with or subsume within the term is intellectual contempt. The theories are pictured as representing a crude form of "psychological indoctrination of the masses" through the manipulation and falsification of the facts and "the extensive use of stereotypes."[57] By inference to the Soviets, any knowledgeable schoolboy should be able to perceive the fallacies of the theories and to treat them with the disdain they deserve. However, since the proponents of the theories "pretend to a progressive outlook" and engage in "shameless speculation on universal ideals, practically implemented in the socialist countries (the so-called method of 'stolen slogans')," the effect can be "to dull the political awareness and paralyze

---

[53]*Ibid.*
[54]From the editorial "Man-Science-Technology," introducing a new series of articles on the scientific-technological revolution, *Voprosy Filosofii*, No. 8, 1972, p. 34.
[55]Serebriannikov, *op. cit.* [60]
[56]*Ibid.*
[57]G. Shliapnikov, "The Myths of Imperialist Propaganda," *Kommunist*, No. 4, March 1970. [30]

the working people's will in the struggle for socialism."[58] This "bourgeois propaganda" may therefore impart to the "politically naive reader or listener unfamiliar with the theory of communism and the practice of the building of socialism" a negative image of communism and its future.[59]

Actually, the extent and nature of the Soviet reaction to the convergence doctrine make clear that the Soviet leadership is deeply concerned to safeguard against any possible adverse impact both within and outside the Soviet Union.

With respect to the Soviet Union, two groups are viewed as particularly vulnerable to the appeal of convergence: the youth and the intellectuals. Soviet leaders have consistently warned that both groups are primary targets of Western ideological subversion.[60] Thus in a speech to the Moscow City Party organization Brezhnev said, "Our enemies in the imperialist camp seize with the utmost tenacity upon any manifestation of ideological immaturity or faltering on the part of particular representations of the intelligentsia."[61] This line was also reflected in the Soviet press where, for example, *Izvestiia* warned that "reaction is trying to separate the intelligentsia, and particularly the student youth, and to counterpose them to the working class, using petit bourgeois radicalism and the absurd idea that in the modern era the working class has allegedly lost its revolutionary force. . . ."[62] The Soviets are apprehensive that convergence ideas will sow seeds of an "individualist 'consumer' psychology, which will stifle revolutionary ideals and socialist convictions . . . of the population, especially of young people, including those in the socialist countries."[63] Again, in a speech on October 11, 1972, Politburo member D.A. Kunayev accused the West of seeking "to galvanize rationalistic moods and to introduce into the consciousness of our people the ideology of indifference to politics, egoistic consumerism and money-grubbing, relying much on the younger generation," and noted that "we still have not gotten rid of all kinds of antisocial elements and bearers of vestiges of the past."[64]

Soviet officials are very alert to the possible appeal of convergence ideas among Soviet scientists. N.V. Podgornyi, member of the Politburo and Chair-

[58]CC-CPSU Theses commemorating the 50th anniversary of the October Revolution, *Pravda*, June 26, 1967. [3]

[59]Shliapnikov, *op. cit.* [30]

[60]For example, see Brezhnev's speech at the October 25, 1968 Plenum of the Komsomol Central Committee; Politburo member P.Ye. Shelest's speech to Ukrainian students on February 18, 1968; First Secretary of the Komsomol Central Committee Ye. Tiazhelnikov's article in *Komsomol'skaia Pravda*, June 26, 1969; Candidate Politburo member P.M. Masherov in *Sovetskaia Belorussiia*, September 27, 1970; First Secretary of the Azerbaidzhan Party Central Committee G.A. Aliyev in *Bakinskii Rabochii (Baku Worker)*, November 2, 1971.

[61]Radio Moscow, March 29, 1968.

[62]Iu. Frantsev, Member of the Academy of Sciences of the USSR, "One Leninist Page," *Izvestiia*, January 21, 1969. [8]

[63]M. Iovchuk, "Leninism and the Contemporary Struggle of Ideas in Philosophy," *Kommunist*, No. 2, January 1970. [25]

[64]*Kazakhstanskaia Pravda*, October 12, 1972.

man of the Presidium of the USSR Supreme Soviet, in a speech to the Academy of Sciences, has called attention to the need for Soviet intellectuals, "under conditions of a sharp aggravation of the ideological struggle in the historical competition between the opposed social systems . . . more actively to counteract and unmask various bourgeois theories . . . inimical to Marxism-Leninism."[65] The "convergence" theories did indeed strike a responsive chord among some Soviet scientists in the 1960s, the most notable case being that of nuclear physicist Andrei Sakharov who advanced his own theories of convergence and rapprochement between the systems. Sakharov's writings were published in the West[66] and also clandestinely circulated in the Soviet Union. Other Soviet scientists have in exchanges with Western counterparts indicated considerable interest in the possibilities of convergence.[67] Peter Kapitsa, Director of the prestigious Institute of Physical Problems of the USSR Academy of Sciences, has publicly as well as privately subscribed to a number of the views voiced by Sakharov.[68]

The very content of Soviet attacks on convergence is indicative of the leadership's concern to hold such wayward Soviet intellectuals in line. Illustrative is that the resolution of the Presidium of the USSR Academy of Sciences on November 27, 1969, dealing with the "basic directions of the scientific-research work and objectives" of the Academy's Institute of Philosophy, included the statement: "A most important problem is the criticism of the theory of 'convergence' of the two systems, 'the single industrial society,' and other similar ideological conceptions."[69] M.V. Keldysh, President of the USSR Academy, in his speech to the Academy's meeting which celebrated the 100th anniversary of Lenin's birth, left no uncertainty as to the direction studies of the problem would take:

> In light of the Leninist analysis of the basic contradictions between capitalism and socialism, in their social-economic principles, and in their attitudes toward scientific-technological development, with complete definitiveness appears the groundlessness of contemporary technocratic conceptions and of the theory of "convergence" of the two systems, the theory of "the single industrial society." Imperialism turns scientific-technological achievements not to the welfare of the people but to their oppression, to the preparation and waging of destructive wars in the name of preserv-

[65]N.V. Podgornyi, speech delivered April 2, 1970, to the Lenin jubilee session of the General Meeting of the USSR Academy of Sciences; reported in *Vestnik Akademii Nauk SSSR* (Bulletin of the Academy of Sciences of the USSR), No. 5, May 1970. [34]

[66]See the *New York Times* translation of Sakharov's *Progress, Coexistence and Intellectual Freedom* (New York: W.W. Norton and Co., 1968). [7]

[67]See on this matter Foy D. Kohler and Mose L. Harvey, "Soviet Science and Technology: Some Implications for US Policy," *Orbis*, Vol. XIII (Fall 1969).

[68]*The New York Times* on October 9, 1969, reported that in an interview Kapitsa had stated that only through convergence along lines advocated by Sakharov "can the two great powers avoid a fatal clash."

[69]*Voprosy Filosofii*, No. 3, 1970, p. 141. [20]

ing its power and the achievement of world hegemony, for the struggle against the socialist and the national-liberation movements.[70]

The receptivity shown by some elements of the Soviet intelligentsia to the ideas of an expansion of the spheres of peaceful coexistence and of some form of convergence of the systems as a way of achieving peace and increasing contacts between the Soviet Union and the West evidently remain and will continue to remain a focal point of attention by the Soviet leadership. An editorial in *Pravda* published in the aftermath of the 1972 Moscow Summit Meeting warned that:

> Our society's mighty ideological political unity dooms to defeat any attempt by imperialism to influence the Soviet people. However, it would be erroneous not to see that individual politically immature people still fall under the influence of bourgeois propaganda and are provoked to antisocial acts. We must resolutely expose bourgeois slander against communism and the Soviet Union and suppress any ideological diversion by imperialism.[71]

The Soviet cultural and literary intelligentsia, as distinct from the scientific-technical, are the object of especially sharp attention. "In the situation of the acute ideological struggle," the Party "gives all-round consideration to the specific features of artistic creativity and literary affairs" and "resolutely opposes anarchist arbitrariness and subjective capriciousness and advocates exactitude and clarity of ideological position."[72] Westerners, and particularly those representative of the "new Left," who "hide behind a concern for the 'purity of art' " are said to be trying "to teach us tolerance, non-violence, and liberalism toward the peddlers of bourgeois ideology and of 'Western ideological baggage'. . . and at the same time . . . to call upon our intelligentsia to be intolerant toward writers and pamphleteers who are consistently defending party positions."[73] Such Westerners express their "solidarity with intellectual criminals condemned by the Soviet courts."

> The West stubbornly seeks "opposition" to Soviet power—for more than 50 years incidentally—invariably expressing wish for reality. [Soviet] apostates and the rabble of the literary fringe at ideological warfare factories are transformed into "unrecognized" national "geniuses" and the Westerners place in their servile open mouths what they would like to hear from the Soviet writers and artists without the prefixes "pseudo" and "circum."[74]

Westerners like to claim, it is said, that Soviet artist-writers are torn between two loyalties, the patriotic and the liberal. But the ones they identify in this

---

[70]*Pravda*, April 3, 1970. [33]
[71]Editorial, "Pressing Tasks of Ideological Work," *Pravda*, July 8, 1972. [88]
[72]Editorial, "The Unity of Communists' Convictions and Actions," *Kommunist*, No. 13, September 1971. [65]
[73]V. Bol'shakov, "Pandora's Box," Part II, *Komsomol'skaia Pravda*, August 26, 1970. [40]
[74]*Ibid.*

regard "have neither the moral nor the legal right to bear this high title," but are persons "whom 'liberal loyalty' and more exactly adherence to bourgeois ideology have led to the open betrayal of their motherland and . . . who objectively play into the hands of our ideological enemies either in search of cheap popularity or through political infantilism."

The ideological deserters, both in the literal and in the figurative sense of this word, deserve only the scorn of the people they have betrayed. They cannot hide from this scorn either by the "martyr's" crown of thorns manufactured in the Western ideological workshops or by the laurels of a "national genius" or a "great writer" also prepared there. One must always realize who is giving those crowns and laurels, and why.[75]

Along with their sensitivity to domestic vulnerabilities, the Soviet leaders also show concern that the theories of "convergence" could adversely affect Soviet control over the East European community of states. The Soviets claim to see the Western policies of "bridge-building" to the Soviet bloc countries of Eastern Europe as a practical and tactical application of the "convergence theory" to specific ends. A *Pravda* article asserted that

The "convergence" theory serves as some sort of pseudo-scientific foundation for the tactics of making advances to individual socialist countries, for "building bridges" and "filling up ditches," in order—with the help of "silent counterrevolution"—to wrest these countries from the socialist communities, to restore capitalism in them, and to undermine the might of world socialism.[76]

The director of the Institute of the USA of the Academy of Sciences of the USSR, G.A. Arbatov, while acknowledging that the Johnson administration's policy of "bridge building" initially "could still be perceived by many as a form of answer to the call for peaceful coexistence which was issued by the socialist states," asserted that it soon became "a platform for the initiation of subversive activity directed toward the destruction of the socialist commonwealth and subversion of the socialist social system."[77] Similarly an article in *Kommunist* attacked "bridge-building" as "aimed at interfering in the internal affairs of the socialist countries, exacerbating 'psychological warfare,' encouraging anti-socialist, nationalist tendencies, disuniting the socialist countries, and subverting the world positions of socialism."[78] Moscow uses the abortive attempt at liberalization in Czechoslovakia under Dubcek in 1968

---

[75]*Ibid.*

[76]A. Rumiantsev, M. Mitin and M. Mshveniyeradze, "The Urgent Questions of the Struggle against Anticommunism," *Pravda*, October 13, 1969. [17]

[77]G.A. Arbatov, "American Foreign Policy at the Threshold of the 1970s," *S.Sh.A.: Ekonomika, Politika, Ideologiia*, No. 1, January 1970, p. 25. [24]

[78]B. Tomashevskiy, "The Leninist Principle of Peaceful Coexistence and the Class Struggle," *Kommunist*, No. 12, August 1970. [42]

as its most favored example of the West's "attempt at the practical implementation of such plans."[79]

> ... in the situation obtaining ... in Czechoslovakia, the ideas raised up on the shield of the antisocialist forces served as nothing more than ... a smokescreen for the criminal plans and actions of the counterrevolution. And in the face of a direct threat to the cause of socialism, the question is resolved by real opposition to those forces that hide behind this screen and mask themselves with it.[80]

Furthermore, the Soviet spokesmen charge that convergence theories aim at undermining Soviet and communist appeals both in the advanced countries of the West and in the developing countries, in order to weaken the worldwide "anti-imperialist" struggle. Exploiting the convergence theory by all possible means, it is said, its authors try to weaken the class struggle in the developed countries by encouraging the masses to think thus: "Why wage such a struggle if capitalism is developing in the same way as socialism and when, somewhere along the way, will merge with it!"[81] The authors of the theory are similarly said to be trying to undermine the will of the peoples of the Third World to seek their liberation and to take the non-capitalist path of development: "Why must you strive toward socialism when even its citadel, the USSR, is compelled to return to 'the proven practice of capitalist management' after half a century of experimentation?"[82]

Evidently of great importance in the Soviet view is the possible impact on both workers in capitalist countries and peoples of the Third World of the efforts of the proponents of convergence to refurbish and "prettify" capitalism and to make it appear that its ultimate demise can be prevented. Thus, Moscow devotes unending attention to refuting the contention of "bourgeois theoreticians" that capitalism is undergoing a fundamental change, and that in the process it is becoming oriented toward human well-being:

> The synthetic bourgeois doctrine of "people's capitalism," supplemented by the conception of the "affluent society," was formulated on the basis of these apologetic conceptions. In the reformist literature this state is characterized by dissemination of theories of the "transformation" of capitalism, of its transition to "democratic" or "humanistic" socialism.[83]

Certain actions undertaken by capitalist governments, Soviet writers acknowledge, have had the effect of ameliorating the life of some workers, but these measures are said to be merely temporary palliatives, the effects of

[79]Platonov, *op. cit.*, p. 40.
[80]Major General K. Bochkarev, "V. I. Lenin and the Defense of the Achievements of Socialism: The Great International Duty," *Krasnaia Zvezda*, February 14, 1969. [11]
[81]Shliapnikov, *op. cit.* [30]
[82]Radio Moscow, September 22, 1967. [4]
[83]Semenov, *op. cit.* [58]

which will be reversed in the long run. In the past, for example, colonialism permitted raising the workers' standard of living in "imperialist" countries, at the expense of the workers in the colonial dependencies. Today, the capitalists are turning to economic integration as a means of making the capitalist system better suited to the contemporary world. But,

> . . . integration does not eliminate the contradictions and crises, anarchy and disorderly development of capitalist production and the struggle among imperialist countries for the division of markets and spheres of influence, inherent in capitalism. It does not soften social antagonisms. All these basic vices of the capitalist system are reemphasized by integration, reappearing on a new scale and in different forms.[84]

"Contemporary imperialism," Soviet writers charge, "has a series of new traits." Here they cite the trend toward economic planning—"state financing of programs for industrial development and scientific research," "programs of economic development," "rational forms of [economic] direction"—but they credit this trend with nothing more than "multiplying the preconditions for socialism," thereby vindicating Lenin's "bold conclusion" that "some basic characteristics of capitalism have begun to turn into their antithesis."[85]

Soviet writers say that technical progress, rationalization, and intensification of labor have increased the profits of capitalist businessmen, making it possible for them, "under the pressure of the toilers' demands . . . to allow some rise in wages, hoping by this to fill the workers with the illusion of the community of interests of labor and capital."[86] Thus,

> the increased number of people owning automobiles, refrigerators and washing machines was interpreted as the advent of a "consumer society" in which, allegedly, the basic needs of the toiling man are satisfied, for which reason there would be no grounds for social conflicts and for the class struggle.[87]

But this "known rise in the living standard of the toilers, achieved by their unyielding struggles, has not resulted in the ideological-psychological integration of the working class into capitalist society. . . ."[88] Moreover, despite the gains capitalism has achieved, its exploitative nature, according to Soviet spokesmen, is unchanged:

> Even in the most developed capitalist countries, millions of people suffer the torments of unemployment, want and insecurity. Con-

---

[84]M. Maksimova, "World Capitalist Economy and the Processes of Economic Integration," *Kommunist*, No. 16, November 1971, p. 86.

[85]Mitin, *et al.*, *op. cit.*, p. 7. [48]

[86]A. Veber, "Crisis of the Anti-Workingclass Policy of the Bourgeoisie," *Pravda*, November 3, 1971. [72]

[87]CC-CPSU Secretary and Candidate Politburo member Boris N. Ponomarev, "Topical Problems in the Theory of the World Revolutionary Process," *Kommunist*, No. 15, October 1971. [70]

[88]Veber, *op. cit.* [72]

trary to assertions about the "revolution in incomes" and "social partnership," capitalist exploitation is in fact increasing.[89]

Thus, although "all sorts of sops are used" by contemporary capitalist monopolies to lure workers away from class struggle to "class collaboration,"

> ... even the worker who is corrupted and deceived for a time, succumbing to the cult of things and imagining himself to be "middle class," still remains a worker and comes in the end into open collision with capital.[90]

Therefore, the Soviets contend, not only has there not been a deproletarianization or "embourgeoisement" of the working class, as the Western theoreticians of "industrial society" assert, but, on the contrary, new groups, such as the intellectuals, have been "proletarianized." Among these new groups which are also contributing to the broadening of the social base of labor are the "farmers and handicraftmen who are being ruined, [and] large sections of the office workers and technicians . . . [who] are being increasingly exploited."[91]

Thus, conclude these Soviet spokesmen, the " 'one world' about which bourgeois ideologists talk profusely, in fact turns out to be the very same capitalist society with those traits inherent to it—predominance of private property, social division of labor, struggle of antagonistic classes and exploitation of man by man."[92] Moreover,

> the fact that the very attempts to adapt to the new circumstances and above all, to the scientific and technical revolution, are of a limited nature without affecting the exploiting nature of the capitalist socioeconomic system, is of decisive significance. In the final account, these attempts have led not to the strengthening of capitalism but to further deepening of its basic contradictions and antagonisms.[93]

# IV

## MOSCOW'S USE OF "CONVERGENCE"
## TO ITS OWN ENDS

Despite the posture of outrage that Moscow has assumed in its reaction to Western convergence theories, the Soviet leadership gives evidence that it finds the development and popularity of such theories in the West useful

---

[89]A. Gorokhov, "The Communist and Working-Class Movement in the Capitalist Countries at the Present Stage," *International Affairs* (Moscow), No. 11, November 1971, p. 57.
[90]S. Epstein, "Is the Working Class Turning Bourgeois?" *Novoe Vremia* (New Times), No. 28, July 15, 1970.
[91]*Ibid.*
[92]Mitin, *et al., op. cit.*, p. 7. [48]
[93]Ponomarev, *op. cit.* [70]

to its own purposes and that it is intent upon exploiting this situation in a variety of ways.

For one thing, the leadership is taking advantage of "the exceptional exacerbation of the ideological struggle" which it sees as motivating the "convergence movement"[94] as the point of departure for a major campaign for a "rejuvenation" of ideological education in the Soviet Union. Citing Brezhnev's call at the 1969 international conference of parties for "a most active offensive against bourgeois ideology" with its newly created "special pseudo-culture designed to befuddle the masses,"[95] party spokesmen have repeatedly and increasingly exhorted those responsible for questions and activities relative to doctrine and ideology not only to concentrate all-out efforts on refuting "the new myths of imperialist propaganda," but also on raising to higher levels understanding of the "richness and eternal validity" of Marxism-Leninism and "its all-conquering nature." Thus a *Pravda* editorial of November 23, 1970, insisted that in the face of any attempted "perversion of our revolutionary theory," it is necessary "to raise the level of ideological work and to foster in communists and all Soviet people ideological staunchness and implacability." A great role in the process of "political hardening" is played by improvement in theoretical work. "The profound creative study of revolutionary theory spiritually arms communists and enables them to work ever more actively and effectively against" modern manifestations of hostile ideology.[96] A subsequent editorial by the main Party organ called for "the positive development of new theoretical problems" in combination with "offensive criticism of modern bourgeois theories and revisionist and reformist concepts." To this end, *Pravda* asserted, it would be necessary to rely on the fundamentals of Marxism-Leninism, "reveal its universal, international significance, and enrich the great revolutionary teaching of modern times with new conclusions on the basis of profound analysis of the latest data of science and social practice."[97]

Altogether, it might be said that to the Soviets the emergence of convergence theories in the West has provided a much needed foil against which to stimulate and add variety and even a degree of zest and meaning to what had long been one of the dullest and most sterile aspects of Soviet life: the massaging of hackneyed "doctrinal questions." However, far more important than this strictly ideological role is the political role which the Soviet leadership has made convergence serve.

---

94 Mitin, *et al., op. cit.* [48]
95 *Pravda*, June 8, 1969. [13]
96 "Implacability Toward Bourgeois Ideology," *Pravda*, November 23, 1970.
97 *Pravda*, August 15, 1972.

23

The most constant of the themes running through Soviet commentaries on the various theories Soviet authorities associate with or subsume within the term "convergence" is that at issue is a new and particularly insidious form of ideological attack on the USSR. The authorities emphasize, of course, that the Western target is communism generally, that is, the total of the socialist states, their systems and their relationships with each other, as well as the whole of the world-wide cause of Marxism-Leninism. However, as an editorial in *Sovetskaia Rossiia* put it,

> As is known, the spearpoint of imperialism's attack is aimed against the Soviet Union, and this is understandable. Our country is the motherland of socialism, the leading force of the world socialist system. It gathers all anti-imperialist forces around itself. All the progressive people of the world are drawn to it. In it they see the inevitable and imminent future of all the world's working people. Our leading people and the guiding force of Soviet society—the CPSU—are the mind, honor, and conscience of our time.[98]

Moscow's evident purpose is to utilize the "convergence movement" to provide a cutting edge to its contention that the USSR continues under siege by an implacable and dangerous enemy despite the Soviet claim that "capitalist encirclement" is a thing of the past and the more recent claim that the balance of world forces has now irrevocably shifted in favor of the USSR. The matter, as the Soviets see it, has again been well stated by *Sovetskaia Rossiia*:

> Imperialism's ideological subversions against the forces of peace, democracy, and socialism are waged with special intensity. The weaker imperialism, which is hated by the peoples, becomes, and the more positions it loses, the more actively its ideological machine operates. All enemies of the world's revolutionary renewal—from the magnate of capital to patent fascists, from colonialists and landowners to the reactionary military and nuclear maniacs—have now united against socialism and the revolutionary movement under the common black banner of anticommunism. Despite the fact that historically imperialism has lost the ideological fight against the world of socialism, and despite the fact that popular movement toward socialism is invincible, this does not mean that the danger from imperialism's subversive actions is past, or that its struggle against the forces of progress and socialism cannot do great harm. It would be a profound and dangerous error to assume imperialism's automatic bankruptcy; today's true reality is such that imperialism is like a strong and infuriated beast which, although deprived of its former invulnerability and having had some of its fangs drawn in the struggle against the new order, nevertheless is still capable of causing incalculable harm and suffering to mankind. . . . The struggle between imperialism and socialism has not been halted for a single day. It cannot be halted because the bourgeoisie will not voluntarily renounce its dominance and because it rightly sees in socialism its deadly enemy. Bourgeois doctrines and various myths replace old ones but their aim remains the same—to overthrow socialism

---

[98]*Sovetskaia Rossiia*, August 27, 1970.

073324

wherever it has conquered and to prevent the victory of revolution in countries where capital holds sway.[99]

Soviet Defense Minister Grechko attempted to give concrete substance to the same argumentation in his speech at the 24th Party Congress: "US imperialists' preparations for aggression have never ceased"; instead, "the forces of reaction are already nurturing plans for their next campaign against the Soviet Union and other socialist countries and are again trying to unleash a still more destructive war." Nevertheless, according to Grechko, the "insolvency" of US hopes of operating from a "position of strength" has been shown "both by past experience and by the course of modern events: the Soviet Union, together with other socialist states, is capable of replying to force with still greater force." But the imperialists have not given up. They are desperately resorting to new stratagems: Among other things, "propaganda warfare occupies a most important place in the imperialists' arsenal of means of aggressive policy."[100] In other words, as another military leader expressed it: Although "imperialism has irretrievably lost its dominant position in the world, . . . during the time of its decline and death throes it has become even more predatory and dangerous. . . . [And] the most important place in the vast system of measures taken by the imperialist states in preparing for war against the countries of the world socialist system is occupied by espionage, subversive activities and ideological diversion."[101]

Having an "enemy" who, despite his alleged loss of position after position and the alleged inevitability of his ultimate defeat, can still be pictured as both unrelenting in his purpose ("stops at nothing," according to *Kommunist*[102]) and capable of posing grave dangers (before us "stands the last but mightiest of all existing exploiter systems," according to Brezhnev[103]) appears in the view of the present leaders as essential now as at any time in the past. The importance of the matter for the Kremlin is that the threat posed by such an enemy provides it with a basis not only for legitimizing the perpetuation of its monolithic hold on power but also for justifying the arbitrary ways in which it uses power at home and abroad.

The Soviet authorities have gone to great extremes to make credible their assertions as to the seriousness of the danger which the enemy with his new theories and methods now poses. If in the face of existing "world realities" the enemy resorts to indirect methods—has "shifted the center of gravity

---

[99]*Ibid.*

[100]*Pravda*, April 3, 1971.

[101]Major General L. Fil'chenko, "Be on Guard," *Kryl'ia Rodiny* (Wings of the Motherland), No. 7, July 1969, p. 2.

[102]Editorial, *Kommunist*, No. 14, September 1970.

[103]Report to the 24th Party Congress, *Pravda*, March 31, 1971. [55]

to circuitous ways"[104]—he has "in no way renounced [his] basic objectives."[105]

The strategic idea of "eliminating" socialism [has] remained the same. It is a question of new methods for its implementation, aimed at promoting in the USSR and other socialist countries a process of "erosion of socialism," of undermining their unity and thus preparing the necessary conditions for the implementation of the so-called "quiet counterrevolution." The period encompassing the decade of the '60's was precisely characterized by the dissemination of the renovated ideological and propaganda schemes; they were based on the former strategic line of the imperialist politicians, a line which, however, was to be pursued not through a frontal attack but through more refined maneuvering.[106]

As a matter of fact, the Soviets insist, the battle between the socialist world and the capitalist world "has never before been as fierce as today, and our enemy has never before introduced such vast resources and such subtle methods into this battle." Further, "it can be stated that both in terms of its scale and its aims the present ideological war, which is being waged against socialism by the ruling circles of the imperialist powers, is a variety of the imperialist expansion which has been particularly active in recent years."[107] Here it is important that, as is explained in more detail below, the Soviet leaders have adopted the practice of identifying with the "new Western theories and myths" that relate to convergence or deideologization the whole range of developments and movements in the world which they consider inimical to Soviet interests and pretentions, including the gamut of revisionist doctrines that have emerged from within the communist movement itself. The argument is that "Modern anti-communism is a multiplan phenomenon." "In order to ideologically disorient people" the imperialists are trying to mobilize and bring together "all possible anticommunist movements, from right-wing opportunist to ultra-leftist movements" and to use them in concert with their new "concepts which oppose . . . Marxist-Leninist ideology."[108]

According to Soviet argumentation, the Western purpose in its "ideological" campaign goes far beyond any mere "struggle for men's minds." The purpose relates directly to subversion, to sabotage, to espionage, to undermining the Soviet system and the Soviet relationship with other socialist countries. "The stake," according to Brezhnev, is "toward the decay of the

---

[104]Iu. Kashlev and E. Yermolayev, "The Anatomy of Anticommunism," *Kommunist*, No. 9, June 1970, p. 125.
[105]V. Bol'shakov, "The Subversive Strategy of the War of the Minds," *Pravda*, January 13, 1972. [77]
[106]Khromushin, *op. cit.* [68]
[107]A. Yakovlev, "The 24th Party Congress: Problems of Ideological and Educational Work," *Kommunist*, No. 10, July 1971, p. 42.
[108]V. Kortunov, "The Triumph of Marxist-Leninist Ideas and the Maneuvers of Anticommunism," *Kommunist*, No. 8, May 1970. [35]

communist and the entire revolutionary movement from within."[109] The
charge is that while trying to depict their theories of convergence and their
policies of bridge-building as confirmation of their abandonment of an aggressive course, the imperialists' actual aim is "to insure favorable conditions
for imperialism in the event of a direct clash with socialism."[110]

> . . . imperialism in its subversive activity against the socialist
> countries gambles primarily on the "erosion," the "washing away,"
> the "loosening up," the "emasculation" of Marxism-Leninism. . . .
> To sow doubt regarding the ideals of communism, distrust, to spread
> rumors and slander, to stir up nationalist tendencies, to encourage
> private-ownership instincts and aspirations for the so-called "soft
> life," to play on ambition, individualism, on disaffection, and on
> doubt—on whatever they please if only to recruit into the anticom-
> munist camp as many sympathizers as possible from among the
> citizens of the socialist countries—that is what all their theorizing
> and all their practice which is based on it amount to.[111]

In engaging in "combat operations" of this new type, the Soviets assert,
the enemy recognizes that he cannot rely merely upon "his own efforts and
means." He recognizes that he must penetrate the USSR and the other socialist countries and combine "efforts of antisocialist forces acting outside and
inside the country selected as the target for . . . ideological subversion."[112]
Brzezinski, for example, is said to encompass within his theories a far-reaching
program for penetrating the socialist countries.

> For the purposes of the most rapid realization in life of his anti-
> communist dreams, Brzezinski recommends in a most active
> manner the utilization of all forms of contacts and cooperation
> between the capitalist countries and the socialist ones, believing
> that with the assistance of "building bridges" it will be possible
> to achieve together with the exportation of industrial goods also
> counterrevolution.[113]

Thus, according to G.A. Arbatov, Director of the Soviet Academy of Sciences' Institute of the USA, "such forms of international intercourse" as
trade, cultural and scientific-technical ties, etc., "which . . . have enjoyed
a good reputation for centuries" are, when "passed through the meat grinder"
of the convergencists and bridge-builders, "immediately turned into their
antipode, into sinister weapons of subversive activity."[114]

[109]Speech at the World Conference of Communist and Workers' Parties, *Pravda*, June 8, 1969.
[13]
[110]Bochkarev, *op. cit.* [11]
[111]V. Bol'shakov, "Pandora's Box," Part 1, *Komsomol'skaia Pravda*, August 25, 1970. [39]
[112]*Ibid.*
[113]V. Bol'shakov, "The Subversive Strategy of 'the War of the Minds,' " *Pravda*, January 13,
1972. [77]
[114]Arbatov, *op. cit.*, also singled out Brzezinski as one who "especially tried this field: In his
lips, even . . . peace and the normalization of the world situation should further the subversion
of world socialism." [24]

The US ideologists and propagandists are pictured as targeting on every possible opening, real or imagined, in the USSR and other socialist countries. "They stubbornly search . . . for food to slander the socialist system,"[115] counting on "dissidents" in Soviet society—that is those who are "ideologically unstable, those torn from the people,"[116] and on "every kind of renegade and degenerate."[117]

In order to drive home their points regarding the imminence and seriousness of the Western (US) threat under "the new conditions" . . . and at the same time to use this threat to instill greater militancy in the Soviet population and to extend and strengthen Party control over all elements of Soviet society, the leadership has launched a vigorous campaign of political vigilance and stepped up ideological indoctrination. The rationale is simply and straightforwardly stated:

> Under conditions of extreme ideological struggle between capitalism and socialism and of constant attacks against our country and party from bourgeois ideologists and right and "left" opportunists, there is a need from us, the Soviet people, for constant vigilance and sharp reaction to any manifestations of indifference to politics, narrowminded attitudes, and nihilistic attitudes toward the achievements of socialism. We must always keep our powder dry, ready to counter the penetration of bourgeois and revisionist views into our environment. In his report devoted to the Leninist jubilee, CPSU Central Committee General Secretary L.I. Brezhnev warned on behalf of our party that underestimation of the danger of bourgeois ideology and revisionism is impermissible. Comrade Brezhnev pointed out: "Experience has shown that the poisonous seeds of ideological vacillation, indifference to politics, and lack of principle can grow on the soil of this kind of underestimation. Communists are obligated to learn from Lenin conviction and ideological steadfastness, fervor in the struggle against any perversions of our revolutionary theory, and implacability toward any manifestations of old world remnants in the consciousness of our socialist society's citizens."[118]

The vigilance campaign calls for tirelessly resisting "all sorts of bourgeois ideology no matter what stylish or glittering uniform it wears," for unceasing watchfulness as against Western penetrative and subversive efforts and activities, for the "unmasking" of all unorthodox views no matter how "innocent" their guise, and for the all-round intensification of the political education of the masses.[119] The campaign was given the highest endorsement by a resolution of the CPSU Central Committee of April 10, 1968,[120] and has

[115]I. Aleksandrov, "The Poverty of Anticommunism," *Pravda*, December 17, 1970. [45]
[116]V. Bol'shakov, "The Subversive Strategy of 'the War of the Minds,' " *Pravda*, January 13, 1972. [77]
[117]Aleksandrov, *op. cit.*
[118]*Sovetskaia Rossiia*, August 27, 1970.
[119]See for example the *Pravda* editorial of November 23, 1970.
[120]*Pravda*, April 11, 1968.

steadily grown in scope and intensity. Typical of the appeals was Politburo member P.Ye. Shelest's assertion that "political vigilance, hatred of the class enemy and readiness to stand in defense of our socialist Motherland, must be increased among our people."[121] While condemning the Western theories that would ideologically disarm the Soviet people,[122] Soviet editorials have called for instilling in the people "two feelings—fervent and tender love for the Motherland and hatred, burning hatred for those who try to weaken our might or delay the victorious march toward communism."[123] In 1970 the campaign was intensified by warnings to Party organizations that they "must not permit even a shadow of liberalism" in ideological matters,[124] and that the West is "scavenging for booty among rotten isolated individuals who are ready to sell anyone and anything for a foreign mess of pottage . . . having recourse to the services of all kinds of criminal elements, all sorts of renegades, drones, scoundrels, and swindlers, and even persons in whom only psychiatrists could be interested."[125] This left no doubt as to how the leadership was prepared to view and treat those who may succumb to Western ideological blandishments. The intensity of the campaign has been sustained after the May 1972 Moscow Summit Meeting. For example, in July 1972 *Pravda* devoted two editorials to the question of "political vigilance" and to the need for "irreconcilability" in the struggle against all "alien" manifestations which "can harm our society's social and moral political unity."[126]

The calls for ideological vigilance have been accompanied by increasingly strident warnings against foreign spies and saboteurs and against contacts of Soviet citizens with foreigners. Numerous articles by KGB or border security force commanders have been published describing alleged efforts by foreign spies and other subversive elements to penetrate the Soviet Union.[127] The Soviet population has been repeatedly warned of foreign agents in the guise of tourists and students. Thus, it is said that US intelligence agencies dispatch to the USSR "their secret agents and diversionists disguised as press representatives, businessmen, tourists and athletes."[128] No less a person than the Chief of the Main Customs Administration of the USSR Ministry for Foreign

---

[121]Radio Kiev, October 17, 1969. [18]

[122]*Kazakhstanskaia Pravda*, October 12, 1972, as cited in FBIS *Daily Report: Soviet Union*, October 24, 1972, p. J-5.

[123]Editorial, "Revolutionary Vigilance," *Sovetskaia Rossiia*, March 11, 1969.

[124]*Pravda*, November 23, 1970.

[125]Aleksandrov, *op. cit.*

[126]*Pravda*, July 8, 1972; July 13, 1972. [88]

[127]For example, see G. Alkanov and V. Liadov, "Secrets of the Intelligence Service," *Novoe Vremia*, No. 38, September 18, 1970, p. 29; Lt. Colonel F. Nikitin, "Our Civilian Duty," *Trud*, November 26, 1970; E. Maksimov, "On the Vigilant and the Careless," *Sovetskaia Rossiia*, December 3, 1970.

[128]Fil'chenko, *op. cit.*

Trade presented a bill of particulars in an article published in September 1972 of attempts by foreign tourists to smuggle subversive literature, including religious books and pamphlets, into the Soviet Union.[129] Americans and other Westerners are charged with being especially active "with respect to Soviet citizens who travel abroad for various types of forums, conferences, symposiums, cultural affairs, and athletic events. By various means they attempt to gain from them intelligence information or to recruit them as their intelligence agents." Above all, "they seek various types of simple-minded loudmouths, those with a weakness for self-acclaim, souvenir collectors, people who have a tendency for the overuse of alcohol and others who are dissolute in a moral sense."[130] Special concern has even been expressed over the need to insure that children of Soviet citizens who had been stationed abroad "adopt the proper tone" in describing their experiences to their classmates by presenting "first" the seamier side of conditions in foreign countries, and that parents whose children have foreign pen-pals or exchange stamps and coins "warn their children that under the guise of a stamp or coin collection the children might sometimes encounter, especially among foreigners, speculators and other suspicious people."[131]

The US Embassy in Moscow is also marked for intensive watchfulness. A special role in "this warfare in peacetime" is said to be given to "the so-called specialists in Soviet affairs" who are working in the Embassy, "primarily its 'cultural section'—actually the representatives of the United States Information Agency, which is actively used by US intelligence."[132] Countless attempts at "subverting" Soviet citizens, particularly intellectuals, are cited in the press, but far more important would seem the charge that "it is not by chance that in recent years every group of American scientists and postgraduates spending a long time in the USSR has turned out to contain persons who were being actively used by the US Embassy in Moscow for conducting so-called secret operations."[133] Further to the same point is Soviet emphasis on the fact that personnel in the cultural section of the US Embassy "have direct relations with the USSR-US scientific and cultural exchange programs," a situation that is seen as bringing into question the sincerity with which promotion "of American-Soviet relations in the sphere of science and culture" is being developed.[134]

---

[129] G. Chmel, "Lying Contraband," *Komsomol'skaia Pravda*, September 15, 1972.

[130] Fil'chenko, *op. cit.*

[131] V. Iarnatovskaia, "To Raise Internationalists," *Uchitel'skaia Gazeta* (Teachers' Gazette), May 25, 1971.

[132] A. Grachev and Iu. Bobrov, "Mr. Russell and Others," *Literaturnaia Gazeta* (Literary Gazette) May 5, 1971.

[133] *Ibid.*

[134] *Ibid.*

Concomitant with the overall vigilance and indoctrination campaign, the Soviet leaders are conducting a special "military-patriotic" education campaign of the youth designed as it is said to compensate for its lack of experience of the older generation's "school of hate" and hardships. Starting in the first grade of school, the stated aim of this campaign is to instill in the youth of the nation Soviet patriotism, which is defined as "undeviating" loyalty to the Communist Party, communist ideology, and the Soviet Motherland; "love" for the Armed Forces and readiness to defend the Soviet Union; and devotion to "socialist internationalism," that is, unity among the Soviet people and support for Soviet allies and the global revolutionary and national liberation movement. It is asserted that "one of the effective means of combatting amoral behavior is Soviet patriotism, which unites people in one working family and protects them from corrupt bourgeois morality."[135] In line with the militant struggle against foreign ideologies, military-patriotic education of Soviet youth seeks to instill "a conscious hatred of the enemies of communism," for, it is asserted, "fervent love for the socialist Fatherland is inconceivable without irreconcilable class hate for its enemies."[136]

In this vein the program seeks to portray the US as persistently threatening war and at the same time condemns "bourgeois pacifism" which argues that war is either unthinkable or that it would result in the simultaneous destruction of capitalism and communism." The "task of military-patriotic education," states an article in April 1972, "is to prepare the youth morally, politically, psychologically and physically for the difficult trials a new war would bring in its wake."[137] The military-patriotic education program among youth has been endorsed by Brezhnev and in resolutions of the 23rd and 24th CPSU Congresses. It is, as General Yepishev, Chief of the Main Political Administration of the Soviet Armed Forces, has described it, "a protracted and many-faceted process which occurs in successive generations and which begins with the school desk and the Pioneer detachment and group, and then runs through all the conscious activity of a person . . . so as to inculcate in a Soviet man such a manner of thinking whereby his conduct, in carrying out the creative tasks, and his exemplary actions under combat conditions be a profoundly understood necessity."[138]

---

[135]Editorial, "Guard Your Honor in Your Youth," *Sovetskaia Rossiia*, September 3, 1969.

[136]Resolution of the Seventh Plenum of the DOSAAF Central Committee, May 25, 1971; Lt. Colonel V. Demin, "Hate for the Enemy—An Inseparable Aspect in the Patriotism of Soviet Soldiers," *Kommunist Vooruzhennykh Sil*, No. 13, July 1969, p. 26; see also Colonel N. Dovbnia, "Attention, Propagandists," *Kommunist Vooruzhennykh Sil*, No. 19, October 1970, p. 72.

[137]Major General I.A. Gubin, Chief of the Political Directorate of the Baltic Military District and Member of the Central Committee of the Lithuanian Communist Party, *Kommunist* [Vil'nius], No. 4, April 1972, p. 32.

[138]General of the Army A. Yepishev, "On the Question of Morale, Political and Psychological Troop Training," in *Vazhnyi Faktor Boegotovnosti* (An Important Factor in Combat Readiness), (Moscow: Voenizdat, 1972), p. 7.

From the standpoint of the Soviet system, the Kremlin uses the alleged Western ideological offensive and its own vigilance and indoctrination campaign to justify intensification of its various restrictive and control measures. Safeguarding the Soviet system, according to a major article in *Trud*, is required not only of officials of the party and government but also of every Soviet citizen: "The Soviet people's sacred obligation is to guard reliably party, state, and military secrets, display political awareness in appraising international events and facts from daily life, strengthen labor discipline, strictly guard and account for secret materials, look after personal documents, and firmly and unswervingly do what is entrusted to a citizen in the Motherland."[139] The enemy is said by Soviet commentators to be especially interested in matters related to military-industrial potential. To achieve his purposes, he not only employs various clandestine methods and direct scientific and technical contacts, but also makes great use of "open sources." A vast network of US specialists, backed by specialists in other Western countries, is pictured as engaged in "processing, analyzing and compiling official data drawn from newspapers, journals, books, manuals, the publications of academies of sciences and of scientific research institutes, dissertations, statistical administration reports, government resolutions, the recording of radio and television broadcasts, and also talks by radiotelephone to troop units, geological parties, scientific expeditions, construction sites, and so forth."[140] Soviet citizens are warned "most categorically" that the misuse of open sources of information "represents a serious danger" to the state. While it is impossible to renounce altogether scientific and technical publications, "it is within our power . . . to reduce the damage inflicted by them on our country's interest."[141] To this end, attention is constantly called to the necessity under conditions of increased interchanges with the West for strictest regard to the decree, first adopted in 1947, "On Liability for Divulging State Secrets."[142] This decree defines as a state secret all information of a direct military character, a fantastic range of information of an economic character, information on discoveries, inventions and improvements of both a military and nonmilitary character, and so on.[143]

Scientific and technical personnel of all pursuits and at all levels are especially admonished to avoid any unnecessary revelations not only through publications but also through "blabbering" in contacts with foreigners either at

---

[139]F. Nikitin, "Our Civilian Duty," *Trud*, November 26, 1970.
[140]F. Sergeyev, "Without Leaving the Study," *Nedelia*, No. 47, November 16-22, 1970.
[141]*Ibid.*
[142]Nikitin, *op. cit.*
[143]On this decree see Foy D. Kohler, *Understanding the Russians: A Citizen's Primer* (New York: Harper and Row, 1970), pp. 96-98.

home or abroad:[144] "Unfortunately, blabbers, gullible people, drunkards, and people with poor moral qualities are still encountered among us. . . . Blabbers are incapable of keeping thoughts and information secret, and hence hostile intelligence services have long sought them out and pinned great hopes on their loquaciousness."[145]

Aside from exercising more effective control over the dissemination of information by scientists and technical personnel, the Soviet leadership has used the "ideological offensive" of the West as justification for greatly extending and tightening direct party control over all aspects of scientific-technical work in the USSR. The 24th Congress of the CPSU accorded primary party organizations the right of control over the administration of all scientific-research institutes and higher schools.[146] While a number of objectives were intended to be served by this far-reaching measure, one of the most important was clearly to achieve greater "ideological purity" within the scientific-technological community.

> Particular significance in the ideological work of the party organization of the scientific institutions attaches to the scientific workers' education in the spirit of militant implacability toward any manifestation of bourgeois ideology. It is important always to remember that our class enemy—imperialism with its anticommunist ideology—uses our slightest miscalculations to its own ends. An underestimation of the danger of bourgeois ideology and revisionism is inadmissible. Experience shows that the poisonous seeds of ideological hesitations, indifference to politics and lack of principle can grow up on this soil.[147]

A number of particular scientific institutes, including that with which "dissident" minded physicist Andrei Sakharov is associated, have been singled out for special attention with respect to ideological laxity.[148] Also Soviet leaders at the highest level have called on various institutes and organizations having to do with the social sciences for a new order of ideological devotion and effectiveness, particularly with regard to dealing with the new Western theories regarding convergence.[149]

---

[144]See Mose L. Harvey, Leon Goure and Vladimir Prokofieff, *Science and Technology as an Instrument of Soviet Policy* (Monographs in International Affairs, Center for Advanced International Studies, University of Miami, 1972, pp. 90-92.

[145]Nikitin, *op. cit.*

[146]See Harvey, Goure and Prokofieff, *op. cit.*, pp. 80-84, for a full discussion of this important decision.

[147]V. Yagodkin (Secretary of the Moscow CPSU Gorkom), "Party Life in the Scientific Collective," *Kommunist*, No. 11, July 1972.

[148]*Ibid.* Also see the *Pravda* editorial "Implacability Toward Bourgeois Ideology," November 23, 1970.

[149]See for example, M.A. Suslov, "The Social Sciences are the Party's Combat Weapon in the Building of Communism," *Kommunist*, No. 1, January 1972 [78]; B.N. Ponomarev, "Topical Problems in the Theory of the World Revolutionary Process," *Kommunist*, No. 15, October 1971 [70]; *Kommunist* editorial, "The Unity of Communists' Convictions and Actions," No. 13, September 1971 [65]; M.A. Suslov, Pre-election Speech in Leningrad, *Pravda*, June 10, 1970 [38]; and N.V. Podgornyi, Speech at General Meeting of the USSR Academy of Sciences, *Vestnik Akademii Nauk SSSR*, No. 5, May 1970 [34].

Meanwhile, of course, the leadership uses the ideological situation as justification for ever tightening control, to the point in some instances of new levels of repression, in the literary-artistic area.[150]

The emergence of "new stratagems" in imperialism's (the US) drive against the USSR, at the center of which Moscow places "the theories of convergence," has provided the Kremlin with what appears to be a welcome opportunity to place all its enemies in one basket, or to tar them all with one brush so to speak. It is not only that, as was emphasized in Section II above, "convergence" is made to encompass a wide range of different and sometimes conflicting specific theories, as for example those of John Kenneth Galbraith, Zbigniew Brzezinski, and Herbert Marcuse. It is also that any activity or movement which the Soviet authorities oppose at home or abroad is in one way or another tied in with the objectives and methods of this "new form of anticommunism." "Unquestionably," according to Soviet spokesmen, "the theory of convergence is influencing the ideological positions of various types of renegades from Marxism-Leninism."

It supplies the right-wing renegades with an entire assortment of economic models "combining" socialism with capitalism. As to the "left-wing" revisionists, vulgarly interpreting socialism in a bureaucratic-barracks spirit, they essentially act as procurers of additional arguments used by the bourgeois theoreticians on the unacceptability of socialism "in its pure aspect." Meanwhile, like the supporters of the theory of convergence, they slanderously depict the development of the USSR and the other socialist countries.[151]

Revisionism, it is said, "has never been original or self-dependent." It has always "shone with reflected light while borrowing and adopting bourgeois ideologies."[152] The lot of the modern revisionists, "as of all renegades who betray the cause of the working class," is "a downward path from ideological capitulation to capitalism to ideological sabotage against socialism."[153]

The "cohorts of anticommunism" are presently attempting "to activate all of the former ideological tendencies hostile to Leninism: Trotskyism, Menshevism, anarchism, and so forth."[154] But their prime aim in their "ideological crusade" is to join forces "with the Peking leaders."

The anti-Sovietism of the Peking leaders naturally brought them to the anticommunist mud just as the partisans of "Human socialism." Such is the logic of the class struggle which is incompatible with the position of a detached onlooker with various types of agreements with imperialism at the expense of betraying the interests of the working class of all toilers.

---

[150]See for example *Pravda* editorial, "Pressing Tasks of Ideological Work," July 8, 1972. [88]
[151]*Kommunist*, No. 13, September 1971. [64]
[152]V. Cheprakov, "The Monopolies' Advocates," *Izvestiia*, October 23, 1971. [69]
[153]*Ibid*.
[154]Kortunov, *op. cit.* [35]

We are convinced of this by the fate of the "dissidents" and the "liberals," who began with the revision of Marxism and ended with the transfer of support to the anticommunists, to the enemies of the working class. We are convinced of this also by the current position of the Peking leadership, which is forming an alliance with USA imperialism also in the struggle against the national-liberation movement and in the ideological war against the USSR, other socialist countries, and against the international communist and workers' movement.[155]

Of another order is the Soviet attempt to tie into "the anticommunist" efforts of the West any stirrings among ethnic minorities in the Soviet Union. The Americans are said to be especially diligent in their efforts to stir up and capitalize on separatist "nationalist" sentiments within the USSR, as well as in the socialist world generally, [156] as, for example, through using Ukrainian Émigré organizations.[157] These and other such organizations, pretending a "blood brother" relationship with particular ethnic groups within the USSR, play upon such things as the legitimate aspirations of these groups to maintain their distinctive "national culture." Among other things, "they counterpose any work of the literary and artistic representative of our national republics, work imbued with pride for their [own] people, to internationalism and Soviet power."[158] The object, according to Soviet authorities, is to exacerbate and exploit "any manifestation of bourgeois nationalism, race hatred, and chauvinism."[159] "It is precisely on nationalist trends, particularly those taking the form of anti-Sovietism, that bourgeois propaganda is now gambling most enthusiastically in the struggle against socialism and the communist movement."[160]

Special emphasis is placed on Zionism as a tool of the US in its design to undermine Soviet society. "Zionism acts as one of the militant detachments of international imperialism, and leans on many different organizations in many countries."[161] The "international complicated system of Zionist organizations and their plurality and superficial diversity cover up a giant capitalist enterprise created on a world scale,"[162] which is said to be dominated by the United States and to work in close collaboration with the CIA.[163] The organizations are undertaking to step up sharply "anti-Soviet and anti-socialist subversive

[155]V. Bol'shakov, "The Subversive Strategy of 'the War of the Minds,' " *Pravda*, January 13, 1972. [77]

[156]Tomashevskiy, *op. cit.* [42]

[157]V. Bol'shakov, "Pandora's Box," Part 2, *Komsomol'skaia Pravda*, August 26, 1970. [40]

[158]*Ibid.*

[159]Ye. Yevseyev, "The Zionists' Ideological Master Keys," *Sovetskaia Belorussiia*, August 18, 1972.

[160]Brezhnev, Report to the 24th Party Congress, *Pravda*, March 31, 1971. [55]

[161]M. Mitin, "Zionism: A Variety of Chauvinism and Racism," *Pravda*, December 18, 1971.

[162]Yevseyev, *op. cit.*

[163]V. Bol'shakov, "Zionism Under the Banner of Anti-Communism," *Pravda*, January 16, 1972.

activities." They spend "huge sums" on these activities and on "evolving allegedly new 'theories' of building socialism on an anti-Marxist basis, that is theories related to 'convergence.' "[164] The Zionists, it is charged, "have fabricated a so-called Jewish question in the USSR, crudely distorting the position of Jews in our country";[165] they stage provocations against Soviet institutions abroad . . . hold noisy anti-Soviet gatherings, pass resolutions calling for an all-out crusade against the USSR."[166] "What is more," the Zionists are seeking to recruit anti-Soviet forces within the USSR itself; they admit to the aim "to penetrate the structure" of the Soviet state.[167] In striving "to establish connections between Israel and the Jewish population" in the USSR "the Zionists stop at nothing."[168] The Executive Committee of the World Zionist Organization (WWZO) in collaboration with the CIA "has sanctioned a campaign of subversive measures . . . against the Soviet Union." The calculation, it is said, is "to establish some sort of Zionist 'underground' in the USSR . . . [with] particular attention to work among young people of Jewish origin—millions of dollars have been allocated from WZO coffers to organize this infamous campaign."[169]

The Soviet authorities charge that the US similarly seeks to exploit other religious groups in its efforts to penetrate the USSR. According to the Chairman of the USSR Council of Ministers Committee for Religious Affairs, V.A. Kuroyedov, religions and churches of all denominations "are assigned a large role in implementing the policy of building bridges . . . with the aim of 'diluting' and 'softening' communism." Large research centers, Kuroyedov says, have been set up in the US and other countries "to study religious attitudes in the USSR," and "all kinds of international organizations 'for the defense of Christian civilization,' saving the Orthodox churches of the USSR from annihilation, and other [such causes] are springing up like mushrooms."

> The purpose of all these activities is on the one hand to form public opinion in foreign countries against the Soviet Union, and on the other to exert a definite, that is anti-Soviet, influence over the believers in our country and to influence them to religious fanaticism.[170]

While insisting that "the clergy as a whole support the Soviet government and foreign policy," Kuroyedov admonished that "as they say, it is a small

[164]*Ibid.*
[165]Mitin, *op. cit.*
[166]V. Bol'shakov, "Zionism Under the Banner of Anti-Communism," *Pravda*, January 16, 1972.
[167]*Ibid.*
[168]TASS International Service in English, January 17, 1972.
[169]V. Bol'shakov, "Zionism Under the Banner of Anti-Communism," *Pravda*, January 16, 1972.
[170]V.A. Kuroyedov, "The Instigators," *Izvestiia*, October 18, 1969.

flock that does not have a black sheep." There are among us, he added, "church officials and officials close to the church who, for careerist, mercenary, and sometimes to a certain extent, political aims, infringe the legislation on cults and try to arouse dissatisfaction . . . among the believers." As an example, Kuroyedov cited "a group of so-called 'initiators' who tried . . . to seize control of the Evangelical Christian Baptist Church . . . [and who] came up with an adverturist program which demanded abolition of all the laws governing religious cults and the atheistic education of students and unlimited freedom to propagate religion everywhere, including streets, squares, parks."[171]

Another aspect of Moscow's use of "convergence" theories and "bridge-building" policies to its own end involves an exercise in what might be called "reverse English." While firmly rejecting the validity of these theories and policies and generally treating them as diabolical in purpose and use, the Soviets profess to see an opportunity to turn to "progressive benefit" the concern of certain types of Western intellectuals to find theories and policies, no matter how fallacious in the Soviet view, intended to lead to stable peace and cooperation between East and West. In this connection, Soviet analysts draw distinctions between the motives of various Western proponents of convergence and bridge-building:

> . . . some do not care about ideological conciliation. For them it is only a tactic, a clever gimmick for the purpose of weakening the influence of communist ideology in the bourgeois countries and to camouflage ideological subversion against the socialist countries. Others, sincerely seeking a path to firm peace, mistakenly see it in a "common ideology." Among them are many prominent scientists, partisans of peace, opponents of militarism and war from among the worldly and religious pacifists. It is important to note these distinctions.[172]

Thus, for example, it is said that "the position occupied by J. Galbraith does not cause indignation in itself," since his basic aim is "to refute the idea of an inevitable clash conditioned by the difference between capitalism and socialism, to put an end to the arms race, and to 'give impetus' to widespread international cooperation." However, "blurring the differences between the two socioeconomic systems does not promote the implementation of this task, sows illusions and vain hopes, and ultimately makes peaceful coexistence more difficult."[173] Still, these "progressive" bourgeois elements "who seek to find new approaches to peaceful coexistence" are seen as offering promising targets for Soviet influence. A Decree of the Presidium of the

---

[171]*Ibid.*

[172]Paiusov, *op. cit.* [63]

[173]Gromeka and Vasilyev, *op. cit.* [52]

Academy of Sciences of the USSR quite openly instructed the Academy's Institute of Philosophy to pursue:

> research on social differentiation taking place among the scientific intelligentsia of capitalist countries, the uncovering of the possibility of attracting to the side of the progressive forces its best representatives, the working out of a system of convincing arguments for this wavering part of the intelligentsia which can exert a real influence on its spiritual development.[174]

As explained by *Voprosy Filosofii*, "the Leninist idea about the needs to realize in this or that form a 'union' with the progressive . . . representatives of bourgeois culture remains extremely urgent also in this day." A number of circumstances "push many of the best representatives of the intellectuals, scientists and philosophers toward Marxism." It is the responsibility of Soviet Marxists "to assist them in understanding the complex collisions in the contemporary world . . . and to carry on with them a dialogue which attracts them to the side of fighters against imperialism."[175]

In any event, according to Soviet commentators, Western intellectuals will inevitably come to realize that their theories and hopes for "convergence" of the systems are false, that efforts at rationalizing and "humanizing" the capitalist system are doomed to failure, and that the Soviet Union will win its struggle with capitalism and build the triumphant communist society. Thus, the intellectuals will increasingly come to identify with the Soviet line:

> The progressive intelligentsia in the bourgeois countries is one of the detachments of the great army of liberation and peace. It can follow no other path than that of alliance with the international working class which struggles under the banner of the Marxist-Leninist ideology.[176]

---

[174]Decree of the Presidium of the Academy of Sciences of the USSR, November 27, 1969; in *Voprosy Filosofii* (Questions of Philosophy), No. 3, 1970. [20]

[175]Editorial, "The Philosophical Bequest of V.I. Lenin and the Contemporary Period," *Voprosy Filosofii*, No. 3, 1972, pp. 6-7.

[176]Paiusov, *op. cit.* [63]

# CONVERGENCE
## OF COMMUNISM AND CAPITALISM
# THE SOVIET VIEW

## PART TWO: DOCUMENTATION

# Soviet Periodicals Cited in Documentation

*Ekonomicheskaia Gazeta (Economic Gazette)*—Moscow—Weekly economic newspaper of the CC-CPSU.

*International Affairs*—Moscow—English-language monthly journal of the All-Union Society "Znaniye" (Knowledge).

*Izvestiia (News)*—Moscow—Daily of the Soviet government.

*Komsomol'skaia Pravda (Komsomol Truth)*—Moscow—Daily of the Communist Youth League (Komsomol) Central Committee.

*Kommunist (Communist)*—Moscow—Major theoretical journal of the Central Committee of the Communist Party of the Soviet Union (CC-CPSU), published 18 times per year.

*Kommunist Vooruzhennykh Sil (Communist of the Armed Forces)* —Moscow—Semimonthly military-political journal of the Main Political Administration of the Soviet Army and Navy.

*Krasnaia Zvezda (Red Star)*—Moscow—Daily of the Soviet Ministry of Defense.

*Partiinaia Zhizn' (Party Life)*—Moscow—Semimonthly political journal of the CC-CPSU.

*Pravda (Truth)*—Moscow—Authoritative daily of the CC-CPSU.

*Pravda Ukrainy (Ukraine Truth)*—Kiev—Daily of the Ukrainian Communist Party and government.

*Sel'skaia Zhizn' (Rural Life )*–Moscow—Daily newspaper of the CC-CPSU.

*Sovetskaia Latviia (Soviet Latvia)*—Riga—Daily of the Latvian Communist Party and government.

*Sovetskaia Rossiia (Soviet Russia)*—Moscow—Daily of the Russian Republic Bureau of the CC-CPSU.

*S.Sh.A.: Ekonomika, Politika, Ideologiia (USA: Economics, Politics, Ideology)*-Moscow–Monthly journal of the Institute of the United States, USSR Academy of Sciences.

*Vestnik Akademii Nauk SSSR (Herald of the Academy of Sciences of the USSR)*—Moscow—Monthly journal of the USSR Academy of Sciences.

*Voprosy Ekonomiki (Questions of Economics)*—Moscow—Monthly journal of the Institute of Economics of the USSR Academy of Sciences.

*Voprosy Filosofii (Questions of Philosophy)*—Moscow—Monthly journal of the Institute of Philosophy of the USSR Academy of Sciences.

*Za Rubezhom (Life Abroad)*—Moscow—Weekly newspaper of the USSR Union of Journalists.

**1. L. F. IL'ICHEV,** *CC-CPSU Secretary until 1965, speech at CC-CPSU Plenum,* **PRAVDA,** *June 19, 1963:* Some time ago there appeared a theory according to which socialism and capitalism, despite their inherent difference, would develop in the same direction, that "the forced economic imperatives of universal industrial development" little by little will lead to the "hybridization" of the two systems, to their "synthesis," to the formation of a unified "mixed" society by means of "the internal alteration of socialism" and some "modernization of capitalism." Before us is blunt social demagogy. The ideologists of imperialism speculate on socialist terminology, they are not beyond "appropriating" some ideas of socialism in order to trick the toiling people, to lead them astray with pseudo-socialist slogans, since they do not have in their hearts the positive ideals which could promise the people any prospects of hope toward the future. Like every reactionary concept, these "newest" fabrications of anticommunism do not have any future whatever.

**2. L. I. BREZHNEV,** *Central Committee accountability report to the 23rd CPSU Congress,* **PRAVDA,** *March 31, 1966:* Combatting bourgeois ideology, revisionism, dogmatism and reformism is of the utmost importance. We should never lose sight of the fact that imperialism is our class enemy. It conducts subversive activities against the socialist system, its principles, its ideology and its morals. The giant imperialist propaganda machine corrupts the individual and attempts to distract the people from politics. In all circumstances, the struggle against bourgeois ideology must be uncompromising, because it is a class struggle, a struggle for man, for his dignity and freedom, a struggle to invigorate the positions of socialism and communism, in the interests of the international working class.

. . . . . . . . . . . . . . . . . . . . . . . . . . . . . . . . . . . . . . . . . . . . . . . . . . . . . . . . . . . . . . .

Marxism-Leninism took shape and developed as a science in irreconcilable struggle against all sorts of distortions, against the ideology of the exploiting classes. It has always deeply analyzed objective historical processes and the class struggle, worked out the theory and tactics of revolution on this basis, and lit the way for the building of a new society. In this lies the vital force, the immortality of the great communist teaching.

**3. CENTRAL COMMITTEE OF THE CPSU,** *Theses commemorating the 50th anniversary of the October Revolution,* **PRAVDA,** *June 26, 1967:* The ideological struggle in the world arena is growing increasingly sharper. The greater the success scored by socialism, the deeper become the contradictions of world capitalism and the more refined become the methods used by the imperialists in their struggle against communism. Bourgeois propaganda has been trying to obscure the principal social antagonisms and evils of the modern capitalist world, to dull the political awareness and paralyze the working people's will in the struggle for socialism. Imperialist ideology has been trying to inject the idea of individualism into the minds of the masses, to distract them from politics and the solution of fundamental social problems. Its stake is on a revival of the prejudices and remnants of the past in the minds of men. It is an important task of communist education to fight the influence of alien morals and traditions and to overcome the negative phenomena in the thinking and behavior of men.

There can be no question of neutrality in the struggle against bourgeois ideology or anticommunism. The struggle against bourgeois ideology and anticommunism is one of the most acute aspects of the class struggle; it is a struggle for man, and for the triumph of freedom and progress for mankind.


*4. V. KORTUNOV, ZA RUBEZHOM, No. 39, September 1967, summarized by MOSCOW TASS INTERNATIONAL SERVICE, September 22, 1967:* "The closer we approach the 50th anniversary of the Great October Socialist Revolution the more heated the ideological struggle around this historical event becomes," writes V. Kortunov in the 39th issue of *Life Abroad.* In his article, he analyzes the reasons and aims of this anti-Soviet and anticommunist campaign mounted by imperialism on the threshold of October.

On the eve of the 50th anniversary of the October Revolution, Kortunov remarks, literally all sides of the communist ideology and the socialist realization are under fire; the economy, the state structure, culture and foreign policy. Anticommunism is throwing all its resources into the fray. Everything is mobilized in order to use all means to distort the true meaning of the events of the past half century, blacken the great cause of socialism, and distract the attention of the world public from the very fact of the 50th anniversary of the Socialist Revolution. The leaders of the anti-Soviet and anticommunist campaign are the high governmental organs of the United States, West Germany, and other imperialist powers.

The most fashionable conception of modern anticommunism, writes Kortunov, is the theory of so-called "convergence"—according to which socialism and capitalism will, in the course of time, allegedly lose their antagonistic character and start to evolve toward each other. From this antiscientific reasoning, the authors of the theory of "convergence" draw a conclusion concerning the necessity of spreading the principle of peaceful coexistence to the field of ideology.

"Talks about the rapprochement of socialism and capitalism," says the article in this connection, "are nothing but camouflage with which they wish to hide the true class aim of imperialism, imperialism's treasured dream of breaking loose and absorbing socialist society."

The efforts of those who direct the ideological machine of imperialism are directed toward proving that Marxism has allegedly become obsolete, and is not suitable for the 20th century; that Leninism, having played a definite historical role in Russia, has turned out to be unsuitable for developed capitalist countries, the author continues. Any new turn of events, any new word in the creative development of Marxism-Leninism, is treated as a "crisis" in communist outlook. The actions of any apostates of Marxism, those of the Mao Tse-tung group in China, for example, are depicted as a "crisis" for communist ideology as a whole.

. . . . . . . . . . . . . . . . . . . . . . . . . . . . . . . . . . . . . . . . . . . . . . . . . . . . . . . . . . . . . . . . . . . . .

All these arguments, Kortunov writes, are completely included in the general theory of the "convergence" of the two systems, and are, in essence, brought into the open for the propaganda concerning the eternal nature of the principles of capitalism. To a large extent they are intended for the countries of Asia, Africa, and Latin America, as if to say to their population: Why must you strive toward socialism when even its citadel, the USSR, is compelled to return to "the proven practice of capitalist management" after half a century of experimentation?

5. *L. I. BREZHNEV, report at the joint jubilee meeting of the Central Committee of the CPSU, the Supreme Soviet of the USSR, and the Supreme Soviet of the Russian SFSR, in commemoration of the 50th anniversary of the October Revolution, PRAVDA, November 4, 1967:* Pressured by the class struggle, imperialism is maneuvering, making partial concessions and widely resorting to social demagogy. The aggravation of inner contradictions and socialism's achievements in the competition with capitalism are compelling the bourgeoisie to lean more and more heavily on state-monopoly regulation of the economy in order to mitigate crisis phenomena and maintain rates of production growth. As it loses its colonies, imperialism switches to more crafty and subtle methods of exploiting other peoples. It spares no effort or resources in the battle for the minds of people. Socialism's growing influence is making the imperialists constantly adapt their ideological weapon, their propaganda to the changing situation.

All politically conscious participants in the revolutionary movement take into account these phenomena in the camp of their adversary and the complexity of the situation in which the class and liberation struggle is taking place today. They chart the most effective ways of this struggle and work to rally all the forces into a united anti-imperialist front.

43

**6.  Lieutenant Colonel D. VOLKOGONOV, Candidate of Historical Sciences,
"The Most Critical Front of the Class Struggle," KRASNAIA ZVEZDA,
November 14, 1968:** The most important feature of the modern tactics of
imperialism is to be found in the fact that now one rarely encounters open
appeals to overthrow socialism. On the other hand, with the aim of restoring
capitalism, they are making attacks on the leading role of the communist
parties, the alliance of the working class and the peasantry, and on the dictatorship of the proletariat. The policy for weakening the positions of the world
socialist system and tearing away its individual links has found its most cynical
expression in Bonn's so-called new Eastern policy and in the "bridge-
building" policy proclaimed in Washington, London, and other capitals of
the NATO countries.

Bourgeois ideologists are advancing every conceivable pseudoscientific
theory for the sake of achieving their aims and for the struggle with revolutionary ideology. The most fashionable of them is the theory of rapprochement,
capitalism's "convergence" with socialism. Here they fuse such varieties of
it as the "mixed society," the "industrial society," the theories of "democratic capitalism," a "state of universal prosperity," and so forth.

"Theories" have appeared in the West which maintain that the growth of
technical opportunities for intercourse and information is leading to a "de-
ideologization" of society and appearance of man's uniform (regardless of
his social system) technical rational thinking, "free of ideology."

This theory has but a single aim—to hypnotize peoples' class and social
vigilance, create the illusion that the path toward truth lies in renouncing
any class position, and attempt to drag "the Trojan horse" into the heart
of red ideology and to paralyze the revolutionizing influence of Marxism-
Leninism.

**7.  Academician ANDREI D. SAKHAROV, PROGRESS, COEXISTENCE
AND INTELLECTUAL FREEDOM, translated by The New York Times (New
York: W. W. Norton and Co., 1968), pp. 81-85:** Having examined in the first
part of this essay the development of mankind according to the worse alternative, leading to annihilation, we must now attempt, even schematically, to
suggest the better alternative. (The author concedes the primitiveness of his
attempts at prognostication, which requires the joint efforts of many specialists, and here, even more than elsewhere, invites positive criticism.)

In the first stage, a growing ideological struggle in the socialist countries
between Stalinist and Maoist forces, on the one hand, and the realistic forces
of leftist Leninist Communists (and leftist Westerners), on the other, will lead
to a deep ideological split on an international, national, and intraparty scale.

In the Soviet Union and other socialist countries, this process will lead first to a multiparty system (here and there) and to acute ideological struggle and discussions, and then to the ideological victory of the realists, affirming the policy of increasing peaceful coexistence, strengthening democracy, and expanding economic reforms (1960-80). The dates reflect the most optimistic unrolling of events.

The author, incidentally, is not one of those who considers the multiparty system to be an essential stage in the development of the socialist system or, even less, a panacea for all ills, but he assumes that in some cases a multiparty system may be an inevitable consequence of the course of events when a ruling Communist party refuses for one reason or another to rule by the scientific democratic method required by history.

In the second stage, persistent demands for social progress and peaceful coexistence in the United States and other capitalist countries, and pressure exerted by the example of the socialist countries and by internal progressive forces (the working class and the intelligentsia) will lead to the victory of the leftist reformist wing of the bourgeoisie, which will begin to implement a program of rapprochement (convergence) with socialism, i.e., social progress, peaceful coexistence, and collaboration with socialism on a world scale and changes in the structure of ownership. This phase includes an expanded role for the intelligentsia and an attack on the forces of racism and militarism (1972-85). (The various stages overlap.)

. . . . . . . . . . . . . . . . . . . . . . . . . . . . . . . . . . . . . . . . . . . . . . . . . . . . . . . . . . . . . .

In the fourth stage, the socialist convergence will reduce differences in social structure, promote intellectual freedom, science, and economic progress and lead to creation of a world government and the smoothing of national contradictions (1980-2000). During this period decisive progress can be expected in the field of nuclear power, both on the basis of uranium and thorium and, probably, deuterium and lithium.

. . . . . . . . . . . . . . . . . . . . . . . . . . . . . . . . . . . . . . . . . . . . . . . . . . . . . . . . . . . . . .

If such an all-encompassing scientific and technological revolution, promising uncounted benefits for mankind, is to be possible and safe, it will require the greatest possible scientific foresight and care and concern for human values of a moral, ethical, and personal character. (I touched briefly on the danger of a thoughtless bureaucratic use of the scientific and technological revolution in a divided world in the section on "Dangers," but could add a great deal more.) Such a revolution will be possible and safe only under highly intelligent worldwide guidance.

45

The foregoing program presumes:

(a) worldwide interest in overcoming the present divisions;

(b) the expectation that modifications in both the socialist and capitalist countries will tend to reduce contradictions and differences;

(c) worldwide interest of the intelligentsia, the working class, and other progressive forces in a scientific democratic approach to politics, economics, and culture;

(d) the absence of insurmountable obstacles to economic development in both world economic systems that might otherwise lead inevitably into a blind alley, despair, and adventurism.

Every honorable and thinking person who has not been poisoned by narrow-minded indifference will seek to insure that future development will be along the lines of the better alternative. However only broad, open discussion, without the pressure of fear and prejudice, will help the majority to adopt the correct and best course of action.

*8. Academician Iu. FRANTSEV, "One Leninist Page,"* **IZVESTIIA,** *January 21, 1969:* In the present plans of the bourgeois politicians and ideologists, a particular place is given to the rightwing and "leftwing" revisionists who verbally adhere to Marxism-Leninism, but in fact reject the most important principles of this revolutionary teaching and replace it by reactionary bourgeois ideological dogmas which are veiled by "Marxist" phrases. Under the pretext of "improving" Marxism-Leninism and "liberalizing" socialism, the revisionists are essentially preaching reconciliation with the bourgeoisie, with its class interests, and with bourgeois ideology in the spirit of the convergency theory—the rapprochement of capitalism and socialism—which is in fashion today in the West, and urge reconciliation with prejudices and reactionary fantasies.

Nevertheless, a serious miscalculation lies in all the imperialist maneuvers and subterfuges, and in their plans for ideological diversions against the socialist countries and the revolutionary movement as a whole. First, they do not take into account that the struggle against capitalism is a historic necessity of social development. The imperialists' maneuvers can delay this process in this or that of its links, but they are incapable of "reversing" it, just as they cannot "eliminate" those reasons which during many years have prepared and which now stimulate the growth of the revolutionary forces.

*9. Academician Ye. M. ZHUKOV, "Leninism and the Present Day,"* **VESTNIK AKADEMII NAUK SSSR,** *No. 1, January 1969, pp. 18-26:* Bourgeois and reformist sociologists try to deny the very existence of the proletariat drawing falsified conclusions from the fact of structural changes taking place in the working class. In fact those structural changes indicate something altogether different—an unceasing expansion of the ranks of the working class, that is, in the final account a continuous growth of its proportion in contemporary society. An objective process of elevation of the role of the working class on both national and international scales is occurring before our eyes.

The "theory" of the "deproletarianization" of the workers in highly developed industrial countries which is being spread by the bourgeois ideologists passes off what is desired by the capitalists as the real thing. In spite of all the hopes to dissolve the working class into a more amorphous social stratum, to "divorce" its petty-bourgeois mass and by the same token weaken its revolutionary potential—none succeeds in "calling off" the class struggle. The class struggle takes place in very varied forms. One must note that strikes—the classical form of the struggle of the proletariat against exploiters —shake the soil of all capitalist countries, including the most developed.

Unavailing also are the attempts of bourgeois ideologists to use the scientific and technical revolution to weaken the class self-consciousness of the workers, primarily on this basis, that it leads to an obliteration of the boundaries between workers and the engineering and technical intelligentsia. However, under the conditions of the capitalist world the scientific and technical revolution is turning more and more in another direction. It leads to the ejection of large masses of the working people from the process of production, to a growth of unemployment and, in the final account, an aggravation of the class struggle. No "refutations" can shake the truth of this position, that capitalist productive relations have been transformed into shackles on the development of productive forces.

Objective economic laws intrinsic to the bourgeois system make a radical change of its exploiting nature by reformist methods impossible. At the same time it is obvious, however, that the working class and all the working people are deeply interested in the implementation of reforms which ease the conditions of organization and the struggle of the masses. Therefore the working class regards the struggle for reform within the framework of the capitalist system as one of the means helping a successful struggle for socialism. Under the conditions of contemporary state-monopolistic capitalism the working class, at the head of all the antimonopolistic forces, is securing a curb of the anti-popular policy of the monopolies, the elimination of the commanding position in the life of a country, and replacement of the power of monopolies by democratic conditions as an important prerequisite for acceleration of the socialist revolution.

The mission of the revolutionary replacement of capitalism by a new social order has been entrusted by the entire objective course of the historical process to the working class, which emerges and develops simultaneously with the emergence of industry—a necessary material prerequisite of socialism.

. . . . . . . . . . . . . . . . . . . . . . . . . . . . . . . . . . . . . . . . . . . . . . . . . . . . . . . . . . . . . . .

Leninism is the sharpest weapon of the working class. It is natural that the forces of international reaction are deeply interested in depriving the proletariat and all the working people of that weapon, in distorting the principles of Leninism, and in weakening its effect on the world-wide revolutionary process.

The open and hidden opponents of communism and their willing or unwilling allies—opportunists of both the right and the left—are intensifying their attacks on Leninism, having become aware of its very great revolutionizing and organizing importance in the political and ideological struggle that is taking place. Attempts are being made from various sides to discredit Leninism, to interfere with its effect on the broad masses of the working people and to poison them with the venom of skepticism and disbelief in socialist ideals.

The name of Lenin is infinitely dear to all progressive mankind. Therefore far from always do the enemies of Leninism speak up openly against Lenin. Their most widespread method is to represent the fundamental positions of Lenin as obsolete and unacceptable in the present situation.

In one case it is asserted that the changes which have occurred in the world since Lenin's death allegedly have led to a weakening of the class contradictions and even to a gradual obliteration of the boundaries between capitalism and socialism. The bourgeois liars and their yes-men from among the revisionists assert that within the capitalist society elements of socialism, of a planned economy are growing, that a transformation of capitalism is occurring, that capitalism is losing its negative qualities and, consequently, the need for a socialist revolution, for dictatorship of the proletariat and for a revolutionary party of the working class "disappears."

. . . . . . . . . . . . . . . . . . . . . . . . . . . . . . . . . . . . . . . . . . . . . . . . . . . . . . . . . . . . . . .

All the efforts of nationalistic propaganda deriving from bourgeois, reformist and revisionist elements are directed toward the alienation of the socialist states, toward attempts to transform nationalism into the principal means of internal ideological "erosion" of socialist collaboration.

10. *Professor E. MODRZHINSKAYA, "Anti-Communism Disguised as Evolutionism," INTERNATIONAL AFFAIRS (Moscow), No. 1, January 1969, pp. 15-20:* The purely negative approach to Socialism and the denial of its achievements are no longer possible, but admission of its successes, and consequently of the failure of the long anticommunist hysteria, would be tan-

tamount to ideological surrender, and that is a thing imperialism cannot afford. Hence the appearance in the late 1950s and especially the 1960s of new imperialist doctrines purporting to show the ways of further development of the two worlds and the outcome of the competition between capitalism and Socialism. These were inevitably theories of social regress, because bourgeois political thinkers cannot admit any other prospects than the restoration of capitalism in the Socialist countries. But these theories of social regress contain some curious ingredients reflecting the present stage in the struggle between the two systems and the present condition of imperialism in the world.

. . . . . . . . . . . . . . . . . . . . . . . . . . . . . . . . . . . . . . . . . . . . . . . . . . . . . . . . . . . . .

Perhaps the most important thing is that they insist on the inevitable convergence of capitalism and Socialism in the future, thereby paving the ideological way for subversion against Socialism.

Among these theories are the theory of stages in economic growth propounded by Walt Rostow (a well known US reactionary politician and sociologist); the doctrine of the single industrial society, whose most famous propagandist is the reactionary French publicist and sociologist Raymond Aron; the convergence doctrine, and—the capstone of them all—the theory of evolution, which has been elaborated in greatest detail by Zbigniew Brzezinski, Director of the Research Institute on Communist Affairs at Columbia University.

These theories differ in line of argument, basic premises and content, but have in common: (1) attempts to provide an alternative to the Marxist-Leninist theory of social development; (2) a pseudo-liberal form; (3) a reactionary anti-Communist essence; and (4) echoes of reformism and Right-wing opportunist revisionism on a number of key questions. Their authors all try to prove that the Socialist countries are evolving towards capitalism and that radical changes are imminent in their sociopolitical system, changes which are presented as a return to capitalism and are welcomed as steps towards "true democracy." It is perhaps the evolution theory which shows this most fully.

. . . . . . . . . . . . . . . . . . . . . . . . . . . . . . . . . . . . . . . . . . . . . . . . . . . . . . . . . . . . .

The subversive anti-Socialist activity which is being carried by the West according to the recipes of the advocates of "convergence," "industrial society," and "evolution"provides fresh evidence that imperialism has not laid down its arms, but, on the contrary, is fighting fiercely to retain its positions. This bears out Lenin's forecast that, in the transition period, the class struggle would be intensified.

. . . . . . . . . . . . . . . . . . . . . . . . . . . . . . . . . . . . . . . . . . . . . . . . . . . . . . . . . . . . .

The events in Czechoslovakia last summer took a turn that gave the impression of the evolution theory on the point of implementation, thereby testifying to the wisdom of its authors. Brzezinski himself hastened to Prague at the invitation of the Czech liberals.

In the circumstances, there was a surfacing of such political "factors" as the counter-revolutionary parties which had been disbanded by the Government of the people and which expressed the interests of the exploiting groups that had lost their economic and political power.

Having surfaced, these "factors" began to operate "after the Brzezinski fashion." Their main slogans were: liberalisation and democratisation of social life, including calls to oust the Communist Party from political life, to liberalise and democratise international relations, including calls for withdrawal from the Warsaw Pact; to liberalise and democratise the economy, including calls to abolish economic planning and introduce free enterprise (at the first stage of evolution, nothing is to be said of a return of the means of production to their former owners).

. . . . . . . . . . . . . . . . . . . . . . . . . . . . . . . . . . . . . . . . . . . . . . . . . . . . . . . . . . . . . . . . . . . . . . . .

The failure of the attempts by anti-Socialist elements to push Czechoslovakia onto the way of evolution from Socialism to capitalism has apparently done nothing to check the proponents of the evolution theory. They cannot admit defeat, for that is tantamount to suicide. They continue their attempts to cause a "quiet counter-revolution" by their own methods.

*11. Major General K. BOCHKAREV, Candidate of Philosophical Sciences, "V. I. Lenin and the Defense of the Achievements of Socialism: The Great International Duty," KRASNAIA ZVEZDA, February 14, 1969:* The essence of the matter is that, first, having thought to effect a "quiet" revolution in the country, the antisocialist forces in Czechoslovakia not only did not rule out armed violence, but with active help from the West—primarily the United States and the German Federal Republic—made strenuous preparations for it. And if the dark plans of internal and external reaction were frustrated, this was due only to the timely and decisive action by the five socialist countries that went to the aid of the Czechoslovak people. Second—and this is no secret either—in the situation obtaining last August in Czechoslovakia, the ideas raised up on the shield of the antisocialist forces served as nothing more than a cover, a smokescreen, for the criminal plans and actions of the counter revolution. And in the face of a direct threat to the cause of socialism, the question is resolved by real opposition to those forces that hide behind this screen and mask themselves with it.

It should also be noted that the imperialists greatly desire to create as much fog as possible around the real purpose of their tactic of "building bridges" with the socialist world. They are trying to depict this as confirmation that they have given up their aggressive course. In fact this tactic is calculated primarily to insure favorable conditions for imperialism in the event of a direct clash with socialism. Only a blind man could not notice that while activating ideological sabotage, the imperialists are at the same time stepping up their military preparations.

A convincing confirmation of this is the present behavior of the Western powers, primarily the United States and the German Federal Republic. Having suffered defeat in their intrigues against Czechoslovakia, they immediately began to engage in frenzied saber rattling and unleashed a provocative fuss near the borders of the socialist community. As is known, the NATO session that took place in Brussels was conducted in an atmosphere of malicious anti-Soviet hooting and under the banner of a further increase in the arms race and an even greater whipping up of international tension. The impudence to which the NATO hawks have aspired is shown by the provocative statements about the so-called "umbrella," in accordance with which several countries not belonging to the bloc were included in the NATO sphere. It is also shown by the recently completed Reforger-1 large-scale NATO maneuvers close to the Czechoslovak border.

Thus the mask of a love of peace is torn from the tactic of "building bridges," and it is revealed in its aggressive nakedness.

*12. RADIO MOSCOW, discussion of the 1968 invasion of Czechoslovakia, February 22, 1969:* The real meaning of the bridgebuilding doctrine was demonstrated prior to and during the events in Czechoslovakia. At that time imperialism employed the entire arsenal of anticommunist devices—a wide propaganda attack on the socialist system in the Czechoslovak Socialist Republic, contacts with the antisocialist forces, promises of loans and economic help, the rattling of sabers on Czechoslovakia's borders, the sending of ideological saboteurs into the country, brazen misinformation on events, and so on.

The actual ultimate aim of bridgebuilding is the restoration of capitalism in the socialist countries. The timely, resolute action of the five fraternal socialist countries that came to the aid of the Czechoslovak people dealt a crushing blow to the imperialist plans to restore capitalism in the Czechoslovak Socialist Republic. The socialist countries showed that they will not tolerate the export of counterrevolution under the guise of bridgebuilding or any undermining of socialist unity.

In the postwar years this sort of thing has happened on many occasions: a new anticommunist doctrine would be adopted as a weapon, only to be modified following its repeated failures, and, finally, with the US ruling circles being forced to publicly announce its bankruptcy. There is no doubt that this will be the case with the bridgebuilding doctrine, now being modernized.

**13. L. I. BREZHNEV, speech at World Conference of Communist and Workers' Parties, PRAVDA, June 8, 1969:** Anticommunism in the capitalist countries is elevated to the level of governmental policy. The stake towards the decay of the communist and the entire revolutionary movement from within now comprises one of the most important directions of the class strategy of imperialism.

. . . . . . . . . . . . . . . . . . . . . . . . . . . . . . . . . . . . . . . . . . . . . . . . . . . . . . . . . . . . . . . . . . . . . .

The hired ideologists of the imperialists have created a special pseudo-culture designed to befuddle the masses, to blunt their social consciousness. And combating its corrupting influence on the working people is an important area of communist work.

Comrades, we have a powerful weapon against bourgeois ideology. That weapon is the ideology of Marxism-Leninism. We know its potency well. We are witness to the fact that our ideas are spreading more and more among the masses. Marxism-Leninism is on the offensive today, and we must develop that offensive to the utmost. It is more important than ever to recall Lenin's warning that any relaxation in ideological work, that standing aloof from it, redoubles the influence of bourgeois ideology.

. . . . . . . . . . . . . . . . . . . . . . . . . . . . . . . . . . . . . . . . . . . . . . . . . . . . . . . . . . . . . . . . . . . . . .

Communists must be in the van of the fight against imperialism in all sectors, including the ideological sector. We are convinced that by concerted efforts imperialism can be decisively defeated in all areas, a world-wide victory thereby achieved for the cause of the working class and all other working people.

**14. Iu. KASHLEV, "Tactics of the Doomed: How the West Tries to Modernize the Old Doctrine of Ideological Subversion," IZVESTIIA, August 19, 1969:** In his speech at the international conference of communist and workers' parties CPSU Central Committee General Secretary L. I. Brezhnev described how in the ideological struggle against communism, "imperialism cannot count on success by openly proclaiming its real aims. It has to create a system of ideological myths, concealing the real meaning of its intentions and lulling people's vigilance."

One of these ideological myths that has been widely advertised by bourgeois propaganda in recent years is the myth that the capitalist world is sincerel seeking to broaden its links with socialist states and proposes building broad "bridges" between the two systems to exchange cultural values, ideas, and so forth. In reality the anticommunist doctrine of "bridges" is the latest perfidious subversion of imperialism aimed at the "erosion" of socialism and against the unity of the socialist system.

Recently, particularly in connection with the U.S. President's world tour, the expression "bridgebuilding" has again flashed strongly through the American press. Almost immediately after the new administration took office, there began, as it were, a public debate of the "bridges" doctrine as the most important factor in the U.S. aggressive policy in relation to socialist countries. The last time there was such an active debate about this doctrine was in the fall of 1968 when, under the influence of events in the Czechoslovak Socialist Republic, many American politicians and ideologists increasingly recommended a "reappraisal" and a "modernization" in the light of the "new experience."

What caused this flood of attention to the theory and practice of "bridgebuilding"? Let us recall that the doctrine originated with the speech made in May 1964 by President Johnson at the Virginia Military Institute. Johnson then urged "building bridges" to European socialist countries in order to facilitate "increasing their independence" and "to open the minds of the new generation . . . to the values of Western civilization."

. . . . . . . . . . . . . . . . . . . . . . . . . . . . . . . . . . . . . . . . . . . . . . . . . . . . . . . . . . . . . . . . . . . . . .

As everybody knows, throughout the entire postwar period up to the end of the fifties, American foreign policy with regard to the Soviet Union and other socialist countries was most clearly expressed by the doctrines of "containment" and then "rolling back" communism. At that time they banked on the "position of strength" policy, nuclear blackmail, and unleashing a frontal "psychological war" against socialist states. In the imperialist propaganda of the time the so-called "troglodyte" anticommunism prevailed, characterized by crude attempts to denigrate the socialist system and by open appeals to the public of socialist countries for uprising, sabotage, and so forth.

. . . . . . . . . . . . . . . . . . . . . . . . . . . . . . . . . . . . . . . . . . . . . . . . . . . . . . . . . . . . . . . . . . . . . .

The "bridgebuilding" doctrine contains additional to this buildup of propaganda capacities a whole series of theories and concepts aimed at insuring the ideological "disarming" of socialism in the face of imperialism. The basic and sole sense of these theories, despite their great number and outward variety (the "convergence," "stages of economic growth," "deideologization," the "technetronic" age, and other such theories) boils down to the fact that in the process of industrial development socialism and capitalism assume common features and in the final analysis meet halfway and form some form of "hybrid society," in which ideology, having lost its former significance, "will disappear."

. . . . . . . . . . . . . . . . . . . . . . . . . . . . . . . . . . . . . . . . . . . . . . . . . . . . . . . . . . . . . . . . .

The culmination of the 5-year history of "bridgebuilding," which largely decided its future fate, was 1968 and in particular the events in Czechoslovakia. It was in Czechoslovakia that the ultimate aim of this imperialist doctrine was unequivocally demonstrated in practice: Creating with the aid of ideological and political pressure conditions for restoring the capitalist system in socialist countries and their rupture from the socialist community. For this purpose imperialism used the entire modern arsenal of anticommunist means, including a broad propaganda attack and subversive diversionary-ideological actions against the socialist system in Czechoslovakia, outwardly concealed in phrases about "the new model of socialism."

. . . . . . . . . . . . . . . . . . . . . . . . . . . . . . . . . . . . . . . . . . . . . . . . . . . . . . . . . . . . . . . . .

Thus the arguments about "modernizing" the compromised "bridges" policy clearly conceal the strivings of reactionary U. S. politicians and ideologists to keep as weapons the doctrine's main components and to step up the ideological struggle against the Soviet Union, the entire socialist camp, and the world communist movement.

This is a hopeless course. The experience of recent years must have convinced its supporters of the fact that socialist countries are watching imperialism's ideological intrigues vigilantly and will not permit the export of counterrevolution under the umbrella of "bridgebuilding." This was said in the speeches of comrades L. I. Brezhnev, W. Gomulka, G. Husak, W. Ulbricht, and other leaders of the fraternal parties of socialist countries at the International Conference of Communist and Workers' Parties. The anticommunist tactics of "bridgebuilding" will suffer the same wretched fate as its predecessor doctrines of "containing" and "rolling back" communism.

Imperialism's latest attempts "to modernize" and refashion its struggle tactics against socialism again show that socialist countries and all communists must constantly be on the alert, keep a careful watch on the subversive ideological activity of the class enemy, and always remember that the successes of socialism, its influence on world events, and the effectiveness of its struggle against imperialism depend on the cohesiveness of socialist countries as the most important guarantee of the present and future victories of communism.

*15. Professor G. CHERNIKOV, Doctor of Economic Sciences, "The Theory of Convergence Is the Tool of Anticommunism," PRAVDA, September 16, 1969:*

In creating a whole system of ideological myths like the theory of convergence, imperialism is thus striving to cloud the real purport of its intentions and blunt the people's vigilance. For this reason, as CPSU Central Committee General Secretary L. I. Brezhnev stressed at the international conference of communist and workers' parties, "it is impossible to win victory in the struggle against imperialism and to achieve the consolidation of the unity of our movement and all anti-imperialist forces without developing a most active offensive against bourgeois ideology." It is on such class-irreconcilable positions that our party stands: It resolutely exposes the various bourgeois theories which propagate both hatred for socialism and anticommunism and try to mask or deny the progressive decline and historic doom of the capitalist system.

Whatever the subjective motives of any particular advocates of convergence may be, this theory is objectively designed to further the working class's ideological and political disarmament.

16. *Colonel V. BONDARENKO, "Scientific and Technical Progress and the Ideological Struggle," KRASNAIA ZVEZDA, October 3, 1969:* The modern stage of scientific and technical progress has gigantically extended man's potential to master the forces of nature and his potential to create enormous material wealth. At the same time the unprecedentedly rapid development of science and technology is accompanied by very marked advances in the social sphere. The scientific and technical revolution has become one of the chief platforms of the competition between the capitalist and socialist systems.

Therefore there is nothing fortuitous in the fact an acute ideological struggle has developed around this problem. The explanation of its essence and nature, of the prospects of the scientific and technical revolution, and of its social consequences—all this is the sphere of the most bitter clashes between Marxist and bourgeois ideologies.

. . . . . . . . . . . . . . . . . . . . . . . . . . . . . . . . . . . . . . . . . . . . . . . . . . . . . . . . . . . . . . . . . . . . .

A second group of bourgeois ideologists, whose views are clearly apologetic regarding capitalism, also take an antiscientific position. The representatives of this trend attempt to show that a certain upsurge in capitalist production in connection with the scientific and technical revolution is proof of the "continuous and increasing progress" of capitalism and the soundness of its foundations.

In order to defend capitalism's basic principles they think up all kinds of theories. Among these the most widely disseminated principle is the theory of "the stages of economic growth" of the American W. Rostow, and the theory of a "unified industrial society" of the Frenchmen F. Perroux and R. Aron. The authors of these theories claim to have made an "objective and impartial" study of social development, but in fact they distort reality, force facts to fall into a preplanned pattern which justifies capitalism in all ways, and strive to conceal from their peoples capitalism's ferocious countenance and its historic doom.

What for instance, does W. Rostow preach? In his book "The Stages of Economic Growth," with its pretentious subheading "A Noncommunist Manifesto," he attempts to dethrone the Marxist-Leninist teaching on socioeconomic formations by substituting the "theory of stages." The criterion of the stage at which this or that country is, W. Rostow claims, is the level of development of technology and consumption.

This theory completely avoids the question of production relations which, taken together, form society's economic basis.

. . . . . . . . . . . . . . . . . . . . . . . . . . . . . . . . . . . . . . . . . . . . . . . . . . . . . . . . . . . . . . . . . . . . . . . . . . . . . . . . .

Thus, all elements of scientific and technical progress are closely linked with society's social development. To alienate science and technology from the complex social processes, as bourgeois theoreticians and ideologues do, means to ignore the true dialectic of social development and metaphysically to coarsen, oversimplify, and deaden the real mutual ties.

It is not merely a question of the theoretical untenability of bourgeois sociology. It is important to see the real class state of affairs behind its conclusions, along with those social forces which are interested in them.

Among the conclusions of bourgeois sociology which studies the problems of scientific and technical progress, the antiscientific idea which says that the process of industrialization allegedly gives rise to "similar living conditions" under capitalism and under socialism has recently been heard. Representatives of this viewpoint, basing their arguments entirely on technical and economic indexes, assert that in proportion to the leveling out of such indexes in countries of the two opposed social and political systems, the "boundaries" between socialism and capitalism will be "erased." These arguments form in general terms the essence of the notorious bourgeois theory of "convergence."

The very birth of this "theory" reflects on the one hand both the terror of the imperialists in the face of socialism's growing popularity and the attempt to enter the same circle as it, and on the other hand it signifies the continuing aspiration to whitewash monopolist capitalism, and to prove some sort of transformation of it into a totally different society. It is not by accident that in his arguments W. Rostow generally avoided the term "capitalism," which has been compromised.

From the theory of "convergence," the mythical, peaceful coming together of socialism and capitalism "at a single point," the conclusion is drawn that radical differences between them and also between the socialist and bourgeois ideologies do not now play any role. Thus, on the basis of a distorted interpretation of scientific and technical progress is born yet another theory that is fashionable in the West—the theory of "de-ideologization." This theory sows the illusion that the way to truth lies through the denial of any class position, but in fact it has its spearhead pointed against Marxism-Leninism, and it pursues the aim of strengthening the corrupting influence of bourgeois ideology.

The conclusions of proponents of convergence are not only theoretically untenable, they distort the real process of the modern scientific and technical revolution. The latter does not save capitalism, but, on the contrary, aggravates all its contradictions, particularly the contradictions between labor and capital, and it revolutionizes social relations.

First of all, the scientific and technical revolution, which is inseparably connected with the gigantic concentration and centralization of capital, leads to a deepening of contradictions between social production and the private capitalist form of appropriation. This brings to light even more the obsolescence of the capitalist relations of exploitation and of the very institution of private ownership, and intensifies the growth of socialism's material prerequisites.

Second, scientific and technical progress and the changes in the social structure of capitalist society evoked by this progress stimulate the formation of the motive forces of the sociopolitical revolution. . . .

The scientific and technical revolution under conditions of capitalism leads to a growth in the number of people in hired labor and to an acceleration in the process of the proletarianization of the broad masses of working people. This takes place not only through the expropriation of the monopolies' petty proprietors but also through lowering to the proletarian's level a growing proportion of the scientific and technical workers and employees. Between this section of the population and the workers former contradictions are increasingly disappearing and new preconditions are being created for their joint action against the united strength of the bourgeois state and the monopolies.

In this way all arguments about "a unified industrial society," just like the fabrications about the drawing together of capitalism and socialism, are built on sand. Nor do the arguments of imperialism's ideologists, and also of revisionists of all hues about a certain "deproletarianization" of the modern working class, stand up to criticism. On the contrary, facts prove that the scientific and technical revolution is accompanied by an increase in class battles. Suffice it to say that from 1960 through 1968 inclusive more than 300 million people in all participated in the strike struggle in the developed capitalist countries, compared with 150 million in the preceding 14 years.

The development of science and technology cannot weaken this revolutionary class pressure. On the contrary, in the United States, for example, most of the big strikes in the last 10 to 15 years were in one way or another connected with the protest against the harmful consequences for the workers of automation of production. This is not surprising: scientific and technical progress under the conditions of capitalism deepen the social gulf between the monopolist clique and the working class and lead to an increase in unemployment and in the working masses' political lack of rights.

Irrespective of the subjective aspirations of bourgeois theoreticians, their conceptions of scientific and technical progress are directed in the final analysis toward hiding from the peoples the real nature of this process, toward weakening the working masses' revolutionariness, and toward delaying capitalism's hour of doom. But no pseudotheories and no ideological diversions can eliminate the fact that under the conditions of capitalism scientific and technical progress strengthen the necessity for sociopolitical revolution and create the material preconditions for socialism.

. . . . . . . . . . . . . . . . . . . . . . . . . . . . . . . . . . . . . . . . . . . . . . . . . . . . . . . . . . . .

As was observed at the International Conference of Communist and Workers' Parties the broad development of the scientific and technical revolution has become one of the main sectors of the historic competition between capitalism and socialism. L. I. Brezhnev said: "Here the struggle ahead is a long and difficult one. We are full of determination to wage it seriously, in order to show the superiority of socialism in this field also."

*17. Academicians A. RUMIANTSEV and M. MITIN and Doctor of Philosophical Sciences V. MSHVENIYERADZE, "The Urgent Questions of the Struggle Against Anticommunism," PRAVDA, October 13, 1969:* The bourgeois ideologists regard the transference of the ideological struggle into the international communist and workers movement as the most important means of implementing anticommunist strategy. They comprehensively support the "pluralism" of Marxism, encourage the creation of "national Marxisms" and "national communisms," and disseminate the myth about the "erosion" of communist ideology. The struggle against the unity and cohesion of the world communist movement is one of the chief trends of modern imperialism's ideological and political strategy.

. . . . . . . . . . . . . . . . . . . . . . . . . . . . . . . . . . . . . . . . . . . . . . . . . . . . . . . . . . . .

Gambling upon sundering the socialist countries and upon the ideological disarmament of the world communist movement, bourgeois ideologists in recent years have advanced the doctrine of "de-ideologization," according to which the 20th century is characterized as the era of the "end of ideologies," which are allegedly being replaced by the scientific and technical "intellectualization" of social life, by "de-ideologized" societies. This concept finds rich soil, in particular, in the political indifferentism of the philistine strata of bourgeois society.

The very closest examination reveals that the concept of "de-ideologization" is directed primarily against Marxism-Leninism. It is designed to deprive the international communist and workers movement of its cementing unified ideological foundation, to dull the ideological vigilance of peoples who are building socialism and communism. It is intended to justify the escalation of ideological diversions against Marxism-Leninism, and to divert the peoples who have embarked upon the noncapitalist path of development away from the movement toward socialism, wresting from them their spiritual weapon in the struggle for social progress.

. . . . . . . . . . . . . . . . . . . . . . . . . . . . . . . . . . . . . . . . . . . . . . . . . . . . . . . . . . . .

Twenty to 30 years ago any propagator of "convergence" in a capitalist country would have been ostracized. Now it is impossible not to take note of the great achievements of the Soviet Union and the other socialist countries. Today ideologists of imperialism try in every way to adapt themselves to communism's successes. In this lies the sign of our epoch, an epoch in which communism is becoming the decisive force of world development.

However, here one ought to take into consideration the fact that the various "theories of drawing together" are not merely the fruits of idle invention. They are based upon distortions of actual facts of reality which are characteristic of state monopolist capitalism.

. . . . . . . . . . . . . . . . . . . . . . . . . . . . . . . . . . . . . . . . . . . . . . . . . . . . . . . . . . . .

The "convergence" theory serves as some sort of pseudoscientific foundation for the tactics of making advances to individual socialist countries, for "building bridges" and "filling up ditches," in order with the help of "silent counterrevolution" to wrest these countries from the socialist commonwealth, to restore capitalism in them, and to undermine the might of world socialism. The well-known American anticommunist ideologists Z. Brzezinski and S. Huntington openly acknowledge: "The majority of the theories of so-called convergence in reality postulate not the convergence but the absorption of the opposing system."

**18. P. Ye. SHELEST, Member of the CC-CPSU Politburo, RADIO KIEV, October 17, 1969:** Political vigilance, hatred for the class enemy, and the readiness to stand up in defense of our socialist motherland must be increased among all our people.

**19. Marshal of the Soviet Union I. KONEV, "Carrying on the Valiant Exploit," IZVESTIIA, November 15, 1969:** A cruel ideological struggle between the two opposed social systems—socialism and capitalism—is taking place. A great propagandist campaign is being conducted against us: People are slandering us and besmirching our heroic deeds. An enemy is an enemy. It is essential that every Soviet citizen be tempered and ready for the clash with the class enemy. V.I. Lenin stressed on more than one occasion that we must accompany our steps toward peace with complete military readiness. Lenin's words are the sacred behest to our party, to our people and to our state.

**20. Decree of the PRESIDIUM OF THE ACADEMY OF SCIENCES OF THE USSR (November 27, 1969), "Concerning the Basic Directions of Scientific Research Work and Problems of the Institute of Philosophy, USSR Academy of Sciences," VOPROSY FILOSOFII, No. 3, 1970, p. 141:** A most important problem is the criticism of the theories of "convergence" of the two systems, "the single industrial society," and other similar ideological conceptions.

. . . . . . . . . . . . . . . . . . . . . . . . . . . . . . . . . . . . . . . . . . . . . . . . . . . . . . . . . . . . . . . . . . . . . . . . . . .

[The Institute of Philosophy of the Academy of Sciences of the USSR is instructed to pursue] research on social differentiation taking place among the scientific intelligentsia of capitalist countries, the uncovering the the possibility of attracting to the side of the progressive forces its best representatives, the working out of a system of convincing arguments for this wavering part of the intelligentsia which can exert a real influence on its spiritual development.

**21. Lieutenant Colonel N. PONOMAREV, Doctor of Philosophical Sciences, "The Struggle of the Communist Parties against Right and 'Left' Opportunism," KOMMUNIST VOORUZHENNYKH SIL, No. 24, December 1969, p. 12:** The communists are waging a resolute struggle against the classless approach to the problems of our time and against the opportunists' attempts to deny the fundamental opposition of the two social systems and to counterpose to the Marxist-Leninist doctrine on socioeconomic formations the now fashionable bourgeois theory of "convergence"—the coming together of the social systems —or a geopolitical, nationalist, and sometimes even racist approach. The world today is the arena in which the most acute struggle of the two social systems is carried out, and any attempts to deny this fact give the right and "left" opportunists away completely as the accomplices of imperialism.

**22. Ia. SEMENOV, "Peaceful Coexistence and the Revolutionary Struggle,"** **PRAVDA UKRAINY, January 8, 1970:** The policy of peaceful coexistence means neither the maintenance of the political status quo nor the weakening of the ideological struggle. In the struggle of ideas there is not, and cannot be, any reconciliations and agreements.

The policy of peaceful coexistence is directed against reactionaries of all hues and meets the common interests of the world revolutionary struggle against all forms of oppression and exploitation. It furthers the strengthening of friendship among people and aids the development of fruitful economic, scientific and technical, and cultural cooperation between countries with different social systems in the interest of mankind's social progress.

**23. P. N. DEMICHEV, Candidate Member of Politburo and Secretary of the** **CC-CPSU, speech reported in PRAVDA, January 21, 1970:** Representing the USSR as an aggressive state, the enemies of communism thus hope to burden the USSR with the responsibility for the international crises which result from the policy of aggression, the export of counterrevolution, and the suppression of the liberation movement of the peoples. In addition, imperialist circles would like a free hand to deal with small and weaker peoples, isolating them from the USSR and other socialist countries by means of slander and by encouraging nationalist prejudices. The concentrated expression of this, the new, imperialist tactical device, is the notorious doctrine of bridgebuilding, the so-called convergence theory, the rapprochement of socialism and capitalism, and the imaginary concept of national models of socialism.

**24. G. A. ARBATOV, Director of the Institute of the US of the USSR Academy** **of Sciences, "American Foreign Policy at the Threshold of the 1970's," S.Sh.A.:** **EKONOMIKA, POLITIKA, IDEOLOGIIA, No. 1, January 1970, pp. 21-34:** Another innovation of American foreign policy strategy in the 1960's was the policy of "building bridges." At the moment of proclamation, it still could be perceived by many as a form of answer to the call for peaceful coexistence which was issued by the socialist states—it is not by chance that at first it was taken under critical fire by the extreme rightists in the United States itself (it should be said that such a meaning is read into this policy by some representatives of liberal circles even today).

Soon, however, the policy of "building bridges" appeared in a different aspect—in essence in the form of a platform for the initiation of subversive activity directed toward the destruction of the socialist commonwealth and subversion of the socialist social system.

The inspirers of this policy displayed a surprising capability to distort and misconstrue the meaning of any ideas which they touch. Even such forms of international intercourse as trade, cultural and scientific-technical ties, etc., which are generally accepted and have enjoyed a good reputation for centuries, when passed through the thinking meatgrinder of these people, are immediately turned into their antipode, into sinister weapons of subversive activity.

Z. Brzezinski especially tried this field. In his lips, even . . . peace and the normalization of the world situation should further the subversion of world socialism. "Only in an international situation free of tension," he announces; "can those hidden roughnesses and contradictions from which the East suffers become politically important." The relaxation of international tension, according to his statement, "invariably throws the challenge to communism." [*Alternative to Partition*, New York, 1965, p. 121].

Such statements and declarations require an extremely sober approach. First, it is necessary to see that they simply contain a lot of irresponsible propagandistic chatter. Irresponsible especially because they try to make the objective of minor and rather unscrupulous speculation in this case problems which have a direct relation to such large political problems of modern times as preserving peace and normalizing Soviet-American relations. (Attempts to place their kind of "signpost" on all ideals and demands in general which enjoy the broad support of the masses became one of the main directions of imperialist propaganda. It tries in every way to instill that not only peace, the weakening of international tension, and the development of economic, scientific-technical, and cultural contacts with the West but even the raising of the well-being of the workers, the increase in the education and culture of the peoples of the socialist countries, and the development of socialist democracy are proceeding to the detriment of socialism, furthering its "erosion." The intent of such ideological diversions is obvious—to appropriate for themselves and portray in the form of something foreign and even harmful for socialism namely those ideals and principles which strengthen the magnetic force of this social system and arouse newer and newer millions of people for the anti-imperialist struggle.)

Meanwhile, statements like those presented above tell with sufficient eloquence about those intentions to which the policy of "building bridges" has been tied by many of its inspirers—particularly antisocialist plans having in mind the undermining of the socialist system and inflicting damage on socialism.

**25. M. IOVCHUK, "Leninism and the Contemporary Struggle of Ideas in Philosophy," KOMMUNIST, No. 2, January 1970, pp. 47-59:** In essence, the "leftist" opportunists who, Leninism notwithstanding, perceive "the revolutionary dialectic" in perpetual and allegedly increasingly stronger social cataclysms—even under the conditions of socialism—set out along the same path. Thanks to the dialectical materialist comprehension of modern social development, Marxist-Leninists refute these fabrications and prove that socialism is being developed on the basis of the resolution and surmounting of the internal nonantagonistic contradictions, and of the struggle of the new against the old.

On the other hand, reformist and rightist revisionist elements assert that scientific-technical progress and the changes in social and spiritual life associated with it eliminate the antagonistic contradictions and class conflicts in the capitalist world, and that later these changes will make possible an "integration" between the socialist and capitalist systems; and they dismiss the question of the necessity of socialist revolution. Life testifies to the contrary, confirming Lenin's thesis on the insurmountability of the social antagonisms under imperialism—antagonisms that grow increasingly deeper under the conditions of modern scientific-technical progress—and on the inevitability of socialist revolution in some form.

Not abandoning its aggressive aspirations with respect to the socialist world, imperialist reaction and its theoretical adherents are placing their main hopes on the "erosion" of communist ideology, the "softening" of Marxist theory, and the "integration" of the socialist countries' peoples' world outlook with the bourgeois world outlook. Counting on the liquidation of Marxism "in a peaceful way," bourgeois philosophers and sociologists, as is clear from the concepts of R. Aron, D. Bell, P. Sorokin, and other ideologists of anticommunism, are preaching the "inevitable end of ideology" as a result of the modern scientific-technical revolution. They refer to the urbanization processes occurring in "modern industrial society" and to the increase in the general educational level, the sharp absolute and relative increase in the number of nonmanual workers, and the introduction into people's lives of equipment and so-called mass media (radio, TV, and cinema) linking with this the hope that an individualist "consumer" psychology, which will stifle revolutionary ideals and socialist convictions, will become embedded in the consciousness of the population, especially of young people, including those in the socialist countries.

There has been an intensification in the bourgeois and reformist ideologists' attempts to "snuff out" the proletariat's revolutionary spirit and cast doubt on its ability to change modern society radically.

**26. I. DVORKIN,** *Doctor of Economic Sciences, "The Scientific-Technological Revolution and Bourgeois Political Economy,"* **EKONOMICHESKAIA GAZETA,** *No. 3, January 1970:* Bourgeois theories of the technologization of political economy, of the "industrial society" and "convergence," which were widely espoused in the '60s, endeavor to influence the minds of the people in the capitalist countries, as well as in the socialist countries, to blunt their vigilance, their revolutionary consciousness, to compel the broad masses to accept in sweetened form the ideology of the monopolistic bourgeoisie. One cannot renounce these theories with definite adeptness, resourcefulness, calculation of the psychology of the "mass reader," who does not possess a solid ideological background. It is therefore necessary for Marxist-Leninists to carry on a resolute struggle against them, tirelessly expose them, to give deep analysis to the genuine regularities of the development of the contemporary epoch.

**27. G. KHROMUSHIN,** *Candidate of Economic Sciences, "The Tactics Are New, the Aims the Same,"* **SOVETSKAIA ROSSIIA,** *February 8, 1970:* The opposition of two world systems—capitalism and socialism—is the main factor of modern history. With the strengthening of the world socialist system and the growth of the Soviet Union's might, the forces of imperialist reaction, without renouncing military, economic, and other methods of struggle against socialism, are moving the center of gravity to ideological diversions and to intensifying the scope of anticommunist propaganda. Therefore, as Comrade L.I. Brezhnev emphasized in his speech at the international conference of communist and workers' parties, "It is impossible to win victory in the struggle against imperialism and to achieve the strengthening of the unity of our movement and all anti-imperialist forces without deploying a most active attack on bourgeois ideology."

Thus, the "new theories" appear as a successive ideological diversion against world socialism. They are called upon to convince the East European socialist countries of the inevitability of renouncing the general law-governed patterns of socialist building, to push them onto the path of capitalist development while maintaining at first their socialist signboards, which would thereby lose any real significance; to isolate them from the Soviet Union, which is building a communist society, and at the same time weaken the world communist movement. Alongside its broad attempts to discredit the "Soviet model of socialism" modern anticommunism is attempting in every possible way to debunk the world historical significance of Leninist teaching on the proletarian revolution and the building of socialism. The traditional theses are being restored to the effect that Leninist teaching is a "specifically Russian" phenomenon, that Leninism, they say, is merely a "pragmatic adaptation" of Marxism to the Bolsheviks' political aims, and so forth.

**28.  P. MASHEROV, Candidate Member of the CC-CPSU Politburo and First Secretary of the Belorussian CP Central Committee, "The Leninist Party and the Constructive Activity of the Masses," KOMMUNIST, No. 3, February 1970, pp. 11-24:** The main reason for the sharpening of the ideological struggle is found, unquestionably, in the realm of material social relations among people, in the characteristics of our epoch and in the social processes underway. We are witnessing a revolutionary breakdown of age-old exploiting social orders, unparalleled in terms of scale and depth, and the confirmation of entirely new relations among people, generated by the new communist world. The revolutionary process has spread over the entire planet, over all its continents. It has assumed a global nature. Contradictions among classes, above all between the working class and the imperialist bourgeoisie, have reached their highest peak. Internationally the main contradiction of the epoch is revealed in the competition and the struggle between the two world systems: the socialist and the capitalist. Clearly losing its competition against socialism, capitalism is resisting with the fierceness of the doomed. It is clutching at any means and, along with military-political adventures, is channeling ever greater efforts into its subversive political and ideological struggle against the socialist countries and the communist movement, placing particular reliance on ideological diversions. That is precisely why the ideological struggle between the two systems has assumed such a sharp nature.

**29.  EDITORIAL, "Leninism and the Revolutionary Renovation of the World," KOMMUNIST, No. 4, March 1970, pp. 3-13:** The reactionary ideologists are devoting tremendous efforts to prove that as a society capitalism is allegedly subject to constant renovation and improvements. To this effect they have fabricated, and continue to fabricate, various "doctrines" and "theories." In the past few years one after another, many high-sounding verbal formulas have been presented to our contemporaries, like a kaleidoscope: "the free world," "people's capitalism," "the democratic West," the "social partnership society," the "general welfare society," the "great society," the "theory of stages," the "theory of convergence," etc., etc. There is no doubt that many other fashionable slogans and political, economic and sociological terms and elaborations will appear. This entire masquerade is needed by the imperialists to display an imaginary progress of capitalism and create the appearance of its renovation whereas, essentially, its purpose is to safeguard, to perpetuate its foundations and to mislead the masses of people dissatisfied with it.
. . . . . . . . . . . . . . . . . . . . . . . . . . . . . . . . . . . . . . . . . . . . . . . . . . . . . . . . . . . . . . .

The Marxist-Leninist analysis of the class battles in capitalist countries made by the International Conference of Communist and Workers' Parties confirms that they will not be extinguished, as the revisionists claim, but will acquire an even broader scope and a sharper nature under the influence of the stifling atmosphere of the omnipotence of the imperialist monopolies which are provoking the indignation of the popular masses. This state of affairs entrusts the communist parties working in the imperialist countries where the class antagonisms are displayed in their most naked and sharp form and which, at any time, may turn into major revolutionary actions of labor against capital, with particular responsibility.

**30. G. SHLIAPNIKOV *"The Myths of Imperialist Propaganda,"* KOMMUNIST, *No. 4, March 1970, pp. 123-127:*** Of late the anticommunists have tried ever more frequently to attack Marxism-Leninism from the positions of the allegedly inevitable "de-ideologization" of social life in the capitalist and socialist societies. The supporters of this "theory" pretend to be against all ideology since, allegedly, ideology hinders the development of the "industrial society."

The thesis of the inevitable "de-ideologization" of social life, proclaimed by imperialist propaganda, means in fact the recognition of the helplessness of the bourgeoisie in the field of positive ideas. It has an entirely clear class content. The true sense of this thesis was revealed by the double-dyed anticommunist Z. Brzezinski who claims that the USA has allegedly already given an example (?!) of de-ideologization, which should be now followed by the Soviet Union and the other socialist countries. In this manner the struggle against "ideology" in general means in fact the imperialist desire ideologically to disarm the peoples of the socialist countries and the toiling masses in the capitalist countries and to deprive the international communist movement of its common ideological foundations.

The concept of "de-ideologization" is the basis for other imperialist "scientifically oriented" social doctrines. This applies, above all, to the theory of "convergence," which calls for the gradual converging of capitalism with socialism and their merger, subsequently into a single "de-ideologized" highly developed industrial society. It is clear that this superficially compromising "doctrine" proclaimed by the imperialist ideologists is based not on their good life and that it had been dictated by the tremendous international increase in socialist popularity.

Trying somehow to adapt to the new circumstances in the world some of the bourgeois ideologists are trying to exploit for their class purposes the illusion of the similarity among many processes related to the scientific-technical revolution in the capitalist and the socialist worlds, totally ignoring the conflicting nature of the two socio-economic systems.

V. Kortunov's and G. Khromushin's books adequately prove that the concept of "convergence," actively preached by noted imperialist ideologists (W. Rostow, A. Schlesinger, R. Aron and others) is a concealed attempt in the defense of capitalism. Investigated, the "hybrid society" turns out to be a typical capitalist system with all its inherent characteristics: private ownership of producer goods, cruel exploitation of man by man and irreconcilable struggle among antagonistic classes.

It is not by accident that the imperialist ideologists consider the abandonment by the socialist states of such basic principles as the leading role of the Communist Party in society and the socialist economic planning and their substitution with capitalist enterprise activities and the free play of political forces an absolute prerequisite for such a "convergence." The absorption of socialism by the opposite social system is the true meaning of such a "convergence."

Convincingly criticizing the "convergence" theory, V. Kortunov draws the conclusion of the global anticommunist direction of this reactionary bourgeois view. "Exploiting the 'convergence' theory by all possible means, its authors try to weaken the activity of the class struggle in the developed capitalist countries (why wage such a struggle if capitalism is developing in the same way as socialism and when, somewhere along the way, it will merge with it!), undermine the efforts for the building of a new society in the socialist countries (in any case the future does not belong to communism but to some kind of hybrid industrial society!) and weaken the striving of the young national states to take the non-capitalist path of development (in any case, whatever the path, the common objective has been predetermined by the conglomerate of socialism and capitalism!)."

With the proclamation of this "theory" the bourgeois ideologists would like to see socialism adopt an "ideological corporation" with capitalism.

. . . . . . . . . . . . . . . . . . . . . . . . . . . . . . . . . . . . . . . . . . . . . . . . . . . . . . . . . . . . . . . . . . . .

Regardless of the attempts made by the bourgeois apologists to "renovate" the unattractive face of capitalism and find ways to subvert the great attractive force of the ideas of Marxism-Leninism and despite the variety of methods used in ideological diversions, steadily improved by the tremendous imperialist propaganda machinery, the Western ruling circles are far from able to boast with their "successes" in the struggle against communism. The fraternal peoples of the socialist comity and the international communist movement remain highly vigilant toward the subversive imperialist activities and firmly reject all "ideological compromising" with the bourgeoisie. The Moscow Conference of Communist and Workers' Parties proved the high level of unity of the communists from various countries in the anti-imperialist struggle and buried the hopes of the bourgeois ideologists and politicians for a split in the international communist movement.

. . . . . . . . . . . . . . . . . . . . . . . . . . . . . . . . . . . . . . . . . . . . . . . . . . . . . . . . . . . . .

We must not forget, however, that sometimes behind the seeming lack of system and even the contradiction in the statements made by the bourgeois ideologists the experienced guiding hand of the ruling circles in the imperialist countries is felt behind the variety of "theories" and "doctrines" and the refined methods and means of imperialist propaganda. The ideological struggle against communism with the help of the mass information and propaganda media in the main imperialist countries has been raised to the level of state policy.

The bourgeois ideologists are actively working on various methods for the psychological indoctrination of the masses, carefully concealing the interests which are in reality served by imperialist propaganda. Shameless speculation on universal ideals, practically implemented in the socialist countries (the so-called method of "stolen slogans") and the arbitrary juggling of facts taken out of context are characteristic features of the reactionary propaganda which stems from the fact that considering today's abundance of information the common man finds it difficult to check the accuracy of one or another news. Imperialist propaganda extensively uses stereotypes. A tremendous number of books, articles and radio and television broadcasts, motion pictures and other materials are created in such a way as to impose the stereotype of the communist and of communism which, by the mere mention of such words, would create a negative reaction in the politically naive reader or listener unfamiliar with the theory of communism and the practice of the building of socialism.

. . . . . . . . . . . . . . . . . . . . . . . . . . . . . . . . . . . . . . . . . . . . . . . . . . . . . . . . . . . . .

The common feature of all these examined works is that they analyze the imperialist ideological "theories" and "doctrines" in the light of the historical doom of the capitalist system. At the same time, their authors justifiably remind us that in some directions of the ideological struggle imperialism will nevertheless succeed, even though temporarily, to energize its subversive activities. This fact once again confirms the need to wage an aggressive struggle against anticommunism, to defeat imperialist ideological diversions and skillfully to expose its propaganda myths.

*31. Review of book by Iu. S. Meleshchenko and S. V. Shukhardin,* **Lenin and Scientific-Technical Progress,** *Moscow, "Nauka," 1969, in* **VESTNIK AKADEMII NAUK SSSR,** *No. 3, March 1970, p. 129:* The global character of the contemporary scientific and technical revolution is clearly shown in the book. It influences all countries, is manifested in all spheres of activity of people. Opening up before mankind are unprecedented possibilities of transformation of nature, of the creation of enormous material wealth, of revelation of all creative capabilities of the personality. However, under the conditions of capitalism the achievements of the scientific and technical revolution are used to increase the profits of the monopolies and intensify the exploitation of the working people; they not only aggravate all the previous contradictions of capitalism but generate new ones.

In our view it would have been desirable to reveal in more detail the essence of various bourgeois theories of "social partnership," the "super-industrial society," the "second industrial revolution," and of "convergence," in which attempts are made to conceal the capitalistic character of use of the achievements of scientific and technical progress. That is only briefly mentioned in the book. However it would have been possible on the latest data to show how valid today are the words of Lenin, who as long ago as September 1913, in the article "Civilized Barbarity," wrote "Everywhere, at each step you meet problems which mankind is completely able to solve *at once.* Capitalism prevents that."

*32. "Leninism–The Ideological Weapon of the Working People,"* **VESTNIK AKADEMII NAUK SSSR,** *No. 3, March 1970, pp. 3-13:* An international theoretical conference convoked by the USSR Academy of Sciences and the academies of sciences of Bulgaria, Hungary, the German Democratic Republic, Poland, and Czechoslovakia conducted its work in Moscow on 19-23 January. The conference, on the theme "The growth of the role of Leninism in the contemporary epoch and criticism of anticommunism," was dedicated to the centennial of V. I. Lenin's birth.

Eminent workers of the international communist movement, leading Marxist theoreticians and well-known Soviet scientists assembled in the auditorium of Moscow University.

. . . . . . . . . . . . . . . . . . . . . . . . . . . . . . . . . . . . . . . . . . . . . . . . . . . . . . . . . . . . . . . . .

Anticommunism is not a new phenomenon. As is well-known, it arose even at the dawn of the working-class movement. With the appearance of the "specter of communism" all the black forces of reaction began to unite under the banner of anticommunism. Gradually anticommunism has become more and more also a political weapon of the rulers of the capitalist states, one aimed not only against communist ideas but also against socialism and communism as a new social system coming to replace capitalism. At the same time anticommunism is the ideological base of the reactionary internal policy of the imperialistic antidemocratic forces. Anticommunism also is the screen and the banner of the most aggressive, adventuristic foreign policy measures of imperialism.

Contemporary anticommunism is a multifaced phenomenon. It also is the political activity of various imperialist organizations. It also is an extreme expression of bourgeois ideology. Anticommunism applies new methods, especially making use of nationalism, which is also a base of anti-Sovietism, to undermine the forces of socialism.

. . . . . . . . . . . . . . . . . . . . . . . . . . . . . . . . . . . . . . . . . . . . . . . . . . . . . . . . . . .

P. N. Demichev characterized the essence of the ideological struggle in the contemporary stage. Militant anticommunism has become the main content of the ideology of the contemporary bourgeoisie and its petty bourgeois minions. The struggle against anticommunism under contemporary conditions is a component part of the general struggle of progressive forces for peace and democracy, for socialism and communism. In the course of that struggle communists use as a basis the creative ideas of Marxism-Leninism, scientific methodology, Leninist principles of the struggle against inimical ideological trends.

. . . . . . . . . . . . . . . . . . . . . . . . . . . . . . . . . . . . . . . . . . . . . . . . . . . . . . . . . . .

The protest against imperialist policy and bourgeois social system embraces increasingly wider strata of the population of the capitalist countries, including the intellectuals and the youth. The myths of "people's capitalism," of the bourgeois state as the "reconciler" of the interests of the opposed classes, are being resolved. The persistent unmasking of that demagogy, the revelation of the real nature and anti-popular mechanism of action of the contemporary bourgeois state and, on the other hand, profound analysis of those features and aspects of social life which determine the level of real socialist democracy will help to organize a still more resultful struggle against the ideology of anticommunism.

. . . . . . . . . . . . . . . . . . . . . . . . . . . . . . . . . . . . . . . . . . . . . . . . . . . . . . . . . . .

Representing the USSR as an aggressive state, the opponents of communism hope to thus cast on the USSR the responsibility for international crises which arise as a result of the imperialist policy of aggression, the export of counter-revolution and suppression of the liberation movements of peoples.

The new aspects of anticommunist tactics have found their concentrated expression in the notorious doctrine of "building bridges," in the so-called theory of "convergence," the "rapprochement" of socialism and capitalism, and the devised concept of "national models of socialism." An argumented criticism of those fabrications was given in the report.

The economic, political and military power of socialism, the struggle of peoples for peace, democracy and socialism are fettering the actions of international reaction. Under those conditions imperialism has been required to take a "step backward," to give up brazen methods of open military aggression where it has been clearly doomed to failure.

B. N. Ponomarev dwelt further on some new features of the contemporary tactics of anticommunism, aimed directly against the socialist countries, having distinguished two principal elements: the aim to break up world socialism as a system, on the one hand, and to erode the socialist states in the bourgeois spirit, on the other.

The basic content of the first direction is putting the countries of socialism in opposition to the Soviet Union. Behind that are hidden far-reaching political plans which form the core of the strategy of imperialism and are aimed at changing the main correlation of forces in the world arena. The essence and distinctive feature of the second is emphasis on the "internal evolution" of the socialist states, on their political and ideological "softening." In a socio-political respect those calculations are oriented—in this is their essential new feature—not only toward the residues of defeated exploiter classes and their fellow-travellers but also toward the revisionist and opportunistic elements. Those features of the tactics of anticommunism were clearly manifested in the well-known events in Czechoslovakia.

. . . . . . . . . . . . . . . . . . . . . . . . . . . . . . . . . . . . . . . . . . . . . . . . . . . . . . . . . . . . . .

Anticommunism, B. N. Ponomarev noted, plays the role of the main ideological and political weapon of imperialism also in the zone of national liberation. It is used to hinder the further development and deepening of the revolutionary process in that part of the world. Here the most important goal of anticommunism is to divorce the national liberation movement from other revolutionary forces of the present day, primarily from the socialist countries.

**33.  M. V. KELDYSH, President of the Academy of Sciences of the USSR, April 2, 1970, speech delivered at General Meeting of the Academy, PRAVDA, April 3, 1970:** In light of the Leninist analysis of the basic contradictions between capitalism and socialism, in their social-economic principles, and in their attitudes toward scientific-technological development, with complete definitiveness appears the groundlessness of contemporary technocratic conceptions and of the theory of "convergence" of the two systems, the theory of "the single industrial society." Imperialism turns scientific-technological achievements not to the welfare of the people but to their oppression, to the preparation and waging of destructive wars in the name of preserving its power and the achievement of world hegemony, for the struggle against the socialist and the national-liberation movements.

**34.   N. V. PODGORNYI, speech delivered April 2, 1970, at General Meeting of USSR Academy of Sciences, VESTNIK AKADEMII NAUK SSSR, No. 5, May 1970, p. 7:** One can note with satisfaction the considerable contribution of the Academy in the investigation of new phenomena of the socio-historical development, in the working out of very varied questions in the building of communism. The further development of the social sciences is acquiring special importance now—under conditions of a sharp aggravation of the ideological struggle in the historical competition between the opposed social systems. Scientists working in that area are called upon to more actively counteract and unmask various bourgeois theories, anticommunism, rightist and "leftist" revisionism, and any trends inimical to Marxism-Leninism.

. . . . . . . . . . . . . . . . . . . . . . . . . . . . . . . . . . . . . . . . . . . . . . . . . . . . . . . . . . . . . .

At the same time we have no right to underestimate our opponent in the antagonism of the two social systems. Imperialism, in spite of being weakened by internal contradictions, still has considerable force and possibilities in the area of economics, in science and engineering, resorts to highly sensitive methods in the ideological struggle.

**35.   V. KORTUNOV, "The Triumph of Marxist-Leninist Ideas and the Maneuvers of Anticommunism," KOMMUNIST, No. 8, May 1970, pp. 113-124:** Ever since Marx and Engels developed their grandiose doctrine the bourgeoisie has not even for one day ceased its "sacred persecution" of communism, employing its centuries-long experience in the spiritual enslavement of the working masses, the full force of its economic and political power and every manner of influence on the inner world of man. Bourgeois ideologists and their stooges have "overthrown" Marxism-Leninism a thousand times, have declared it "outmoded" and have buried it. On numerous occasions they have attempted to oppose scientific communism with their concepts of social progress.

. . . . . . . . . . . . . . . . . . . . . . . . . . . . . . . . . . . . . . . . . . . . . . . . . . . . . . . . . . . . . .

Modern anticommunism is a multi-plan phenomenon. It represents the totality of the strategic doctrines, political arrangements, theoretical concepts, and propaganda stereotypes of imperialism in its struggle against the liberation movement both within the capitalist world and on the international arena.

. . . . . . . . . . . . . . . . . . . . . . . . . . . . . . . . . . . . . . . . . . . . . . . . . . . . . . . . . . . . . . . . . . .

In the first postwar years imperialism's foreign policy vis-a-vis the socialist countries was based on the doctrine of so-called "containment" and later "limiting" or "rolling back" communism. At that time imperialism still placed great hopes in implementing against the USSR a policy "from a position of strength."

. . . . . . . . . . . . . . . . . . . . . . . . . . . . . . . . . . . . . . . . . . . . . . . . . . . . . . . . . . . . . . . . . . .

In conformity with this general doctrine of imperialism in those years was its line for the economic and political isolation of the socialist countries which, in its turn, was reinforced in the ideological and propaganda field by the most frantic, straightforward anticommunism, overt appeals for counterrevolutionary coups, and so forth. However, even by the beginning of the 1960's the balance of forces in the world arena had changed in socialism's favor to such an obvious degree that imperialism's ruling circles were themselves obliged to consign the referenced doctrines to the archives. In an extremely short time the Soviet Union restored its economy and made a great leap in the development of science and technology, including military development. The building of socialism was being successfully implemented in a number of European and Asian countries.

Imperialism suffered a new blow of enormous force from another direction also: it was these same years that witnessed the disintegration of the colonial system, which posed on a global scale the question of the selection by dozens of new states of the paths of further development.

Again imperialism was obliged to revise its anticommunist strategy. In 1960 the then U. S. President J. Kennedy stated: "The policy of liberation has proven to be a trap and a delusion . . . . We must now slowly and carefully . . . cultivate the seeds of freedom in any cracks in the iron curtain." Without abandoning attempts at economic and political pressure and military threats and provocations against socialism, imperialism at the same time is promoting the more refined tactic of "building bridges," transferring the center of gravity to the ideological struggle. The policy of "building bridges," ideologically backed up by the so-called theory of the "convergence" of the two systems, has essentially constituted the basis of imperialism's tactical line regarding the socialist countries for the duration of the entire 1960's period. Even today it still remains a part of imperialism's arsenal. However, certain amendments (a more differentiated approach to individual socialist countries and individual categories of the population, a still greater emphasis on inflaming nationalism, and so forth) are being introduced into this policy following the failure of the imperialist circles' plot against the working people of the Czechoslovak Socialist Republic.

The most characteristic feature of the present tactics of anticommunism's ideologists was stressed by Comrade L. I. Brezhnev at the 1969 Moscow International Conference of Communist and Workers' Parties. "Imperialism," he noted, "cannot count on success by openly stating its real aims. It is compelled to create a whole system of ideological myths which blur the real significance of its intentions and dull the people's watchfulness." (*The International Conference of Communist and Workers' Parties, Moscow, 1969.* Prague, "Peace and Socialism" Publishing House, 1969, p 203.)

. . . . . . . . . . . . . . . . . . . . . . . . . . . . . . . . . . . . . . . . . . . . . . . . . . . . . . . . . . . . . . .

At the same time, in describing modern capitalism, the bourgeois ideologists attempt not to call a spade a spade, preferring to rely on such finer-sounding, although extremely unjustifiable terminology as the "free world," a "state of universal prosperity," "the great society," and so forth. It is possible to cite literally dozens of concepts circulated by bourgeois propaganda intended to "scientifically" substantiate the idea of capitalism's magical transformation. Among these are the theory of the "deideologization" of social awareness and the theories of the "stages of economic development," "a single industrial society," the "convergence" of the two systems, and so on and so forth.

If one attempts to separate out the main thing in all these and many similar theories, it transpires that the majority of them, beginning with W. Rostow's book *Stages of Economic Growth: A Non-Communist Manifesto,* attempt to inculcate one simple idea, which is precisely that modern capitalism is, properly speaking, no longer capitalism and that it has been "transformed" under the influence of industrialization and scientific and technical progress into a society which is allegedly closer to socialism than socialism itself. Harvard University Professor Adam Ulam, for example, states outright that the West's industrial progress has led to a situation in which the ideals of socialism have merged with the idea of a "state of universal prosperity" and have been realized under the conditions of modern capitalism and that Marxist-Leninist ideology has remained on the wrong side of these ideals.

. . . . . . . . . . . . . . . . . . . . . . . . . . . . . . . . . . . . . . . . . . . . . . . . . . . . . . . . . . . . . . .

In order to ideologically disorient people and distract them from Marxism-Leninsim, imperialism is mobilizing all possible anticommunist movements—from right-wing opportunist to ultraleftist movements—and any concepts which oppose the working classes' Marxist-Leninist ideology. Attempts are presently being made here to activate all of the former ideological tendencies hostile to Leninism which have long since been refuted by life itself—Trotskyism, Menshevism, anarchism, and so forth.

. . . . . . . . . . . . . . . . . . . . . . . . . . . . . . . . . . . . . . . . . . . . . . . . . . . . . . . . . . . . . . . .

American "Sovietologist" Z. Brzezinski advocates a "differentiated approach" with respect to the socialist countries. In his article "Bridge-building: How It Is Presented from Moscow" he writes: "Communism has now assumed such diverse forms that the United States can deal individually with each of the communist regimes, thereby acting in the direction of splitting the communist camp. Such actions comprise the encouragement of nationalism in Eastern Europe, the encouragement of the multiparty system, and the resurrection of the fundamental concepts of a private entrepreneurial economy." (*Freedom's Facts,* August 1968.)

**36.  Academician Ye. M. ZHUKOV, *"Problems in the Study of World History,"* VESTNIK AKADEMII NAUK SSSR, *No. 5, May 1970, p.* 68:** The struggle between the Marxist-Leninist and the bourgeois and revisionist historiography inimical to it is developing primarily on the question of the acknowledgment of the objective regularities of the world-historical process. The opponents of Marxism, as a rule, deny the presence of objective laws of the development of society. For them, acknowledgment of the progressive replacement of socio-economic formations is unacceptable, as it involves a statement of the historical foredoom of capitalist social relations and the inevitability of a transition to other, incomparably higher forms of organization of society.

However, it is characteristic that the most current and "fashionable" bourgeois conception of world history is the quasi-materialistic theory of "stages of growth," proposed by the American W. Rostow. It is reduced to a depiction of the historical process as a successive progressive replacement of the technology of social production. Social relations are completely absent in that scheme.

Also close to that conception are the views of the French bourgeois sociologist R. Aron, who attempts to prove the inevitability of the "rapprochement" of socialism and capitalism on the basis of scientific and technical development, which as it were "deideologizes" a highly developed industrial society, removing the class contradictions in it. In essence it is a matter of "historical substantiation" of the idea of the convergence of socialism and capitalism, designed for the spread of anti-Marxist revisionist views.

**37.  A. Ia. PELSHE, *Member of CC-CPSU Politburo, pre-election speech in Riga,* SOVETSKAIA LATVIIA, *June 4, 1970:*** The capitalist system is losing ground. Its last foundations are crumbling. Its ideologists and troubadors are in a blind alley. Having failed in their predictions of the "imminent collapse of Soviet Power," and in their prophecy that "nothing can succeed without private enterprise," and having abandoned such primitive methods but by no means renouncing their previous intentions, they have begun to use more cunning and refined methods.

Today's subverters of Marxism-Leninism resort to all kinds of devices to plant the seed of confusion in the mind, to present black as white, to unite the ununitable. In other "essays," capitalism is depicted as being "people's" capitalism, as being capable of operating a planned economy. "Common features of modern industrial society" are suddenly discovered. The notorious "convergence theory," whose authors maintain," without any embarrassment whatsoever, that "socialist society is becoming capitalistic," has become popular.

*38. M. A. SUSLOV, Member of Politburo and Secretary of the CC-CPSU, pre-election speech in Leningrad,* **PRAVDA,** *June 10, 1970:* An intensification of the class struggle in capitalist countries is taking place. The proletariat's class battles in those countries are acquiring an increasingly broader, organized, and military nature. The working class is again demonstrating its leading role in the revolutionary process and is completely upsetting the bourgeois ideologists' false theories on some sort of "modernization" of capitalism, on "popular capitalism," and the theories of rightist and "left" revisionists on the alleged "bourgeoisification" of the working class and on their loss of revolutionary initiative and activity.

*39. V. BOL'SHAKOV, "Pandora's Box,"* Part I, **KOMSOMOL'SKAIA PRAVDA,** *August 25, 1970:* Possessing no other ideology than anticommunism, imperialism in its subversive activity against the socialist countries gambles primarily on the "erosion," the "washing away," the "loosening-up," the "emasculation" of Marxism-Leninism. These are not terms that I have invented. They appeared on several occasions in recent years in the theoretical works of "Sovietologists" and "Kremlinologists" of the most varied caliber. To sow doubt regarding the ideals of communism, distrust to spread rumors and slander, to stir up nationalist tendencies, to encourage private-ownership instincts and aspirations for the so-called "soft life," to play on ambition, individualism, on disaffection, and on doubt—on whatever they please if only to recruit into the anticommunist camp of as many sympathizers as possible from among the citizens of the socialist countries—this is what all their theorizing and all their practice which is based on it amount to.

But how is one to penetrate the minds of the intelligentsia and young people of the socialist countries? How is one to select the master key to the hearts of people? According to the idea of the Western "strategists" it is necessary to propose some attractive system, if not of ideas, then of views, a model of a world outlook seemingly not anticommunist but not antibourgeois either, a "panhuman" world outlook, so to speak. The political essence of this "panhuman" world outlook is very precisely expressed in the concept of so-called "ideological disarmament," in the theories of "convergence" and of a single industrial society, and in the furturological constructions of "de-ideologized worldwide society in the technetronic age," according to Brzezinski, Kahn, and Wiener. The bourgeois modeling of the "future society," whatever the attractive terms by which its contemporary designers operate, remains invariably bourgeois in essence. The ideologists of "humane capitalism" assert that such a system will be formed by the voluntary mutual swallowing up of the two systems—the capitalist and the socialist—at a definite moment in the future.

**40. V. BOL'SHAKOV, "Pandora's Box," Part II, KOMSOMOL'SKAIA PRAVDA, August 26, 1970:** The West stubbornly seeks "opposition" to Soviet power—for more than 50 years incidentally—invariably expressing wish for reality. Apostates and the rabble of the literary fringe at ideological warfare factories are transformed into "unrecognized" national "geniuses" and the Westerners place in their servile open mouths what they would like to hear from the Soviet writers and artists without the prefixes "pseudo" and "circum". . . . The Western "pastors" teach us tolerance, nonviolence, and liberalism toward all peddlers of bourgeois ideology and of "Western ideological baggage" and insist in every way on the peaceful coexistence of ideologies. At the same time, in their verbal and written recommendations they call upon our intelligentsia to be intolerant toward writers and pamphleteers who are consistently defending party positions. In the West they are called none other than "diehards," that is, "hard-headed conservatives" even when they made an honorable and principled criticism of those shortcomings which we have and which we do not conceal. But the West fears such criticism more than any other varnished literature, for such criticism helps socialism to become stronger. The strategists of the "war of minds" need a criticism which is not creative but destructive, and invariably with an anti-Soviet flavor. . . . "The bourgeois or the socialist ideology. There is no middle way. . . . Therefore, any belittling of the socialist ideology and deviation from it thereby signifies a strengthening of the bourgeois ideology." This is what Lenin taught. His words sound just as topical today.

**41. EDITORIAL, *"Our Strength Is Ideological Steadfastness,"* SOVETSKAIA ROSSIIA, August 27, 1970:** The struggle between imperialism and socialism has not been halted for a single day. It cannot be halted because the bourgeoisie will not voluntarily renounce its dominance and because it rightly sees in socialism its deadly enemy.

**42. D. TOMASHEVSKIY, *"The Leninist Principle of Peaceful Coexistence and the Class Struggle,"* KOMMUNIST, No. 12, August 1970, p. 112:** The notorious American doctrine of "bridge-building" to the socialist countries is also far removed from true peaceful coexistence. There is no doubt that insofar as it reflects the bankruptcy of the former policy aimed at "liberating" the socialist countries with the help of armed aggression and economic blockade, this foreign political doctrine can be viewed as a certain withdrawal of imperialist reaction from its former positions. However, in fact, "bridge-building" is aimed at interfering in the internal affairs of the socialist countries, exacerbating "psychological warfare," encouraging antisocialist, nationalist tendencies, disuniting the socialist countries, and subverting the world positions of socialism. There is no doubt that all this has nothing in common with the principles of peaceful coexistence.

Sometimes the organizers and inspirers of subversive activity against the socialist system allude to the Marxist-Leninist thesis concerning the inevitability of ideological struggle under the conditions of the peaceful coexistence of states with different social systems also. What a crass method! Communists actually proceed from the fact that the peaceful coexistence of the socialist and capitalist states does not signify and cannot signify a deadening of the class struggle between them and reconciliation of the bourgeois and socialist ideologies. But the ideological struggle is a struggle of world outlooks and a struggle of ideas. The attempts of the supporters of the obsolete system to raise lies and misinformation, slander socialism, and the "theoretical" exertions of the professional anticommunists and of various turncoats to the level of ideological struggle merely testify to the profound ideological crisis of the modern imperialist bourgeoisie, the spiritual poverty of its ideologists, and to the historical doom of anticommunism.

**43. S. A. DALIN, *"The 'Industrial Society' and the Working Class,"* S.Sh.A.: EKONOMIKA, POLITIKA, IDEOLOGIIA, No. 9, September 1970, pp. 38-50:** The socioeconomic consequences of the scientific and technical revolution have proved to be so substantial that bourgeois economists and sociologists have had to engage in extensive theoretical reflections on the problems of the further development of capitalism. The theory of the "industrial society," with which they attempt to answer the current questions of contemporary capitalist reality, has made its appearance as a result.

In the imperialist countries the scientific and technical revolution is taking place under conditions of contemporary state-monopoly capitalism, the theory of which was worked out by V. I. Lenin more than 50 years ago. These five decades have wholly confirmed Lenin's doctrine. Much of what bourgeois economists previously denied they must now admit in one way or another under the pressure of inexorable facts. The statements of K. Marx and V. I. Lenin are therefore frequently cited in the theories of the "industrial society." But all of this is done in order to oppose the Marxist-Leninist doctrine of state-monopoly capitalism in a new way (for the umpteenth time!) with still another theory, which goes by the name of the "industrial society."

Its birthplace is France, and its authors are French economists and sociologists: Jean Fourastie, Raymond Aron, and Jacques Ellul. But upon closer examination it is not difficult to see that their conceptions are based mainly on American economic theories, if we do not speak of the Englishmen J. Keynes and Colin Clark. Having migrated from France to the United States, the theory of the "industrial society" seems to have fallen upon fertile soil and received an American interpretation in such books as *The New Industrial State* of John Galbraith, *Problems of Industrial Society* by William Founce, and *One Dimensional Man: Essays on the Ideology of Advanced Industrial Society* by Herbert Marcuse.

. . . . . . . . . . . . . . . . . . . . . . . . . . . . . . . . . . . . . . . . . . . . . . . . . . . . . . . . . . . . . . . .

As treated by its theoreticians, "industrial society" is a society in which the absolute majority of the population is concentrated in the cities and is no longer bound up with agriculture, but with industry. A decisive role in present-day industry is played by the most recent engineering and technology, which supposedly have predetermined both the enormous size of corporations, and also the transfer of management of industry from hands of capitalists into the hands of the technically educated managers, who in their activity are no longer guided by an aspiration to extract maximum profit, but by the aspiration to achieve certain "social goals." Present-day engineering, according to these theoreticians, calls for production planning on the scale of the entire state and therefore a restriction and even suppression of the spontaneous operation of the market. As a result of technological development, there is less need for workers who do physical work, and the numbers and importance of mental workers increase. The conclusion is therefore drawn that society is undergoing a process of "deproletarianization," and since the interests of mental workers do not oppose the interests of the managers, the development of "industrial society" is accompanied by gradual extinguishment of the class struggle. On the whole the "industrial society" is supposedly no longer capitalist, but is a new social formation that approaches a socialist formation.

This in short is the content of the theories of "industrial society," in which capitalism is defended by being denied.

. . . . . . . . . . . . . . . . . . . . . . . . . . . . . . . . . . . . . . . . . . . . . . . . . . . . . . . . . . . . . . . .

Though many authors on "industrial society" do not use the term "scientific and technical revolution," it occupies a central place in all their theoretical constructions. Properly speaking, the theories of "industrial society" are a kind of distorted reflection of the scientific and technical revolution in the consciousness of certain strata of contemporary capitalist society. Engineering and technology are the starting point of these theories. They are the criterion which makes it possible to establish that by "industrial society" they do not mean capitalism of the twentieth century in general, but precisely postwar capitalist society.

The theoreticians of "industrial society" ascribe an all-determining role to present-day engineering and technology. For example, the present monopoly corporation arose, according to them, not as a result of concentration and centralization of capital, but to meet the demand of present-day engineering. Galbraith writes that machines and complex technology "required enormous investments of capital . . . . The possibility and need to organize big business arose out of these changes." It turns out that the capital for large investments is lying about in the street and anyone can pick it up as long as there is engineering. In actual reality before contemporary engineering could come into being, sufficiently large capital had to be accumulated in order to apply that engineering.

. . . . . . . . . . . . . . . . . . . . . . . . . . . . . . . . . . . . . . . . . . . . . . . . . . . . . . . . . . . . . . . .

Thus, even given the existence of large capital, it is not always profitable under capitalist conditions to use the most refined equipment. Here engineering comes into collision with the social relations within whose limits it is developing. Meanwhile, the theoreticians of "industrial society" assert that the development of engineering does not depend on social relations. For them engineering determines everything: the scale of production, the form of its organization, the management system, the make-up of managers, and even the form of administration of the entire production of society. A number of social processes are portrayed in the theories of "industrial society" as a direct result of engineering, as a direct function of it. Moreover, they assert that this same engineering is giving rise to identical consequences in socialist society as in contemporary capitalist society. On this basis they have built up their theory of "convergence," that is, convergence of the two social systems. In actuality the socioeconomic consequences of the scientific and technical revolution are diametrically opposed under capitalism and socialism. Such consequences as "technological unemployment" or the destruction of the mass of farmers, which is now taking place, are altogether impossible in the socialist system. Under capitalism the scientific and technical revolution is demonstrating more and more the incompatibility between present-day productive forces and the production relations that exist there. Under socialism, though, they create the material and technical foundation for the transition to communism. Consequently, "technology" is bringing about completely different socioeconomic consequences for capitalism and socialism.

. . . . . . . . . . . . . . . . . . . . . . . . . . . . . . . . . . . . . . . . . . . . . . . . . . . . . . . . . . . . . . .

The class nature of the theories of "industrial society" come to the surface most noticeably when their authors declare that technology is deciding everything and the forms of ownership have no importance in this.

Although certain theoreticians of "industrial society" treat technology in the strict sense of the word, most of them use the word "technology" to mean the productive forces in general. Of course the productive forces have decisive significance in the development of society, but this certainly does not mean that production relations are a passive category. They exert an energetic effect on the development of the productive forces. It is therefore impossible to divorce the productive forces from production relations, as the theoreticians of "industrial society" are doing, without revealing the antagonistic contradiction between the movement of the productive forces and the trend of production relations under capitalism.

. . . . . . . . . . . . . . . . . . . . . . . . . . . . . . . . . . . . . . . . . . . . . . . . . . . . . . . . . . . . . . .

As we have already pointed out, the formation of the world socialist system and the aggravation of the class struggle in the capitalist countries have forced the monopolies to make a number of concessions to the working class with regard to wages, social security, etc. But the theoreticians of "industrial society" have represented this result of the class struggle as the transformation of capitalism into the "state of universal prosperity," the "affluent society."

According to their assertions, trade unions are supposedly not necessary in "industrial society," since the class struggle is dying out and "interests which previously opposed one another radically are more and more approaching harmony at the present time." Still another thesis of the theoreticians of "industrial society" derives therefrom: "integration" of the interests of the workers and the ruling elite.

81

Thus, the theories of "industrial society" proceed from the position that the working class consists exclusively of physical workers and they attempt to prove that the scientific and technical revolution, mechanization, and automation of production have brought about a reduction in the size of the working class, "deproletarianization," a decline in the role of the trade unions. According to these theories, along with "deproletarianization" the "new middle class" is growing and is coming to replace both the working class and also the "old middle class," which consisted of the petty bourgeoisie of the city and rural areas.

. . . . . . . . . . . . . . . . . . . . . . . . . . . . . . . . . . . . . . . . . . . . . . . . . . . . . . . . . . . .

In spite of the difference that exists between mental and physical labor, the worker and employee — be he engineer or office worker — do not differ fundamentally from one another at all with respect to the means of production. Membership in a specific class is determined by the relation to the means of production. "The basic feature of the difference between classes," V. I. Lenin wrote, "is their place in social production, and consequently their relation to the means of production."

The privileged position of the intelligentsia was in the past based on its small size and the fact that the demand for its labor exceeded the supply. Now the occupations of mental labor are very numerous, and the supply frequently exceeds demand. This brings about a drop in the value of the manpower of mental workers. Rather frequently the wages of office workers, trade employees, teachers, and persons in other categories of mental work are now even somewhat lower than the average wages of the worker. The work of the beginning engineer in the United States is not remunerated as well as the work of the skilled worker. Thus, the enormous mass of mental workers have been proletarianized, mental work and physical work have not only come closer together in their very nature, but the bulk of employees and workers have come closer together with respect to their material position.

Consequently, not only has there not been a deproletarianization of the working class, as the theoreticians of "industrial society" assert, but, on the contrary, mental workers have been proletarianized. As a result the present-day working class has grown considerably in all respects. . . .

. . . . . . . . . . . . . . . . . . . . . . . . . . . . . . . . . . . . . . . . . . . . . . . . . . . . . . . . . . . .

Theories of "industrial society" constitute a distorted picture of contemporary state-monopoly capitalism, whose development is accompanied by an aggravation of all its contradictions in general and of its class contradictions in particular. In presenting the thesis of "deproletarianization," the adherents of these theories thereby assert that contemporary capitalism is no longer capitalism. In this way they are striving to defend it.

*44. Colonel T. KONDRATKOV, Candidate of Philosophical Sciences, "The Social Nature of War and the Advocates of Aggression,"* **KRASNAIA ZVEZDA,** *December 16, 1970:* In the military theoretical field as in other spheres of ideology, a bitter, uncompromising struggle is going on. Here two viewpoints on war, opposed in their class essence—the Marxist-Leninist and the bourgeois viewpoint—clash with each other.

The bourgeois theorists, confusing and distorting in every way possible the question of the essence and origins of war, direct their poison arrows with particular diligence against the Marxist-Leninist understanding of the social nature of wars and their separation into just and unjust wars. Such a trend in bourgeois falsification and its stirring up in modern conditions are not accidental.

Imperialist reaction does not want to make peace with the course of events in the world arena which is clearly not developing in its favor, is trying to switch over to counterattacks, is preparing for a new world war against the forces of socialism and progress and is rushing into local adventures. With the aim of an ideological cover for their piratical actions, which are arousing the wrath and condemnation of peoples, the imperialist circles and their theorists are seeking justifying reasons and arguments to conceal the unjust nature and reactionary sociopolitical essence of their aggressive wars. This is why the exposing of the antiscientific conceptions of the advocates of aggression and the correct elucidation of the nature of modern wars have an important significance in our times.

. . . . . . . . . . . . . . . . . . . . . . . . . . . . . . . . . . . . . . . . . . . . . . . . . . . . . . . . . . . . . . .

But however zealous the bourgeois ideological arms bearers may be, all their constructions and sophisms vanish into dust when they come into contact with genuinely scientific opinions and the facts of reality.

Lenin's teaching on the social nature of war has gained enormous theoretical and practical significance. It arms the workers with a correct understanding of the class-political and moral makeup of past and modern wars, of their just or unjust nature and serves as the keenest weapon in the unmasking of the bourgeois falsifiers.

. . . . . . . . . . . . . . . . . . . . . . . . . . . . . . . . . . . . . . . . . . . . . . . . . . . . . . . . . . . . . . .

Alongside the bellicose, militarist views on the nature of modern wars, bourgeois pacifist notions have also been propagated in the west. The pacifists morally condemn war and declare it an "absolute evil," and preach utopian projects for the establishment of eternal peace.

. . . . . . . . . . . . . . . . . . . . . . . . . . . . . . . . . . . . . . . . . . . . . . . . . . . . . . . . . . . . . . . . . . . . . . . . . .

The pacifist ideology conceals the origins of wars, and their class essence and nature, thereby disarming the popular masses in the face of the military danger which imperialism bears. Truly, such viewpoints have nothing in common with the Leninist teaching about the social nature of wars.

The right and "left" revisionists regard the social nature of wars from anti-Marxist positions. In particular, the "leftists" regard a world skirmish as a positive historical phenomenon, as a morally justified means of creating a "better society." The Marxists-Leninists refute such adventurist ideas which bring harm to the cause of peace, socialism and the peoples' liberation movement.

To the imperialist policy of aggression and war, socialism poses a policy of peace which is to the highest degree just, a policy of friendship between peoples, a policy of resolute opposition to the forces of militant reaction. "The CPSU Central Committee and the Soviet Government," said Comrade L. I. Brezhnev, "are immutably conducting a policy of peaceful coexistence of states with different social systems. This is our firm line, the founder of our state bequeathed it to us. But let no one confuse our persistence and consistency in this issue with pacifism and with "nonresistance to evil"—to that evil which the imperialist aggressors bear to the people."

*45. I. ALEKSANDROV, "The Poverty of Anticommunism," PRAVDA, December 17, 1970:* The course of the world revolutionary process causes deep alarm to imperialist reaction which is using every means of struggle against the forces of social and national liberation, against peace and socialism. The creative labor of the Soviet people and of the working people of the fraternal socialist countries serves as an inspiring example to the peoples of all continents.

Bourgeois propaganda wages a fierce struggle against the ideas of socialism, striving first and foremost to defile the Soviet system and to slander the historic achievements of our people. One campaign of slander follows another, critics and oracles succeed one another, but the essence of anticommunism as the major trend of the policy and ideology of the imperialist reaction remains unchanged.

. . . . . . . . . . . . . . . . . . . . . . . . . . . . . . . . . . . . . . . . . . . . . . . . . . . . . . . . . . . . . . . . . . . . . . . . . .

While slandering the world of socialism, imperialist propaganda at the same time is making every effort to disguise the exploiting and antipopular nature

84

of the bourgeois system. Ideologists of imperialism realize that against the background of the achievements of the world revolutionary process and the indisputable successes of the countries of the socialist community the embellished facade of the free world is crumbling away and the prestige of the imperialist states is going downhill.

. . . . . . . . . . . . . . . . . . . . . . . . . . . . . . . . . . . . . . . . . . . . . . . . . . . . . . . . . . . . . . . .

Entire groups of pseudoscientists—"Sovietologists"—are producing writings, filled with schemes and models for the annihilation of socialism. The propaganda servants of imperialism are mobilized to help them. In close cooperation with the intelligence services, they stubbornly search in our country for food to slander the socialist system. This is an ungrateful task and obviously beyond their strength. Opposed to imperialism and all its intrigues stand the monolithic Soviet people proud of their achievements, their unity, and of their confidence in the triumph of the exalted ideals which they are upholding.

**46. S. BEGLOV, Doctor of Historical Sciences, "The Minds of People Are a Battle Arena," PRAVDA, December 26, 1970 (review of a book by G. A. Arbatov):** From the insoluble conflict with reality and with life emerge the attempts by the bourgeois theoreticians to distort the very concept of ideological struggle and to ascribe to it an uncharacteristic role and place in modern international relations. One school of bourgeois thought is striving to prove the "unlawfulness" and "illegality" of the ideological struggle, elevating it to the position of prime cause of the contradictions and conflicts in the world arena. From this invented "reason" a bridge is thrown out toward a demand for the "de-ideologization" of international relations, and for peaceful coexistence in the field of ideology. Exposing this false concept, the author of the book stresses that the ideological struggle, in reflecting the split of the world into two systems, is one of the forms of the class struggle in the world arena and within society. This form is important and plays a big role in international relations. But not the ideological struggle, but rather the aggressive policy of imperialism, is the reason for the clashes and armed conflicts which unfold in the international arena.

**47. N. D. GAUZNER, "The 'Postindustrial Society' and the Tendencies in the Socioeconomic Development of the United States," S.Sh.A.: EKONOMIKA, POLITIKA, IDEOLOGIIA, No. 12, December 1970, pp. 37-43:** The theory of the "postindustrial society" is a further development of the theory of the "industrial society" relative to the new conditions and is based on the same methodological foundations. Like the theoreticians of the "industrial society," adherents of the theory of the "postindustrial society," taking their start from Colin Clark, mechanically subdivide the stages of social development as a function of the level of national income, labor productivity, and the branch structure of the economy. In the conception of bourgeois theoreticians the "industrial society" is a society in which the overwhelming majority of the population is concentrated in the cities and is not bound up with agriculture, but with large-scale industry. As for the "postindustrial society," the well-known American sociologist D. Bell, who headed the Year 2000 Commission, for example, sees one of the main features of this society in the fact that most of its gainfully employed population is employed neither in agriculture, nor in industry, but in the service sphere: in trade, finance, transportation, public health, the entertainment and recreation industry, research, education, and administrative bodies.

Both theories view technological progress as an independent process that automatically entails social changes, This approach is particularly distinct in the works of the American professor Leslie White, who asserts that "technology is an independent variable, while the social system is a dependent one." The dialectics of the interaction between the productive forces and production relations, discovered by the founders of Marxism and confirmed by the entire course of history, is completely ignored in the theories of the "postindustrial society." Accordingly, the authors of these theories paint illusory pictures of the unlimited progress of capitalism and do not take account of the acute social problems and contradictions of today and tomorrow. As they see it, it turns out that the "postindustrial society," just like the "industrial" society, is not even capitalist any longer.

. . . . . . . . . . . . . . . . . . . . . . . . . . . . . . . . . . . . . . . . . . . . . . . . . . . . . . . . . . . . . .

Different authors give different names to this "new civilization." J. Ellul calls it the "technological society," D. Bell the "postindustrial society," Z. Brzezinski the "technicoelectronic society" (shortened to "technetronic"). What these theories have in common is that these authors associate the development of the new society not with the transformation of social relations, but derive it directly and exclusively from transformation of the material and technical base of capitalism. "Our society," Z. Brzezinski writes, "is ceasing to be an industrial society. To an ever-increasing degree it is taking shape under the influence of technology and electronics and is becoming the first technetronic society."

. . . . . . . . . . . . . . . . . . . . . . . . . . . . . . . . . . . . . . . . . . . . . . . . . . . . . . . . . . . . . .

Taking their start from actual processes that have been caused by the scientific and technical revolution, the authors of the conception of the "postindustrial society'' present the reader with a camouflaged apology for the present capitalist system. Thus, the actual change in the ratio of the number of workers primarily performing physical labor (''blue-collar workers'') to those performing primarily mental work (''white-collar workers'') to the advantage of the latter is used to support the thesis of ''deproletarianization'' of bourgeois society.

In this connection we should note above all that the ideologists of the ''postindustrial society'' replace the actual changes in the social structure of bourgeois society by shifts in the occupational division of labor. The truly scientific concept of classes is thereby blotted out. But if we do not approach this question from the vantage point of external and formal features, but from the standpoint of the nature of classes, which are distinguished above all by their place in the historically determined system of social production and by other features, as formulated by V. I. Lenin, then it is clear that as the number of engineering and technical workers and employees increases, a process of social differentiation among them is intensifying. The very important changes in the social and economic position of a substantial portion of commercial and office employees and engineering and technical workers are intensifying the tendency for them to draw closer to the proletariat, and in certain cases to merge with it. In the period of the scientific and technical revolution the proletariat, which is not only a product of certain production relations, but also the most important productive force, is becoming more complex and more diversified in its composition. Along with workers performing primarily physical labor, it naturally will include an increasingly large portion of workers performing mental labor.

. . . . . . . . . . . . . . . . . . . . . . . . . . . . . . . . . . . . . . . . . . . . . . . . . . . . . .

On this basis the ideologists of the ''postindustrial society'' are giving a rebirth to the old technocratic theories, which have been long since refuted. They speak of the birth of an omnipotent elite of ''egg-heads'' or an electronic-cybernetic elite, which is taking power over society. In the opinion of Z. Brzezinski, the United States is even now ceasing to be a plutocratic-oligarchic society and is becoming a ''meritocratic democracy.''

. . . . . . . . . . . . . . . . . . . . . . . . . . . . . . . . . . . . . . . . . . . . . . . . . . . . . .

Consequently, powerful productive forces, which are social by nature, which possess colossal potential capabilities for increasing production and making it cheaper, are at the disposition of a diminishing group of monopolists, whose behavior is motivated entirely by the interests of profit and the interests of strengthening the capitalist system. Here lies the basis for the antagonistic nature of the social processes generated by the scientific and technical revolution, which more and more is coming into conflict with capitalist production relations.

"The scientific and technical revolution," it is stated in the basic document of the International Conference of Communist and Workers' Parties, "is speeding up the process of socialization of the economy; in the context of the rule of the monopolies, this is bringing about reproduction of social antagonisms on a still larger scale and with still greater acuteness. Not only are all the previous contradictions of capitalism being exacerbated, but new ones are also coming into being. First, there is the contradiction between the extraordinary possibilities opened up by the scientific and technical revolution and the obstacles which capitalism erects to prevent their use in the interests of the entire society, by turning a large portion of the discoveries of science and enormous material resources to military purposes, by squandering national resources. Then there is the contradiction between the social nature of present-day production and the state-monopoly character of its regulation. Then there is not only the growth of the contradiction between labor and capital, but also the deepening antagonism between the interests of the overwhelming majority of the nation and the financial oligarchy."

. . . . . . . . . . . . . . . . . . . . . . . . . . . . . . . . . . . . . . . . . . . . . . . . . . . . . . . . . . . . .

In the words of D. Bell, the creation of the "effective megalopolises" raises a very important problem for the "postindustrial society," that of new planning which is very far from its old forms, where main emphasis was on capital investments and growth. But this "new planning" comes up against such serious barriers under the conditions of capitalism as private ownership of land, the need to invest enormous amounts of capital that do not directly bring profit.

Portraying the process of social development as an automatic evolution without conflicts toward the "postindustrial society" as the scientific and technical revolution spreads, the bourgeois sociologists announce that the class struggle, and at the same time mass organizations of the working class, are outdated. In the opinion of Galbraith, for example, the trade unions in the "new industrial society" are inevitably to lose their role because of the transfer of power from owners to the "techno-structure," and also because of state regulation of markets, over-all demand, and the dynamics of prices and wages. The inventor of the "technetronic society," Z. Brzezinski, says that " a unifying ideology for political action" is altogether impossible in this society.

**48.** *Academician M. B. MITIN*, et al., SOVREMENNYE BURZHUAZNYE TEORII O SLIIANII KAPITALIZMA I SOTSIALIZMA [KRITICHESKIY ANALIZ] (CONTEMPORARY BOURGEOIS THEORIES ON THE

CONVERGENCE OF CAPITALISM AND SOCIALISM [CRITICAL ANALYSIS]), *Moscow, "Nauka," 1970, introduction, pp. 5-9:* In the contemporary conditions of exceptional exacerbation of the ideological struggle in the international arena, the proper determination of an urgent range of questions, the selection of the most effective methods and means for the successful struggle against anticommunism as the chief ideo-political weapon of imperialism, takes on important significance. The struggle of two opposing ideologies—bourgeois and Marxist-Leninist—serves as a manifestation in the ideological sphere of the fundamental antagonism of the current epoch—the antagonism between capitalism and socialism—and objectively as a manifestation of the directed dynamism of this antagonism, in the process of which communism steadfastly stands as the decisive force of world development.

Anticommunism is the most significant obstacle in the path of socio-economic, political, scientific and cultural progress of the peoples. It is directed towards undermining the unity of all progressive forces of today. The General Secretary of the CC-CPSU, comrade L. I. Brezhnev, in his report at the International Conference of Communist and Workers' Parties in Moscow on June 7, 1969, remarked: "Anticommunism in the capitalist countries is elevated to the level of governmental policy. The stake towards the decay of the communist and the entire revolutionary movement from within now comprises one of the most important directions of the class strategy of imperialism." The struggle against anticommunism—this is an objective necessity of our time.

Contemporary anticommunism presents itself as a rather complex ideo-political phenomenon. It is greatly multifaceted, but it directs its spearhead first of all against the three basic revolutionary forces of the present today—the world systems of socialism, of the international working class, of the national-liberation movement.

. . . . . . . . . . . . . . . . . . . . . . . . . . . . . . . . . . . . . . . . . . . . . . . . . . . . . . . . . . . . . .

Adapting to new conditions, the bourgeois ideologists in a new fashion are formulating a slogan of struggle: "to know not only that *against* which we fight, but also that *for* which it is necessary to fight." Along with "negative" anticommunism, so-called "positive" anticommunism is receiving increasingly wider dissemination, the objective of which is to fill the "vacuum of ideas" in the capitalist countries, the basis of "a positive program of mass action," which maintains the "positive" bourgeois ideas and ideals.

Namely towards this goal they have served to disseminate in recent years different "theories of convergence," which preach the development of the two systems along approaching (convergent) lines towards "one world." Without question, these similar theories are summoned to life by the successes of socialism and the discreditation of capitalism in the eyes of millions of people. The rise of these "theories" signifies that contemporary bourgeois ideologists refuse to acknowledge the clear line of the development of capitalism. They do not see its historical perspectives and therefore try to maintain themselves at the expense of socialism which has caught on to those real historical perspectives which indeed belong to socialism.

The present collection is devoted to a critical analysis of different theories of convergence and is representative of the materials of the All-Union Theoretical Conference organized by the Scientific Council concerning problems of foreign ideological trends, under the Social Sciences Section of the Presidium of the Academy of Sciences of the USSR. The conference drew the great attention of specialists, scientific workers, instructors at *yuzs*, scientific and soviet *aktivs*. Comrades who spoke at the conference emphasized that fifty years ago any preacher of "convergence" in a capitalist country would have been anathematized. Today ideologists of imperialism no longer can ignore the successes of Marxism, of communism, and in every way possible they try to adapt to them. In this is the sign of our era, when communism stands as the *decisive* force of world development. It follows from this to take into account, however, that different "theories of rapprochement" are not simply the fruit of an idle imagination. They are based on distortion of the real facts of life, typical for state-monopoly capitalism.

Contemporary imperialism has a series of new traits. It makes wide use of state financing of programs for industrial development and scientific research, comprises programs of economic development, increasingly implants rational forms of direction into the economy, multiplying the preconditions for socialism. In his time, the skill of a brilliant dialectician allowed V. I. Lenin to draw the bold conclusion that "some basic characteristics of capitalism have begun to turn into their antithesis" [V.I. Lenin, *Complete Collected Works,* Vol. XXVII, p. 385].

But, on the other hand, contemporary imperialism as never before aggravates and carries to the limits the exploitation of the toilers, the alienation of man, the antagonism between the individual and the society, the militarization of the economy, and creates the growing danger of war. . . .

The illusion of "a coming together" of capitalism and socialism lies at the foundation of the faulty theses of the theories of convergence, deludes not only the man in the street, but also many of the honest scientists in foreign countries. Meanwhile, "one world," about which bourgeois ideologists talk profusely, in fact turns out to be the very same capitalist society with those traits inherent to it—predominance of private property, social division of labor, struggle of antagonistic classes and exploitation of man by man.

Along with this, convergence is conceived of as rapprochement along "all lines"—economic, political, social, theoretical, ideological. Often it is accompanied by hypocritical admission of "the great merits of Marx," so that thereupon under the pretense of "objectivity" of analysis, distinctly negative opinions can be expressed in reference to "outdated" Marxism and its revolutionary dialectic.

Theories of convergence serve as the pseudoscientific foundation for the tactic of "the building of bridges" and "the filling of ditches," in order to tear these countries from the socialist commonwealth with the aid of "silent counterrevolution," to restore capitalism in them and undermine the might of world socialism.

The well-known American ideologists of anticommunism, Z. Brzezinski and S. Huntington, frankly admit: "Most theories of the so-called convergence in reality posit not convergence but submergence of the opposite system" [Z. Brzezinski and S. Huntington, *Political Power: USA/USSR,* New York, 1964, p. 419].

The correct position on exacerbation of the ideological struggle must be understood not only in the context of the expansion of the spheres of its influence, but also with regard to the exclusive refinement of methods by which it is conducted by the bourgeois ideologists. A successful criticism of current anticommunist concepts and doctrines requires a sufficiently high culture of thought, theoretical vigilance, principle, based on a class approach.

The book being offered renders aid to the Soviet reader in understanding one of the features of contemporary anticommunism, which consists in the attempt to set off against Marxism-Leninism a series of pseudoscientific social doctrines, arms him with arguments in the struggle against one of the most diffuse anticommunist "theoretical" concepts—the theory of convergence.

**49.  M. SIDOROV, Doctor of Philosophical Sciences, "Lenin on the Irreconcilability of Socialist and Bourgeois Ideologies," LENINISM TODAY, Moscow, Novosti Press Agency Publishing House, 1970, pp. 123-133:** Socialist ideology, from its inception has existed and developed as an ideology opposed to bourgeois ideology and a negation of it. The working class comes out as the attacking class which rejects the old capitalist society that has outlived itself. It is called upon by history itself to carry out a revolution and build a new, classless society. Consequently, it cannot tolerate the ideology that protects the old system.

Socialist ideology scientifically substantiates the laws of the revolutionary transformation of capitalist society and therefore it cannot peacefully coexist with bourgeois ideology. Revolutionary and reactionary outlooks are as mutually exclusive as fire and water, as day and night.

Though obviously losing in the competition with socialism, capitalism does not want to quit the historical arena; it uses the most diverse means of struggle pinning special hopes on ideological sabotage.

In their campaign against socialism bourgeois ideologists strive, above all, to attack Marxism-Leninism, the scientific basis of socialist ideology. They declare Marx's teaching to be "obsolete" and Leninism to be a product of "Russian backwardness," allegedly unsuitable for the West, and so on and so forth.

When direct attacks against the revolutionary ideology of Marxism-Leninism fail imperialist leaders try to achieve their insidious aims through ideologically "eroding" socialism, "softening" the new social system in the socialist countries, weakening their ideological and political might and then effecting their evolution towards capitalism.

. . . . . . . . . . . . . . . . . . . . . . . . . . . . . . . . . . . . . . . . . . . . . . . . . . . . . . . . . . . . . . . . . . . . . . . . . . . . . . .

Bourgeois ideologists have put into circulation the theory of the "convergence" of capitalism and socialism, and also of such modifications as "an integrated industrial society," "mixed society" and so forth. In the opinion of the American economist, J. Galbraith, a multilateral drawing together of the industrial systems takes place at this juncture. He claims that the imperative demands of a technological and organizational order, rather than ideological formulas, determine the economic system of society. Thereby the social revolution is replaced by the scientific-technological revolution. What he ignores is that scientific and technological progress under capitalism, in a society of private ownership and exploitation, serves as a means of enrichment, as a tool of militarism, but under socialism it serves the workingman.

The aspirations for "convergence" find their expression in the conceptions of "ideological disarmament," the "deideologization" of social consciousness. These fashionable theories are actually directed against the Marxist-Leninist world outlook with its consistent party and class approach to phenomena of social life. The same purposes are served by the propagation of "pure democracy," abstract freedom and abstract humanism.

The Marxist-Leninist parties are waging a resolute and irreconcilable struggle against all the theories which disarm the working people in their fight for emancipation from all forms of oppression.

Present-day bourgeois ideologists are trying to thrust on Communists the idea of peaceful coexistence of ideologies under the pretext that the peaceful coexistence of the two systems, championed by the Communists, is impossible without the peaceful coexistence of the communist and bourgeois ideologies. Yet, Communists, proceeding from some well-known theses set forth by Lenin, consider that peaceful coexistence does not mean reconciliation or a waning of the ideological struggle. The struggle between the two ideologies—socialist and bourgeois—was, is and will be irreconcilable. As long as there are classes and the class struggle, the working class will not reject its views, its aims or its class ideology.

Peaceful coexistence does not extinguish or cancel out class struggle—it is a new form of class struggle employed by the working class and the socialist countries in the world arena. It "cancels" only one type of struggle—war as a means of settling international issues.

*50. MOSCOW TASS INTERNATIONAL SERVICE, Commentary on Western Ideology, January 27, 1971:* Here the Western institutions for psychological warfare concentrated all their efforts on propagating a "synthesis" of socialism and capitalism, and also on some kind of "liberal socialism" which allegedly would choose the "best" from the capitalist system. "Radio Free Europe," for example, breathlessly proved that now when the socialist countries have attained a high standard of industrial development and have in many fields approached the United States and other developed capitalist countries they are entering an "industrial society" common to them and that "the time has come to stand above the sclerotic forms of ideology."

Comrade L. I. Brezhnev said in the accountability report of the CPSU Central Committee to the 23rd Party Congress: "We must always remember that our class enemy is imperialism. It conducts subversive activities against the socialist system, its principles, ideology, and morals. The struggle against bourgeois ideology must be uncompromising under all circumstances, because this is a class struggle, a struggle for man, for his dignity and freedom, for the strengthening of the positions of socialism and communism, a struggle in the interests of the international workers' class."

There have never been and never will be compromises in the ideological struggle, Lenin wrote. "The question can only be put as follows: Either bourgeois or socialist ideology, There is no middle way here." The pie with the putrid filling composed of the theory of "convergence" of socialism and capitalism offered by the bourgeois propaganda cannot deceive anyone. The future is with socialism, while "the ashes of the old world" are left for capitalism. History does not offer any third choice.

*51. G. TROFIMENKO, "Anti-Communism and Imperialism's Foreign Policy," INTERNATIONAL AFFAIRS (Moscow), No. 1, January 1971, pp. 49-54:* Anti-communism is the chief ideological and political weapon of imperialism, underlying the foreign policy of the leading imperialist states.

Under the pretext of fighting world communism, the imperialists are knocking together aggressive military blocs, waging wars against the national liberation movement and carrying out repressive measures against democratic forces. By playing the role of world policeman and suppressing the popular revolutionary struggle, imperialism aggravates international tension. As a rule, the imperialists undertake their peace-menacing actions under the flag of anti-communism.

. . . . . . . . . . . . . . . . . . . . . . . . . . . . . . . . . . . . . . . . . . . . . . . . . . . . . . . . . . . . . . . . .

The "bridge-building" doctrine and its various versions which superseded the "liberation" doctrine were an attempt to consider the patent failures of US anti-communist policy and somehow to adapt the imperialist strategy and tactics to the changed situation in Europe.

While the "liberation" doctrine did not recognise the status quo in Europe, the "bridge-building" doctrine outwardly proceeded from the recognition of the situation and the existing social systems, its ultimate goal being to change the status quo through restoration of capitalism in the socialist countries. While the "liberation" doctrine did not rule out using NATO to achieve this end the "bridge-building" doctrine played down the military means and counted on the "internal evolution" of the socialist states towards capitalism. According to Brzezinski, such "evolution" was to be fostered from above, mainly through seizure of political power by the nationalist elements infected with bourgeois theories of "technocratisation" and "Europeanisation."

The bourgeois theorists completely support the principle of integration of West European states, yet take an entirely contrary stand in the case of the socialist countries of Eastern Europe. For the latter they advocate total seclusion and isolation. With this theory they seek to fan bourgeois nationalism and use it to destroy the unity of the socialist countries.

. . . . . . . . . . . . . . . . . . . . . . . . . . . . . . . . . . . . . . . . . . . . . . . . . . . . . . . . . . . . . . . . .

Such changes in the tactics of the ideological struggle, while preserving the main canons of imperialism, also include expatiations of American propaganda to the effect that today's policy is one of "negotiation not confrontation" with the Soviet Union. It is not hard to discern certain propagandist and diplomatic considerations for the mood of American and world public opinion. Washington has to reckon in particular with the pressures exerted by wide sections of the US community who demand that their government relinquish foreign policy adventures and concentrate on the solution of burning domestic issues, such as abolition of racial discrimination, liquidation of poverty and unemployment. At the same time, the thesis on the transition from confrontation to negotiation signifies that US imperialism acknowledges that the onward march of the USSR cannot be stopped by force of arms.

While displaying a certain willingness for negotiations with the Soviet Union on some problems, in particular on limiting the strategic arms race, the US ruling circles do not at all give up the most active confrontation wherever they hope to succeed. Washington's steps show that it seeks to intensify the political and ideological struggle against the socialist countries.

**52. *V. I. GROMEKA* and *V. S. VASILYEV*, *"Bourgeois Theorists on the Scientific and Technical Revolution,"* S.Sh.A.: EKONOMIKA, POLITIKA, IDEOLOGIIA, *No. 1, January 1971, pp. 56-62:*** The modern scientific and technical revolution is exerting an enormous influence, although in different ways, upon the economic, political, and social life of the capitalist as well as the socialist countries. In the capitalist countries it has sharply exacerbated former contradictions and engendered new ones even more serious and profound in nature and scale. "The scientific and technical revolution accelerates the process of the socialization of the economy; under conditions of monopoly domination this leads to reproduction of social antagonisms on an even larger scale and with even greater acuteness. Not only are all of capitalism's former contradictions exacerbated, new ones are also engendered. These contradictions are primarily the contradiction between the extraordinary possibilities opened by the scientific and technical revolution and the obstacles which capitalism places in the path of their utilization in the interests of the whole of society by devoting a large proportion of scientific discoveries and enormous material resources to military ends and trampling national wealth underfoot, the contradiction between the social nature of modern production and the state monopoly nature of its regulation, and not only the growth in contradiction between labor and capital but also intensification of the antagonism between the interests of the overwhelming majority of the nation and the financial oligarchy." [Documents of the International Conference of Communist and Workers' Parties, Moscow, 1969, p. 15.]

. . . . . . . . . . . . . . . . . . . . . . . . . . . . . . . . . . . . . . . . . . . . . . . . . . . . . . .

*A Frank Apology for Capitalism*

The most zealous defenders of capitalism regard the modern scientific and technical revolution as an "ally" capable of rejuvenating decrepit capitalism and serving as a springboard for a leap into the 21st century. The best-known authors of these fashionable "new" concepts in the United States are Z. Brzezinski, H. Kahn, D. Bell, and A. Wiener.

According to the views of these ideologists of U.S. imperialism, the United States has already experienced the stage of industrial development and is now on the threshold of a new society—the "postindustrial" (technetronic) society.

The specific feature of this stage is the alleged fact that the center of economic and political activity in such a society has shifted from the primary (mining and agriculture) and secondary (industrial production) sectors to the "tertiary" (services) and "quaternary" (science and education) sectors. This change is also accompanied by radical changes in the education system itself, by the spread of cybernetics, the institutionalization of scientific and technical innovation (that is, transformation of the process of the creation of scientific and technical knowledge and its introduction into production into a permanent process), and other things. "U.S. society," Columbia University Research Institute on Communist Affairs director Z. Brzezinski writes, "is emerging from a spontaneous phase of development and entering a more self-controlled phase; it is emerging from the industrial society stage and becoming technetronic before others. This explains at least partially the majority of the cases of a tense atmosphere and disorder."

As we can see, the authors of the apologetic theories of modern scientific and technical progress rely on superficially indisputable facts—reduction in the proportion of those employed in the extraction industries, agriculture, and processing industry sectors at the expense of an increase (absolute and relative) in employment in other spheres of social production. Furthermore, they admit that the rapid rate of modern scientific and technical progress is engendering a need to make some changes in social life and they see the cause of "tension and disorder" in the inadequate rapidness of the implementation of these changes.

However, the essence of these views by no means lies in admitting the need for changes even limited by the framework of capitalism. The main point of the hypotheses of the proponents of the "postindustrial" society amounts to the fact that a "technetronic civilization" is the lot of all mankind and the difficulties being experienced by the United States are allegedly the difficulties of the first country to enter the "new age." They are attempting to pass off one of the most serious social crises in U. S. history as the inevitable consequence of adaptation to the results of scientific and technical development by U. S. society, which is "blazing a trail forward."

Those who predict a "technetronic civilization" have borrowed from Rostow the fundamental idea of his work *Stages of Economic Growth*, which the author himself called a "non-Communist manifesto," but which should have been called an anti-Communist manifesto. The replacement of the Marxist-Leninist concept of the socioeconomic formation by "stages of growth" when explaining historical progress was needed by W. Rostow to demonstrate the "inevitability" of Communism's evolution into capitalism as the socialist countries develop economically. The link between the "latest" theories of D. Bell, Z. Brzezinski, and H. Kahn and W. Rostow's artificial hypotheses is self-evident, but the difference between them amounts primarily to the fact that reference is now made to the role of scientific and technical progress in the development of society.

. . . . . . . . . . . . . . . . . . . . . . . . . . . . . . . . . . . . . . . . . . . . . . . . . . . . . . . . . . . . .

## The Convergence Theory

The efforts of the bourgeois theorists and propagandists to depict the present scientific and technical revolution as a set of factors determining the development of society irrespective of its organizational forms were expressed in the convergence theory, a theory widespread during the 60s which was expressed most fully in the book *The New Industrial State* by well-known U.S. liberal economist J. K. Galbraith. The author attempted to prove his thesis of convergence between the capitalist and socialist economic systems substantiating this by the fact that technical progress allegedly dictates its laws to the development of society.

. . . . . . . . . . . . . . . . . . . . . . . . . . . . . . . . . . . . . . . . . . . . . . . . . . . . . . . . . . . . .

J. Galbraith attempts to substantiate the convergence theory by proceeding from formal symptoms inherent in all developed industrial production, in which some common features are indeed immanent to a greater or lesser extent in an organizational and technical respect. However, the differences between socialist and capitalist organization are obvious even at the enterprise level. In precisely the same way organizational and technical relations in no way coincide with production relations, as J. Galbraith believes. Production relations also include ownership relations. According to the Marxist interpretation, it is precisely in ownership relations that the radical differences between the socioeconomic formations, differences which are also manifested at the enterprise level, rise to the surface. J. Galbraith believes that the differences in the organization of large-scale capitalist firms and Soviet production enterprises vary within negligible limits (in the former case, with consideration of their orientation toward a planned and regulated market, and in the latter, with respect to their orientation toward the state plan). However, this "approximately" identical system of planning and organization oversteps the limits of organizational and technical relations and constitutes the sphere of opposite production relations, that is, relations of ownership in the broad sense of the word.

It should be noted that the convergence theory is interpreted in different ways by its proponents. For J. Galbraith it is intended to refute the "idea of an inevitable clash" conditioned by the difference between capitalism and socialism, to put an end to the arms race and to "give an impetus to widespread international cooperation."

This position occupied by J. Galbraith does not cause indignation of itself. It is indisputable that the most important task facing mankind is to insure peaceful coexistence between the two opposing systems and to put an end to the arms race. But blurring the differences between the two socioeconomic systems does not promote the implementation of this task, sows illusions and vain hopes, and ultimately makes peaceful coexistence more difficult.

However, usually the point of the theory is in no way restricted to an aspiration to "reconcile" capitalism and socialism but amounts to attempting to prove the inevitability of the "identicalness" of the development of these two opposing socioeconomic systems, to extend the capitalist formation's development laws to the socialist mode of production, and thereby to confirm the capitalist system's universality. It is precisely here that the main point and defect of the convergence theory are to be found.

## The Fetishization of Technology and Criticism of Capitalism

The exaggeration of the role of scientific and technical progress—an exaggeration which has gone so far that this progress is regarded as some self-sufficient force capable of "crushing" the individual—has served as the basis for creating of concepts depicting all mankind's future in the most gloomy and pessimistic tones. In the majority of cases such fears and worries are based on the real, pernicious consequences of scientific and technical progress under the conditions of modern capitalism—mass unemployment, the utilization of scientific progress in the interests of the property owners, the indoctrination of public opinion with the aid of modern propaganda media, the threat of thermonuclear war, and so forth.

. . . . . . . . . . . . . . . . . . . . . . . . . . . . . . . . . . . . . . . . . . . . . . . . . . . . . . . . . . . . . . . . .

Only a class approach to the analysis of modern capitalist reality and to the socioeconomic and political consequences of the scientific and technical revolution makes it possible to find the correct rather than partial answers to the urgent questions which life is posing for the development of society in capitalist countries.

## The Renovation of Old Theories

The bourgeois theorists are trying to use the modern scientific and technical revolution to reinforce the theories of "popular capitalism," of the capitalist society of "universal wealth," of "class peace," and other most outspoken "theories" for embellishing the capitalist system. The well-known bourgeois scientist P. Drucker hastens to affirm that new equipment and the growth in the workers' level of education and labor productivity have led to the point where "the class war is overcome" and is nothing but . . . "an importunate specter of the 19th century."

The facts irrefutably testify to the fact that the progress of science and technology by no means leads automatically to social progress but on the contrary is accompanied by an aggravation of the socioeconomic and political contradictions of modern capitalism. What "universal prosperity" can one speak of in the richest capitalist country where 20 to 30 million people are officially acknowledged to be living in poverty and millions of people are hungry? Surely the strike battles of the American proletariat, which is constantly coming out for the maintenance and improvement of its standard of living and against capitalist exploitation, refute the theories of "class peace"?

**53. A. POKROVSKY, "Some Sociological Aspects of the Scientific-Technological Revolution in the Capitalist World," INTERNATIONAL AFFAIRS (Moscow), No. 2, February 1971, pp. 24-30:** Monopoly capital makes use of the achievements of scientific and technical progress for increasing the scale of its robbery of the working class and for stepping up its ideological offensive against the working people. The huge propaganda machine of the present-day bourgeois state has adopted a variety of economic and sociological theories and doctrines preaching the progressiveness of a social system based on private ownership of the means of production.

Bourgeois apologists try hard to show that capitalist society is now renovated, just and flourishing in all respects. They say that this transformation of the "old" "bad" capitalism took place precisely under the influence of the unusual leap in the development of the forces of production attributable to the scientific-technological revolution. The purpose behind such arguments is to convince the working man that he is no longer being exploited, that now there are no classes and no class struggle, that in today's capitalist world no one oppresses anyone, everyone gets the good things of life in almost equal measure and, consequently, that there is no need for social revolution, no need for changing the social formation.

The "old" capitalism—which had thoroughly compromised itself—is referred to by bourgeois politicians and ideologists as a kind of inevitable historical evil which is gone forever. New names are suggested for the present social system in the Western countries, such as "the postindustrial society", "people's capitalism", "collective capitalism" and "neocapitalism."

Doctrines of the "transformation" and "rejuvenation" of capitalism under the impact of the scientific-technological revolution take a variety of forms, primarily in the United States, where a vast school of sociologists and "technocrats", closely connected with monopoly capital, has become adept at apologetics. Considerable effort is expended also by "theorists" in Western

Europe, who import the experience of their Transatlantic colleagues and assemble their own Western European versions and models of "neo-capitalism".

. . . . . . . . . . . . . . . . . . . . . . . . . . . . . . . . . . . . . . . . . . . . . . . . . . . . . . . . . . . . . .

Another widespread form of apologetics of modern industrial capitalism is the concept of the stages of economic development formulated by American sociologist Walt Rostow. In his "theory" Rostow places the United States at the "fifth stage," painting a pretty picture of American capitalism concentrating on the allround satisfaction of popular needs. As indices of society's development he uses the degree of technical modernisation in industry and the level of scientific-technological progress, but ignores the most important, to wit the system of production relations dependent on the nature of the ownership of the means of production.

One of the more recent concepts in bourgeois sociology is the theory of the post-industrial society. Its weakness again is in its ignoring of the difference between social and political structures, taking into consideration only the level of industrialisation (the principle of technological determinism). In analysing the processes in the formation of different types of societies, the post-industrialists take American capitalism as a prototype, treating it as a model for the whole world, thus essentially extrapolating into the future of all mankind. They harp on the idea that the current scientific revolution leads to the perpetuation of the bourgeois system. Herman Kahn and Anthony Wiener, for instance, postulate in their book *The Year 2,000* that governments in post-industrial society can use technical means to directly control people's thought processes.

A number of bourgeois sociologists make out that technical progress brings about the dissolution of the working class within the capitalist system and its loss of vanguard status in the world revolutionary process. This idea is particularly propagated in the theories of Herbert Marcuse.

. . . . . . . . . . . . . . . . . . . . . . . . . . . . . . . . . . . . . . . . . . . . . . . . . . . . . . . . . . . . . .

There are numerous versions of the neo-capitalist notion of scientific-technological revolution. In most Western countries their own proponents try to contribute to tactics and strategy of monopoly capital's ideological offensive. But despite the multiplicity of forms of new and old neo-capitalist doctrines, their essence is the same. These doctrines and concepts and similar trends in "industrial sociology" all serve to fill the order placed with the bourgeois ideologists by modern monopoly capital—an order which the owners of firms and corporations have resorted to in order to create the illusion of "class peace" in an exploitative society in the era of the scientific-technological revolution.

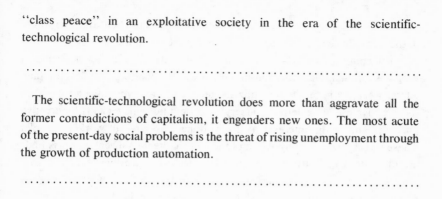

. . . . . . . . . . . . . . . . . . . . . . . . . . . . . . . . . . . . . . . . . . . . . . . . . . . . . . . . . . .

The scientific-technological revolution does more than aggravate all the former contradictions of capitalism, it engenders new ones. The most acute of the present-day social problems is the threat of rising unemployment through the growth of production automation.

. . . . . . . . . . . . . . . . . . . . . . . . . . . . . . . . . . . . . . . . . . . . . . . . . . . . . . . . . . .

The militarisation of science .is a characteristic feature of contemporary capitalism. Achievements in electronics, cybernetics and other new directions in science and technology are placed at the service of imperialism's aggressive plans.

Enormous sums are allocated for the development of new kinds and models of weapons in the imperialist states.

. . . . . . . . . . . . . . . . . . . . . . . . . . . . . . . . . . . . . . . . . . . . . . . . . . . . . . . . . . .

The increasingly rapid rate of scientific and technological progress sharpens the rivalry between different monopoly groups and aggravates inter-imperialist contradictions. The basic stimulus of capitalist production—the extraction of maximum profits—prompts the properietors to improve their equipment and to apply the latest achievements of science to production. Competing firms take every measure to keep their technical and technological secrets from each other, which leads to a steady growth of industrial espionage. One American businessman said that espionage in business is not an ethical problem; it is an established method of business competition.

The competitive struggle has become especially bitter on the world market. US monopolies try to use their superiority in scientific and technological research to grab the key positions in international exchange, try to concentrate in its own hands the basic mass of research in the latest problems of science and production, and to broaden the technical and technological gap between the Old and the New Worlds. There has been a feeling of alarm in Europe for a number of years over the fact that US allocations for scientific research have been four times greater than similar allocations of all the countries of Western Europe combined, and that the Americans are encouraging a brain drain—the migration of scientists and technicians overseas (between 1961 and 1966 alone, 70,000 West European scientists and specialists emigrated to the United States).

The working class and all progressive forces are confident that the future of the technological revolution will ensure unprecedented social progress. The socialist countries are glaringly demonstrating the fruitfulness of technical progress for man. Under socialism there is every opportunity to develop fully all the potentialities of the scientific and technological revolution and to ensure the effective use of modern machinery and scientific achievements for creative purposes and in the interests of the working class and all working people. These possibilities arise by virtue of the fact that technological progress finds an adequate social structure in socialist society. A working people's state possesses the necessary economic and administrative levers for applying the results of the scientific and technological revolution in the interests of all society—so as to satisfy people's material and spiritual needs. With the development of science and technology, physical labour becomes enriched and more creative.

In the socialist world, the intensive development of science and technology and the wide application of the latest achievements to production are both the central economic task and an important political task. Indeed, in the economic competition between the two systems, scientific and technological progress in the socialist countries not only strengthens socialism, it also has an international political and social resonance; on the one hand, it shows capitalism's incompatibility with the humane tasks of ever creative human thought and, on the other, it points to the broad prospects for countries and people during this process and demonstrates the possibilities for an ever fuller satisfaction of the material and spiritual needs of all members of socialist society.

**54. I. Iu. FOMIN, "On the 'Technocratic' Utopia and 'Managerial Revolution,' " S.Sh.A.: EKONOMIKA, POLITIKA, IDEOLOGIIA, No. 2, February 1971, pp. 59-66:** Among the numerous theories designed to conceal the antipopular essence of capitalism, the technocratic concepts of "managerism" and the "managerial revolution" have been widely propagated in postwar America. Arguments about the new role of the "technocracy" in general and managers in particular are one of the methods most frequently used by theoreticians in the West to prove the "transformation" of capitalism under the conditions of the modern scientific and technical revolution. These attempts are aimed at creating the impression that capitalist society is "evolving" and undergoing the sort of changes which make it unlike the old capitalism which compromised itself in the face of the broad masses.

The rapid development of science and technology, the progress of technology and its increasing significance in modern production, and a number of other factors have led to the appearance and relatively wide distribution of different versions of the so-called theory of the "technocracy." Its authors have tried to prove that the old class division of society has become outdated and its "new stratification" has emerged. In contrast to the old division of society on the basis of ownership of production means, a new factor has arisen which has become a determining one in terms of the social grouping of people. This factor is the growing significance of technology. The bourgeoisie, the advocates of this theory maintain, is being replaced by a new group of people, the "technocracy," linked to the technical and administrative management of modern production. These people act only as possessors of special knowledge and are not capitalists.

The appearance and substantiation of the "technocracy" theory is connected primarily with the name of the American, Thorstein Veblen, whose ideas found a particularly broad response among liberal bourgeois economists and the technological intelligentsia during the 1929-1933 economic crisis and subsequent depression. . . .

Pushing off from the fact of the growth of technical engineering workers in production, the advocates of the "technocracy" theory drew the false conclusion that precisely they are the force which is destined to replace the supremacy of the capitalists. These theoreticians sketched out the society of the future, where the leading role would be played not by "greedy" egotistical capitalists but by the "enlightened" servants of production—engineers and technicians. They believed that the engineer was becoming the personification of not only technical progress but also sociopolitical progress. So they treated the growing role of the scientific and technical intelligentsia as a sign of the appearance of a new class. In turn, this delusion was linked to another: the proclaimers of the "technocracy" theory confused two different concepts, mixing up the functions of management of capitalist production with the scientific and engineering work itself. However, the technocrats of the 30's were not united in their views on many questions, including the role of the working class in society's historical fate.

But for the bourgeoisie the main flaw in Veblen's doctrine was the fact that it left no room in the "new" society for capitalist-owners of production means. Therefore, very soon the "technocracy" theory became the object of fierce criticism on the part of such bourgeois authors as, for example, A. Berle. True, the latter does not refute everything but just a few of the technocrats' ideas which are "unacceptable" to the bourgeoisie. He points out that the most important and significant person at the enterprise is not the engineer but the manager, whose activity differs qualitatively from the activity of technical engineering workers.

. . . . . . . . . . . . . . . . . . . . . . . . . . . . . . . . . . . . . . . . . . . . . . . . . . . . . . . . . . . . . . . . . . . . . . . . .

The theory of the "managerial revolution" is directly connected with the whole concept of the "industrial society" of J. Galbraith (as with all other theories on this plane). He writes that in "mature" corporations "capitalists have been simply suspended from power." According to Galbraith the power has passed to the managers in connection with the special role played in a developed "industrial society" by the so-called "technostructure." Its appearance is connected with the development and increasing complexity of technology and the need to plan production. Galbraith's "technostructure" consists of a relatively broad group of people—from the leaders of the largest corporations to the lowest categories of organizational and technical personnel endowed with a variety of technical knowledge and experience. These are all the people without whom modern industrial technology and capitalist programming cannot be implemented. Engineers, production organizers, economists, and finance workers who form part of the technostructure are not only individual people but also an organization to whom the power has passed not only at the enterprise but also in society. Being the synthesis of group individuality, it "far and away transcends the individual as such" and possesses, compared with it, "the advantage of immortality." And further: "When the power is in the hands of a group, it not only passes to an organization but passes to it irretrievably." [J. Galbraith, *The New Industrial State* (Moscow, Russian ed., 1969), pp. 100-101, 107.]

In explaining the motives for the behavior and social thinking of the technostructure, Galbraith has his own approaches but they are fundamentally no different from other technocratic utopias. The technostructure, according to Galbraith strives not for maximum profit "in any event" but for its defined minimum necessary for insuring the maximum growth of the volume of production and sales and also technical progress. Even the monopoly press noted that the author does not make ends meet when the aims of the limitless expansion of sales and the acceleration of technical progress are in fact counterposed to the institution of maximum profit, without a desire for which it is impossible under modern American conditions to accomplish the tasks set by the technostructure.

It should be noted that although Galbraith is an opponent of the financial oligarchy, nevertheless a certain part of it, occupying many important posts in the system of big business, is represented in his technostructure. It is no accident that Galbraith himself is not very satisfied with his technostructure, since, as he realizes himself, it cannot independently formulate broad social

104

methods of approach. The scholar found the solution to this problem by means of idealistic constructions. He believes that the representatives of science must help their former pupils—representatives of the technostructure—and head their movement toward social justice. These attitudes on the part of Galbraith politically disorientate the progressive circles in capitalist countries and replace class struggle with the counter-position of education and ignorance. Galbraith does not separate the lower and middle element of managers from the higher element which implements along with the financial oligarchy the exploitation of the working class and other strata of the population approximate to the working class in terms of their position, although he is essentially the ideologist of the "white collar workers."

. . . . . . . . . . . . . . . . . . . . . . . . . . . . . . . . . . . . . . . . . . . . . . . . . . . . . . . . . . .

Recently there has been an increasingly clearer tendency to limit the group of "powers that be" to a narrow circle of chosen people. For example, Zbigniew Brzezinski maintains that the technocracy, and especially its elite, both has the right to and does in fact lead and determine the development of American society and also of the whole of mankind.

**55. L. I. BREZHNEV, speech at the 24th CPSU Congress, PRAVDA, March 31, 1971:** Comrades, ideological, propaganda, and mass work is an important and responsible sphere of the party's activity. A great deal has been accomplished here, but I must say that we are still not completely satisfied with the state of affairs in this field. The Central Committee deems it necessary to intensify all our ideological work and, above all, to make it more active and purposeful—a propaganda of communist ideals and practical tasks of our construction. In the nearest future one of the central areas of the party's propaganda and agitation mass work must be a thorough explanation to the working people of the sense and significance of the decisions of our congress. To know really how to completely convey to the working masses the full force of our ideological conviction, to approach genuinely and in a truly creative manner the cause of communist education of Soviet man—therein is our main task in this field.

We are living in conditions of unceasing ideological warfare waged against our country and against the socialist world by imperialist propaganda, which is making use of the most refined methods and powerful technical means. All those instruments influencing minds which are in the hands of the bourgeoisie—the press, films, radio—are mobilized to deceive people, to suggest to them the concept of almost heavenly life under capitalism, to slander socialism. The air is literally permeated with various inventions about the life in our country and in the fraternal countries of socialism. It is the duty of our workers of the propaganda and agitation mass front to give timely, resolute, and effective rebuff to these ideological attacks; to bring to hundreds of millions of people the truth about the socialist society, about the Soviet way of life, about the building of communism in our country. And this must be done with conviction, in a convincing manner, with clarity and, I would say, vividly. The voice of truth about the Soviet Union must be heard on all continents of our earth!

Thus, comrades, a substantial part of party work during the period under review has been occupied by problems concerning the sociopolitical development of the Soviet society, the ideological and political education of the working people, the development of science and culture. Substantial results have been achieved in these spheres of communist construction. But more and more complicated tasks face us. We are confident, however, that the party will achieve successes in their solution and will have a unanimous and active support of the whole of our Soviet people. It is precisely because of the cohesion and conscientiousness of the people that our country is strong. The party will unstintingly strengthen this source of our strength, the indestructible ideological-political unity of our Soviet people.

**56.** *V. KORTUNOV, "The Collapse of Imperialist Ideological Myths,"* **INTERNATIONAL AFFAIRS** *(Moscow), No. 3, March 1971, pp. 59-66:* The radical change in the world balance of forces in favour of democracy and socialism has forced the apologists for the bourgeois order to modify the tactics of anti-communism. Fearing (and with good reason) to make an open stand against socialism they prefer to twist and turn, to refrain from calling a spade a spade, and to pour out the old anti-communist concoction from bottles with new labels.

L. I. Brezhnev, exposing the essence of the present tactics and ideological subversion of imperialism against the Marxist-Leninist doctrine, socialism and the liberation movement, told the International Meeting of Communist and Workers' Parties: "Imperialism cannot expect to succeed if it speaks openly of its true aims. It is compelled to create a system of ideological myths to disguise its true intentions and lull the vigilance of the peoples." Bourgeois propaganda has concentrated its main efforts in this direction. It cares little that its myths fail to stand the test of life and go down in the clash with reality. There are always any number of learned professors at hand ready to invent new ones. After all, the whole point of the exercise is not to get at the truth, or to give a true picture of history, but on the contrary to divert people from the truth, to spread plausible illusions, however shortlived, so long as they help to lead them away from the main direction of the liberation struggle and to suggest ideas which poison men's minds and disarm them spiritually.

After the Second World War, especially in the last ten or fifteen years, the ideologists of imperialism and their revisionist yes-men have shown themselves to be exceptionally prolific. They have launched dozens of pseudoscientific doctrines, claiming either to refute or to "improve" the theory and practice of scientific communism, and to whitewash the capitalist system in peoples' eyes. Among them are "people's capitalism," "the affluent society," "the consumer society," "the stages of economic growth," "the post-industrial society," "the single middle class," "convergence," "deideologisation of social life," and many other doctrines, all of which are ambitiously presented as the "last word" in scientific cognition, which allegedly leads Marxism-Leninism in comprehending the new phenomena of present-day reality, like the scientific and technical revolution, state-monopoly capitalism, inter-imperialist integration, and so on, which they say, had noth-been envisaged either by Marx or Lenin.

In effect, however, their efforts amount to an outright distortion of Marxism-Leninism and more or less skillful falsification of reality. The usual method used by the rising lights of bourgeois science is arbitrarily to extract from the the overall process separate phenomena, however important, and to invest them with a significance of their own. Thus, for instance, it has become fashionable in the West recently to expound on the "unexpected" aspects of social life brought about by the scientific and technical revolution, which are said automatically to modify the social nature of capitalism. It is also said that Marxism-Leninism has failed to "take account" of or to "appreciate" these phenomena.

Actually, however, the present-day critics of Marxism criticise their own arbitrary interpretation of Marxism and nothing more. Neither Marx nor Lenin ever claimed to be prophets (even if their fundamental conclusions have proved to be prophetic); they made a study of the historical process as a whole, in its unity and dialectical development. It is this approach (and it is the only possible one for those who really want to understand the regularities of social development) that has enabled Marxism-Leninism to provide exhaustive answers to the fundamental issues of our day, including those connected with the scientific and technical revolution, the development of state-monopoly capitalism, integration, and so on. But that is precisely what the anti-communist ideologists fear most of all, which is why they seek artificially to fragment the coherent process into a multiplicity of isolated phenomena, to range them against each other, and to give each its own interpretation.

. . . . . . . . . . . . . . . . . . . . . . . . . . . . . . . . . . . . . . . . . . . . . . . . . . . . . . . . . . . . . . . . . . . . . . .

The inability of modern capitalism to make full use of the available production facilities, while millions of working people are unable to find jobs, continues to be a chronic and progressive malaise of bourgeois society. Massive unemployment has always gone hand in hand with capitalism. This calamity, which is a constant one for the working people under capitalism, may assume even greater proportions with the growing mechanisation and automation of production on the basis of the latest scientific and technical achievements. Is that perhaps why Western ideologists, while turning technology into something of a fetish, now talk and write more and more about its "destructive" impact, approaching the subject either through the problem of environmental pollution, excessive urbanisation, and the downgrading of the individual in the "machine civilisation"? Bourgeois scientists may put the blame on technology for all sorts of things, but the fact is that technology is in itself blameless. The responsibility for the "destructive" consequences of the machine does not fall on the machine itself, but on the social system which is unable to make reasonable use of it.

In the epoch of its domination, capitalism has managed to boost the productive forces in only a handful of so-called advanced countries, but has proved to be incapable of doing so in vast areas of the globe, and consequently, of making use of its natural resources on a modern technical level. The greater part of the globe consists of economically backward countries, whose native population, like centuries ago, tills the soil with the most primitive implements and, for all the natural resources at its disposal, is time and again unable to subsist on its own. Modern scientific and technical progress has, for all practical purposes, run past that area, because capitalism, which seeks to maintain the vast Afro-Asian continents as its raw material appendages and objects of exploitation, has displayed no interest in their development.

. . . . . . . . . . . . . . . . . . . . . . . . . . . . . . . . . . . . . . . . . . . . . . . . . . . . . . . . . . . . . . . . . . . . . . . .

This inability to resolve the urgent social and political problems has been driving capitalist society more and more into a dead end of contradictions from which it is seeking an exit through stepping up its violence against the working people, violence in every form, including the most extreme, namely, war.

In the 350 years of bourgeois domination, mankind has lost more than 100 million people through war. In the two world wars alone, 60 million died and another 110 million were crippled. Today, imperialism is stepping up the arms race to unprecedented proportions, and is preparing for another war, making use for that purpose of the bulk of its material resources and the latest scientific and technical achievements of human genius.

The whole social practice of the world confirms that nowadays scientific communism alone provides the answers to the basic problems of our day. Under the ideological banner of Marxism-Leninism the Soviet people have gone a long way and have scored epoch-making victories in every economic, political and cultural sphere. Under the ideological banner of Marxism-Leninism, the communist parties have been working out effective programmes in the struggle for social progress. Of all the political parties of the modern world, only the communist parties have clear-cut answers to questions like international security, national liberation, effective struggle against the sway of the monopolies, and the way to prevent imperialism from committing its last and most horrible crime—plunging mankind into the holocaust of a thermonuclear war.

57. *V. KOLOMIITSEV, "Essence of a Sociological Concept" (Review of Alain Touraine,* La Société Post-Industrielle, *Paris, Editions Denoel, 1969),* INTERNATIONAL AFFAIRS *(Moscow), No. 4, April 1971, pp. 101-102:* The theory of the post-industrial society has received strong support in recent years from prominent Western sociologists, including Daniel Bell and other American sociologists. This bourgeois theory, aimed at proving the stability of the capitalist system, asserts that in contemporary capitalist society the class division becomes meaningless and the class struggle—futile. Its proponents bow to technological determinism, trying to prove that the level of industrial development is the only criterion of progress, while the social structure of society is automatically adapted to changes in the level of productive forces.

Alain Touraine, Professor of Sociology at Nanterre University, is one of the staunchest French supporters of the post-industrial society concept. The publishers who put out his latest book in a series of essays on the post-industrial society bill him as a "pioneer sociologist".

. . . . . . . . . . . . . . . . . . . . . . . . . . . . . . . . . . . . . . . . . . . . . . . . . . . . . . . . . . . . . . . . . . . . . . . . .

Alain Touraine's sociological outlines are inconsistent and contradictory. They at times take account of the real contradictions of modern capitalism, and he now and then is critical and writes about social conflicts. Meanwhile, he persistently tries to whitewash and defend the historically-doomed social system. He believes that sociologists should not give way to economists in forecasting and programming the capitalist world's social development. He holds that the Western sociologists' task is to show the nature of social conflicts and to neutralise their affects, which are dangerous to the bourgeoisie.

Prof. Touraine's book shows once again that bourgeois ideologists are trying to reduce the intensity of the class struggle and replace the revolutionary struggle with vague reforms which would not affect the basis of capitalism.

**58.** *V. S. SEMENOV, "Certain Traits of Apologetic Conceptions of Capitalism,"* **S.Sh.A.: EKONOMIKA, POLITIKA, IDEOLOGIIA,** *No. 4, April 1971, pp. 63-68:* With the help of politicians and public figures, ideologists, and scholars, over the last two decades or more the imperialist bourgeoisie has formulated a large number of conceptions whose purpose is to defend the capitalist system and to falsify Marxism-Leninism and has put them to practical propaganda purposes. These are the theories of "people's capitalism," "the affluent society," "stages of growth," "the single industrial society," "the Great Society," "the molded society," "convergence," "the postindustrial society," "the scientific society," and the like.

Bourgeois theories on questions of social development have undergone a definite evolution in recent decades. Originally (in the latter half of the forties and in the fifties of this century), the principal attention of their authors was concentrated on an apologetic evaluation of the internal development of capitalist society. Rather little consideration was given to the external aspect of the interaction between capitalism and socialism.

. . . . . . . . . . . . . . . . . . . . . . . . . . . . . . . . . . . . . . . . . . . . . . . . . . . . . . . . . . . . . . . . .

The synthetic bourgeois doctrine of "people's capitalism," supplemented by the conception of the "affluent society," was formulated on the basis of these apologetic conceptions. In the reformist literature this stage is characterized by dissemination of theories of the "transformation" of capitalism, of its transition to "democratic" or "humanistic" socialism.

. . . . . . . . . . . . . . . . . . . . . . . . . . . . . . . . . . . . . . . . . . . . . . . . . . . . . . . . . . . . . . . . .

In the bourgeois theories concerning the alteration of capitalism which were formulated in the sixties an increasingly large place began to be occupied by a comparison of the development of capitalism and socialism, a comparison whose purpose was to defend the bourgeois system in every way possible. At the end of the fifties the doctrine of the "single industrial society" took shape in bourgeois ideology; this doctrine regards all the industrially advanced countries of capitalism and socialism to be components of some "single" industrial and social entity. Theories of the "mass society," of the "consumer society," etc., became widespread in the United States and a number of other countries. The theory of "stages of growth" was set forth in the writings of the American bourgeois economist and sociologist W. W. Rostow; this theory lays claim to a social-philosophical explanation of world history and of the basic levels and stages of the development of humanity. A set of bourgeois views concerning the processes of the interaction, interrelationship, and prospects for development of capitalism and socialism has taken shape, and it has come to be called the theory of "convergence."

. . . . . . . . . . . . . . . . . . . . . . . . . . . . . . . . . . . . . . . . . . . . . . . . . . . . . . . . . . . . . . . . .

*The Technologism of the Bourgeois Theories and Speculation*
*on Scientific and Technical Achievements*

Bourgeois theories are still a product of their time and of concrete historic conditions, but they are a product which reflects real circumstances in a false and distorted form that is socially beneficial to the bourgeoisie. All of these bourgeois conceptions we have mentioned reflect—primarily in distorted form —technical shifts in the capitalist countries since World War II, and they constitute the bourgeois ideological product of the scientific and technical revolution which began in the middle of the fifties.

The bourgeois theories of the "industrial society," of "stages of growth," of "convergence," of the "postindustrial society," of the "scientific society," and others like them are based on the fact of the scientific and technical revolution in the industrially advanced countries of capitalism and socialism; this is a qualitatively new form of development of the productive forces in the middle of the twentieth century, and it is marked by discoveries and achievements in the fields of cybernetics and atomic energy. . . .

The bourgeois ideologists and theoreticians strive to describe capitalism not in terms of its social traits, nor in terms of the production relations that exist, but in terms of its technical-and-economic indices. They deliberately depart from a social description of capitalist and socialist societies, gloss over the fundamental contradiction between them, detach the productive forces from production relations, and ignore the latter. The launching of the term "industrial society," R. Aron has written, "is for me a means of avoiding the socialism-capitalism conflict from the very outset and of regarding socialism and capitalism as two species of the same genus, the industrial society, for example. . . . I do not ask the question: What are the social consequences of the capitalist system? but I am concerned with the question of the social consequences of industrial society as a whole."

In the present age countries of the two fundamentally opposed systems—the socialist and the capitalist—may, indeed, be industrial. These countries include the USSR and the United States, Czechoslovakia and England, the German Democratic Republic and West Germany. But socialism prevails in some of them and capitalism in the others. In order to correctly describe the socioeconomic nature of these two groups of countries, we must first describe the level of development of productive forces in these countries and, second, accurately describe the production relations that prevail in these countries, i.e., the social system. An analysis of the two aspects of the mode of production—the productive forces and the production relations—is a compulsory condition for proper definition of the socioeconomic nature of any country.

. . . . . . . . . . . . . . . . . . . . . . . . . . . . . . . . . . . . . . . . . . . . . . . . . . . . . . . . . . . . . . .

Vulgar technicism is manifested in the bourgeois authors in that they mechanically and metaphysically draw conclusions from technical development concerning the development of all other aspects of the life of society and of its functioning as a whole. A group of American sociologists is convinced, for example, that the "socioeconomic organization of society will be increasingly standardized from one society to another if societies introduce more and more advanced engineering. Socioeconomic arrangements will differ more and more from one another if their technical achievements are different."

. . . . . . . . . . . . . . . . . . . . . . . . . . . . . . . . . . . . . . . . . . . . . . . . . . . . . . . . . . . . . . . . . . . . . . .

D. Bell asserts that the "postindustrial society" will in approximately 40 or 50 years replace the present "industrial society," which exists in our time in the United States, England, West Germany, France, and the other advanced capitalist countries.

The postindustrial society, according to him, is distinguished from the present industrial society mainly by the different level of technological development. "Whereas the leading figures in the last 100 years were entrepreneurs, businessmen, and managers; scientists, mathematicians, economists, and engineers of the new computer equipment are becoming the 'new' people. The principal institutions of the new society . . . will be intellectual institutes. The leading role will be played not by businessmen or corporations such as we see them today (since production will be routinized to a considerable degree), but by research corporations, industrial laboratories, experimental stations, and universities.

. . . . . . . . . . . . . . . . . . . . . . . . . . . . . . . . . . . . . . . . . . . . . . . . . . . . . . . . . . . . . . . . . . . . . . .

D. Bell and other bourgeois ideologists ignore the content of the process of the transformation of one social organism into another because they are not interested in the actual replacement of the present society in the United States and the other capitalist countries by a society that is really new. The shaping of the new society encompasses an entire set of phenomena: technical, economic, social, political, ideological, intellectual, and psychological. The entire social organism is changing from top to bottom. Its socioeconomic content, its mode of production, its property relations, and the technical-and-economic and social structure of society are changing above all.

This is what is happening in connection with the replacement of capitalist society by socialist society, which is actually being accomplished in history.

Everything in society is being renewed: above all, the "mechanism" which sets it in motion—the totality of production relations. The new method of production ensures both its new growth rates and dimensions and also, which is particularly important, the possibility of scientifically substantiated, proportional, and planned development of production and of the entire social organism as a whole.

. . . . . . . . . . . . . . . . . . . . . . . . . . . . . . . . . . . . . . . . . . . . . . . . . . . . . . . . . . . . . . . . .

For all their technicism and emphasis on the technical aspect, the conceptions of "stages of growth" and of the "industrial" and "postindustrial" societies are shot through with subjectivism, arbitrariness, and idealism. They step aside from what is the main thing in social development, from the patterns that are objectively manifested. This is the fundamental distinction between this kind of bourgeois theory and Marxism-Leninism, which derives the new society not from its desires, not from subjective conjectures, but from the objective tendency in the development of the previous social organism.

Subjective hypotheses are unable to substantiate the emergence of some sort of "new" society, whatever name is given it: the "mature" society, the "industrial" society, or the "postindustrial" society. These arbitrary hypotheses are very far from science, and they run directly counter to it. They cannot serve as the foundation either for truly scientific forecasting or for scientific planning of the development of society.

*Falsification of the Sociopolitical Nature of the Capitalist System*

Although the theoretical conceptions of contemporary bourgeois ideology are chiefly parasites on the progressive changes taking place in engineering and science even in the capitalist countries, their basic purpose is not at all to reveal the significance of scientific and technical achievements, but an attempt to prove that sociopolitical progress is on the rise in capitalist society. In other words, the emphasis on technicism is only a means by which the bourgeois ideologists and theoreticians "reinforce" the unproven thesis of the social and political "progress" of the contemporary capitalist system.

. . . . . . . . . . . . . . . . . . . . . . . . . . . . . . . . . . . . . . . . . . . . . . . . . . . . . . . . . . . . . . . . .

Given the ever greater exacerbation of social problems and contradictions, the main class and political task of bourgeois apologetic conceptions is now to embellish contemporary capitalism from the sociopolitical standpoint. Overemphasizing in every way the shifts in the domain of engineering and science, the bourgeois conceptions put the main emphasis on attempts to prove that major shifts and changes are taking place in the social and political life of the capitalist countries.

The leitmotif of most of these apologetic conceptions is that bourgeois society has altered its social nature. This was asserted by the theory of "people's capitalism." Later the point was to accumulate more and more new adjectives:

the "mature" society, the "great" society, the "molded" society. Whereas emphasis in some conceptions was placed on the supposed prosperity that was coming for all (the "affluent society," the "state of universal prosperity"), emphasis in others was put on the questions of the social unity of people (the "single" industrial society).

But these apologetic inventions are more and more coming into conflict with objective reality. The facts convincingly show that the main cause of the contradictory, morbid, and conflict-torn state of social life in the advanced capitalist countries is not the productive forces of society, but capitalist production relations, the socioeconomic nature of the capitalist system. Under capitalism the productive forces and engineering are still "working," but the system of socioeconomic relations and all social relations is skidding more and more.

### The Aspiration to Adapt Social Currents and Movements to the Purposes of Preserving the Capitalist System

From the standpoint of domestic problems, the class and political purpose of the bourgeois ideological conceptions, particularly the official doctrines, is to defend capitalism, to embellish it, to prove its viability and progressiveness. In what way is this being done? What means and methods are bourgeois authors using in striving to achieve these goals? What is the main issue that reveals the back-room methodology of contemporary bourgeois apologetic doctrines?

. . . . . . . . . . . . . . . . . . . . . . . . . . . . . . . . . . . . . . . . . . . . . . . . . . . . . . . . . . . . . . . .

From the standpoint of the imperialist political and ideological bosses, the best and in practice the most reliable way of defending capitalism is to accommodate the masses of people—with all their moods, moral values, orientations, and behavioral motivations, with all their social actions and acts—to the exploitative capitalist system, to its main principles, standards, values, and ideas. Inculcating conformism, adaptability, the narrow horizons of the man on the street, and petty bourgeois social inaction means blunting the class antagonism, social conflicts, and contradictions that are continuously being generated by capitalism and stemming the tide of social protests and social demonstrations.

The invariable components in the bourgeois apologetic theories have always been and still are the ideas of consumerism, "a tolerable way of life," Philistinism, narrow-mindedness, acquisitiveness, and comfortable existence. This has had an effect on the frame of mind and mode of behavior of a certain part of the workers. V. I. Lenin noted that "the working class has manifested

114

two tendencies in its political and economic activity under capitalism. On the one hand, there has been the tendency to accommodate comfortably and tolerably under capitalism, which was feasible only for the small upper stratum of the proletariat. On the other hand, there has been the tendency to take the lead for all the workers and the exploited masses in the revolutionary overthrow of the rule of capitalism in general.''

Acquisitiveness has recently been advertised with particular insistence in the theories of the "consumer society" and the "mass society." But if, say, we also take the conception of the "Great Society," we also find at its center arguments that assert "universal prosperity," "abundance for all," and the like in the United States.

The thinking man feels uncomfortable in this mass-organized society of consumption, of achieving a "decent standard of living," of the mass pursuit of things and the generally accepted standards of the "American way of life." The result of this has been the appearance of a whole series of ideological and social currents that do not accept this organized and standard way of life, that protest against the fetish of material prosperity alongside spiritual poverty, that protest against the transformation of man into a one-sided being who thinks only of maintaining the standards of ideological and material existence and the established norms and "values" that are imposed on him.

The process of social awakening of ever broader groups of the population is inexorably marching through all the difficulties that confront it. The protest against the entire system of social relations created by capitalism and against the entire way of life advertised by the bourgeoisie is growing. The progressive workers, the advanced representatives of all groups of the workers and the population, the best of whom are members of the communist and worker parties, are marching in the avant-garde of the sociopolitical struggle.

**59. N. I. LAPIN, Doctor of Philosophical Sciences, "An International Meeting of Sociologists: Congress in Bulgaria," VESTNIK AKADEMII NAUK SSSR, No. 4, April 1971, pp. 67-68:** Every four years the International Sociological Association assembles the sociologists of different countries to discuss the most important problems of their science. The regular Seventh International Sociological Congress was held on 14-19 September 1970 in Varna, Bulgaria. Participating in it were 3550 sociologists of over 50 countries. The Soviet delegation, numbering 450 persons, was headed by vice-president of the AS USSR A. M. Rumiantsev.

. . . . . . . . . . . . . . . . . . . . . . . . . . . . . . . . . . . . . . . . . . . . . . . . . . . . . . . . . . . . . . . . . . . .

Soviet and foreign Marxists criticized the latest bourgeois concept of the future which found reflection at the Congress in the reports of the well-known sociologists T. Parsons (USA), I. Galtung (Norway), F. Tenbruck (West Germany), and others. The basis of those concepts is a striving to modernize bourgeois society, to conceal its historical doom and substantiate the "convergence" of capitalism and socialism through the absolutization of some aspect of the social process. Thus, the "theory of the mass society" concentrates attention on planning the needs of the "average man" (more precisely, the average bourgeois); "the theory of the technocratic society" reduces all problems to a need to transfer social control to a selected group of engineers; "the theory of the post-industrial society" advances the role of science to the foreground, etc. The scientific approach to society, however, consists in the fact that it is regarded as an integral social organism. Such an approach permits revealing the radical opposition of the social orders of capitalism and socialism, and by the same token the principal differences in the content and role of the particular problems arising in a given society.

This was demonstrated at the special session on "Leninism and theoretical problems of contemporary social development," in which the introductory speech was made by P. N. Fedoseyev (USSR). Participating in the work of the session were eminent workers of the Communist and Workers' parties of Bulgaria, Cyprus, France, and Tunisia and scientists of Italy, the USA, and other countries. Their reports showed the growing interest of progressive sociologists of the entire world in the Leninist theoretical legacy.


*60. Colonel V. SEREBRIANNIKOV, "The 'Convergence' Theory in Military Uniform," KRASNAIA ZVEZDA, July 8, 1971:* The most important front of the irreconcilable class struggle between capitalism and socialism now runs through the sphere of scientific and technical progress. Sharp ideological skirmishes are developing over its problems and particularly over the question of the social consequences of the development of science and technology. In striving to impose their false, all-egotistical notions upon public opinion, the imperialist ideologists are premeditatedly distorting too the processes which are taking place, under the influence of scientific and technical progress, in military matters.

The aspiration to adapt the "convergence" theory to an explanation of the changes in the armed forces of states with opposed systems is inherent in many bourgeois authors.

Such deductions are devoid of any scientific character. It has long been proved that the nature and purpose of armies are determined by the nature of the social system and the policy and the ideology of the dominant classes. The army is an element of the political superstructure, it is created and directed by the state, and it implements the state's policy.

As for the social consequences of the scientific and technical revolution, they have different directions and natures under the conditions of contrary systems.

Under the conditions of socialism the progress of science and technology accelerates the progressive movement of society, consolidates its unity, and promotes the fuller realization of its historic advantages. Under conditions of capitalism, scientific and technical progress inevitably aggravates the contradictions and deepens the general crisis of this system; the achievements of science and technology, through the fault of imperalism, are directed not toward the good of mankind but are used for barbaric, reactionary purposes. This, naturally, finds its logical reflection in the sphere of military matters too.

Consequently the outwardly similar processes in the development of armaments do not change and cannot change the class-political nature, the essence and the purpose of armies.

Bourgeois ideologists also distort the essence of the changes that are taking place under the influence of the scientific and technical revolution in the personnel, particularly in the officer corps of armies, and in the nature of military activity. Considering the triumph of technology to be the main thing now, they are proclaiming the "end of ideology" and they are bringing to the forefront, as the American sociologist D. Bell does, the "technical approach" to all social questions. According to these opinions, the officers and the military commanders are allegedly transformed into simple executors of established technical norms, into an attribute of the purely "technical-information" administration.

However, the "investigations" of the convergencists are far from inoffensive. It is a question of patent ideological subversive activity which is calculated to blunt the class consciousness of the working people and their vigilance regarding imperialism. At the same time, by such "theories" the bourgeois ideologists are fanning the adventurism and aggressiveness of imperialism, and are spiritually corrupting the soldiers and officers of their armies and preparing them for destructive war. And this is why the task of exposing the apologists of reaction and aggression is so urgent.

*61. Academician T. KHACHATUROV, "Directions of Economic Research in the New Five-Year Plan," VOPROSY EKONOMIKI, No. 8, August 1971, p. 6:* An important section of the general theoretical subject matter is criticism of bourgeois and revisionist concepts, especially those pertaining to the principles of socialist economic development. On the one hand, criticism of "neo-Keynesian" and "neoclassical" theories and the theory of "convergence" will be continued, as will criticism of socioeconomic models of future society as envisioned by bourgeois economists, that is, the society of "universal prosperity," in which a rebirth of the working class purportedly takes place and "true" socialism in a petty-bourgeois sense prevails. On the other hand, criticism of bourgeois and revisionist concepts of the socialist economy, criticism of attempts to prove the need for "commercial socialism," criticism of the rejection of centralized planning, and criticism of the theories of "barrack socialism" are of real significance.

*62. Iu. Ia. OL'SEVICH, Candidate of Economic Sciences, "Methodology of Criticism of Anti-Marxist Concepts of Socialism," VESTNIK AKADEMII NAUK SSSR, No. 8, August 1971, pp. 73-80:* In the book *Prospects for Soviet Society*, written by a group of American sovietologists, there is an attempt to re-evaluate the views of the prospects of socialism which have formed in the last decade in bourgeois literature. In the book it is stated that bourgeois ideologists approach this question from three points of view. Some state that "contemporary totalitarianism," which has been completely reinforced, will actually become permanent and capable of adapting to new requirements without important change in their principles. Others say that the entire "experiment of Bolshevism" is allegedly only a temporary turning on the path to modernization and gradually, they say, the Soviet Union will more and more resemble "American and European society." According to the third, both Western societies and the Soviet Union (as well as the socialist countries in general) are allegedly developing in the direction of a still not clearly defined society of the type of a "hybrid."

. . . . . . . . . . . . . . . . . . . . . . . . . . . . . . . . . . . . . . . . . . . . . . . . . . . . . . . . . . . . . . .

The views of the authors of the book *Prospects for Soviet Society* on the whole can be classed as belonging to the relatively moderate, conservative direction in contemporary bourgeois ideology. True, those "theoreticians" interpret without discernment the path along which the Soviet Union is proceeding and distortedly represent the driving forces of development, but their acknowledgment that socialist society is successfully developing along its own characteristic path is remarkable in itself.

A characterization of socialism and its prospects of a different type is given in a book by two reactionary bourgeois ideologists H. Kahn and A. Wiener entitled *The Year 2000: A Framework for Speculation on the Next Thirty-Three Years*. In discussing the allegedly observed transition in the Soviet Union from "totalitarianism" to "authoritarianism" the authors pessimistically see in that the "phenomenon of convergence," which, it seems to them, "will halt a long time before the achievement of parliamentary democracy."

In their opinion, socialism is most probably doomed almost to social stagnation, whereas before capitalism, especially American capitalism, the rosy prospects of the "postindustrial society" are allegedly opening up.

. . . . . . . . . . . . . . . . . . . . . . . . . . . . . . . . . . . . . . . . . . . . . . . . . . . . . . . . . . . . . . . . . . . . . . . . . . . .

Whereas the bourgeois critics of socialism, emphasizing the difference between socialism and capitalism, start from the thesis of the so-called "advantages" of capitalism, the ideologists of the petty bourgeoisie, on the contrary, attempt to slander socialism, identifying it to some degree with capitalism.

"The antagonism of the forces of capitalism and socialism in the world arena, like attempts of various types of revisionists to emasculate the revolutionary teaching and distort the practice of the building of socialism and communism," it was stated in the report of L. I. Brezhnev at the 24th Party Congress, "requires from us also further intensified attention to problems of theory and its creative development. The repetition of old formulas where they have already become outdated, inability or unwillingness to approach new problems in a new way — all this harms the cause and creates additional possibilities for the spread of revisionist falsifications under Marxism-Leninism. The convincingness of criticism of bourgeois and revisionist attacks on our theory and practice is intensified to an enormous degree when it is based on an active and creative development of the social sciences and Marxist-Leninist theory."

. . . . . . . . . . . . . . . . . . . . . . . . . . . . . . . . . . . . . . . . . . . . . . . . . . . . . . . . . . . . . . . . . . . . . . . . . . . .

In criticizing our opponents it is necessary for us to recall that one of the most important spheres of the struggle against bourgeois and revisionist theories is becoming more and more the functioning of the economic mechanism, which requires special knowledge, especially in the area of administration. At the same time the expanding scientific and technical revolution substantially changes not only the means and methods of production of objects of labor and products of labor, but also the system of technical relations of production. Those objective changes serve as a starting point for a number of new reformist, rightist and leftist reformist concepts of socialism which require special analysis.

In bourgeois political economy one notes a process of transformation of theories of growth (and of long-term quantitative forecasts based on them) into the theory of evolution of socio-economic systems and forecasts based on them of the long-term qualitative change of the structures of capitalism and socialism. The criticism of such "futurological" concepts is impossible without scientific elaboration of the problems pertaining to the gradual transition from socialism to communism.

By starting from what has been said and also with consideration of the organizational structure of our economic science which has formed, it is possible to distinguish the following directions and problems for critical investigations in the given area: problems of methodology and the history of Marxist-Leninist criticism of bourgeois and petty bourgeois economic theories of socialism; criticism of bourgeois and revisionist views of the development of the economy of the countries of socialism; criticism of bourgeois-reformist and revisionist concepts of the "socialist transformation" of the economy of imperialist states; and analysis of non-Marxist concepts of socialism in the developing countries.

63. *Colonel K. PAIUSOV, Candidate of Philosophical Sciences, "What Is Hidden Behind Preaching of a 'Universal' Ideology?"* **KRASNAIA ZVEZDA,** *September 24, 1971:* The adaptation of modern capitalism to new world conditions, the desire of the bourgeoisie to keep the masses under its ideological and political control find expression in the search for new methods and uses of the ideological defense of the old world, in the struggle with communism. One consequence of this is the appearance on the front of the ideological class struggle of the two systems of the so-called 'liberal" or "intellectual" anticommunism.

The peculiar characteristic of the present multi-faceted anticommunism consists in the fact that its representatives do not wish to identify themselves with open reaction. . . . They claim to be "unprejudiced," "objective" and even nearly "respectful" in their approach to Marxism. But this "quiet," "liberal-intellectual" anticommunism is no less dangerous. What they plan is the "erosion" of communist ideology, the implanting of "class neutrality" among the toiling masses, the weakening of their will in the struggle against imperialism.

To this end, in particular, is aimed the concept of "universal" ideology, which, in recent years, is being especially actively developed by bourgeois philosophers and sociologists. The essence of this fashionable theory is trivial in its simplicity. It focuses the attention on the so-called "universal human interests," on abstract "non-class" ideals. Its partisans say: in our century, people, regardless of class, nationality, race or world view, have one common interest — to prevent a nuclear war, with its tragic consequences for mankind, from breaking out. Why not, on the basis of this common interest, rise above class and national contradictions; why not create a universal, global ideology. . . . ?

Along with this the bourgeois ideologues recommend the most varied ways of creating the "universal" ideology. . . . But at the present the predominant [theory] is that of the so-called technological direction of social analysis, which is represented by the American ideologues, D. Bell and D. Hertz and others. They see the path to spiritual universalism on the basis of the "convergence" of the industrially developed countries with opposing social systems.

While demanding the cessation of the struggle of ideas, the supporters of "universal" ideological synthesis are guided subjectively by various motives. In fact, some do not care about ideological conciliation. For them it is only a tactic, a clever gimmick for the purpose of weakening the influence of communist ideology in the bourgeois countries and to camouflage ideological subversion against the socialist countries. Others, sincerely seeking a path to firm peace, mistakenly see it in a "common ideology." Among them there are many prominent scientists, partisans of peace, opponents of militarism and war from among the worldly and religious pacifists. It is important to note these distinctions. But the essence of the matter is that all partisans of a "universal" ideology, regardless of their motives, have one thing in common — the dissolution of socialist into bourgeois ideology.

In what lies the theoretical unsoundness and political harm of this concept? Its methodological basis is bourgeois objectiveness, the denial of the class concept of ideological partisanship. The objectivism arises from an ideological, unrealistic concept of a "universal man." But a "universal man" does not exist. There is specific man as the aggregate of social relations, as the representative of a specific epoch, of his social milieu, of his class. There is also in nature no "universal interest." Common interest exists only as inseparably tied to the particular, to the interests of a specific class, nation, etc. Consequently, the basic assumption of objectivism concerning the possibility of attaining an "objective," "above class" point of view is without foundation. . . .

Under the conditions of the present world which is divided into opposing social systems and antagonistic classes, the political harm of the concept of "universal" ideology lies in that it gives birth to utopian hopes that the cardinal problems of our epoch can be solved by means of a simple agreement of all peoples to do good. The preaching of abstract "above class" ideals, behind the smokescreen with which the bourgeoisie camouflages its class goals, may give rise among some people not only in the bourgeoisie, but also in the socialist countries as well, to unrealizable illusions and dull their vigilance concerning the aggressive plots of imperialist circles.

The danger of the "universalist" ideology consists in the fact that it gambles on the real and vital problems of the present time, on the desire of the peoples for peace and mutual understanding, and hides behind the widely popular principle of peaceful coexistence of states with different social systems, but passes over in silence the fact that this principle by no means implies ideological coexistence. . . .

Ideological "peace," the unification of ideals can signify but one thing: the opposing classes give up their fundamental interests and objectives. But isn't it naive to expect that the bourgeoisie will give up the principles of the capitalist system? Is it possible that the working class will give up its interests which are scientifically expressed in communist ideology?

Experience shows that in our time not a single class shows the least desire to give up its class point of view. Who, then, in the views of the proponents of the "universal" ideological concept will be the bearer of the "global" consciousness? The "universalists" place their hopes mainly in a "republic of the educated," i.e., the intelligentsia. It is alleged that it is less subject to national and class prejudices and can more easily come to an agreement. . . .

The main hope is placed in the technological intelligentsia which, in the opinion of the theoreticians of ideological unification, is the farthest removed from politics. . . .

At the center of the present epoch stands not the intelligentsia but the international working class and its offspring — the world socialist system. The progressive intelligentsia in the bourgeois countries is one of the detachments of the great army of liberation and peace. It can follow no other path than that of alliance with the international working class which struggles under the banner of the Marxist-Leninist ideology. The preaching of intellectual "universalism" feeds the vain hope that it may be possible to persuade the imperialists and militarists to voluntarily give up exploitation, oppression of the masses and aggressive intentions. In order to assure, let us say, peaceful coexistence of states with different social systems, what is needed is not "peace" in ideology, but determined struggle against imperialism.

For a quarter of a century now, mankind has been free of world war. The triumph of the Leninist policy of peaceful coexistence of states with different social systems is based not on ideological tolerance but on the power of the world socialist system. . . .

Under the conditions of the intensification of imperialism's aggressiveness there is no more effective means of preventing a world missile-nuclear war than assisting in every possible way the growth of the economic and military might of the world socialist systems, the unity of all anti-imperialist forces and to put into practice the constructive ideas for the active struggle to strengthen international security which have been proposed by the Soviet Union and other brotherly socialist countries.

**64.** *Review of book by M.B. Mitin,* et al., **Modern Bourgeois Theories on Convergence of Capitalism and Socialism (Critical Analysis),** *in* **KOMMUNIST,** *No. 13, September 1971, pp. 125-128:* The convergence concept was brought into bourgeois sociology from the science of biology where it means the appearance of similar features in different organisms as a result of their adaptation to the same environment. The supporters of this theory claim that a similar process is currently taking place in the two world socio-economic systems, socialism and capitalism. If bourgeois ideologists are to be believed as development takes place in each of these, processes occur which increase the similarity between them [i.e., the systems]. Allegedly, capitalism and socialism are irreversibly progressing toward each other in order to meet at a certain point and converge, i.e., merge once and for all and form a mixed society, a hybrid society, a compromise society, neither socialism nor capitalism but something else endowed with certain elements of both. The careful analysis of such a speculative future society, as presented by the imagination of the bourgeois theoreticians, leaves no doubt that it would remain, essentially, the same old state-monopolistic capitalism. The latter, in the opinion of the supporters of the theory of convergence, needs no more than some partial improvements. They predict that socialism would experience far greater substantial changes. The bourgeois ideologists claim that socialism must abandon the public ownership of capital goods, the leading role of the communist party, etc.—in a word, voluntarily to take the path of gradual capitalist degeneracy. This program was quite clearly formulated in the famous "Two Thousand Words" in which the anti-Socialist elements in Czechoslovakia and their Western inspirers and supporters clearly indicated what they understand by "improvement" and "renaissance" of socialism.

The failure of these plans was also a blow at the convergence theory itself. The events in Czechoslovakia showed that the "quiet" counterrevolution has just as few chances to succeed as open sallies against socialism. The role of the theory of convergence called upon, like a smokescreen, to conceal the undermining by anticommunists of the foundations of the socialist society, was depreciated greatly. We must take into consideration, however, that as long as the anticommunists have not abandoned the hope of "ideologically softening" socialism, in one or another aspect they will continue to utilize the theory of convergence in "psychological warfare." Therefore, the thorough analysis and systematic exposure of this theory completely retain their political urgency.

We should note (as can be well seen throughout the materials of the collection) that the term "theory of convergence" is a collective concept. In the camp supporting this concept various currents, sometimes contradictory, can be detected. However, they are all based on an attempt to refute the historically proved Marxist-Leninist conclusion of the historical inevitability and law-governed nature of the revolutionary replacement of the capitalist system by the socialist system.

. . . . . . . . . . . . . . . . . . . . . . . . . . . . . . . . . . . . . . . . . . . . . . . . . . . . . . . . . . . . . . . . . . . .

In 1960 W. Rostow offered his ambitious concept of the "stages of economic growth." According to Rostow in the course of its historical development all mankind goes through five stages. The final stages—maturity and high mass-consumption—belong to the "single industrial society." According to Rostow the USSR is in the first of these stages while the U.S. and the most developed capitalist countries in Western Europe are in the second. This way an attempt is being made to suppress the fact that socialism is an immeasurably higher level of social development compared with capitalism, eliminate the question of communism as the future of all mankind and replace communism with the chimera of the "single industrial society" and "prove" that in the progress toward this far-fetched objective capitalism is considerably outstripping its opponent.

Such is the soil on which have grown the weeds of the "new" theory on future social progress. The most frank and malicious "Sovietologists" do not conceal the factual purpose of this concept. Thus, together with another professional "Sovietologist," S. Huntington, as early as 1964 Z. Brzezinski frankly admitted that "most theories of the so-called convergence in reality postulate not a convergence but the absorption of the opposite system."

. . . . . . . . . . . . . . . . . . . . . . . . . . . . . . . . . . . . . . . . . . . . . . . . . . . . . . . . . . . . . . . . . . . .

Bearing in mind that the economic side of the convergence theory on the surface is most thoroughly supported in reactionary bourgeois literature, the critical response of the Soviet scientists to this literature has been quite substantial and broad: dozens of solid monographs have been published witheringly criticizing the theory of the "general welfare state," "single industrial society" or "stages of economic growth."

So far the falsifying methods of the anticommunists in the fields of Soviet economics and the economy of the other socialist countries have been studied less. Yet, various "Sovietologists" are actively claiming that the economic reforms now under way in the world socialist system precisely prove a convergence, a sliding toward a market socialism or a mixed socialist society and, in the future, capitalism. Particular emphasis is placed on linguistic similarities and the names given to a number of economic categories, particularly those of profits under capitalist and socialist conditions, totally ignoring the fact that they mean entirely different things.

. . . . . . . . . . . . . . . . . . . . . . . . . . . . . . . . . . . . . . . . . . . . . . . . . . . . . . . . . . . . . . . . .

In J. Galbraith's imaginary hybrid society the power is in the hands of the "elite," the "technocrats." Here the theory of convergence has inherited the concepts of the bourgeois technocrats existing more than one decade and which were quite thoroughly analyzed in our literature.

The scientific-technical revolution was the pretext for the galvanizing and further developing of these views. Its content and social consequences are speculatively interpreted in several directions by the supporters of the convergence theory. Distorting the Marxist thesis to the effect that the development of production forces is at the basis of the changes and the development of production methods, its supporters are trying to prove that the tempestuous technological progress today has an identical impact on capitalism and socialism, being precisely the type of objective force which requires the unification of the social systems, i.e., the type of force leading them toward convergence. What is deliberately ignored is that the production forces influence the socio-political system not directly but through production relations.

Bearing in mind that the scientific-technical revolution creates, as a side product, mass destruction means unparalleled in terms of their destructive force, the proponents of the convergence theory give their theories a certain military-political aspect. They speculate on the most sacred feelings of the people, demagogically using a nonexisting alternative: either the indescribable horrors of a world nuclear war or convergence.

. . . . . . . . . . . . . . . . . . . . . . . . . . . . . . . . . . . . . . . . . . . . . . . . . . . . . . . . . . . . . . . . .

The anticommunists greatly rely on the convergence of ideas, on the allegedly inevitable de-ideologization of the Soviet society and the conversion of our theory into "open Marxism," allowing extensive borrowing from the ideas of right-wing socialists and bourgeois scientists. The views of the authors of the theory of convergence played a major role in the "bridge building" or "moat filling" concepts formulated in the mid-sixties.

Unquestionably, the theory of convergence is influencing the ideological positions of various types of renegades from Marxism-Leninism. It supplies the right-wing renegades with an entire assortment of economic models "combining" socialism with capitalism. As to the "left-wing" revisionists, vulgarly interpreting socialism in a bureaucratic-barracks spirit, they essentially act as procurers of additional arguments used by the bourgeois theoreticians on the unacceptability of socialism "in its pure aspect." Meanwhile, like the supporters of the theory of convergence, they slanderously depict the development of the USSR and the other socialist countries. In conclusion, let us mention the criticism ever more frequently voiced toward the theory of convergence in the anticommunist camp itself. Under conditions marked by the tempestuous development of the world socialist system, demonstrating to the entire world the great vital force and tremendous constructive possibilities of the new social system, the views of the supporters of convergence on the inevitable return of the socialist countries to capitalism appears less and less convincing against the background of the upheavals experienced by contemporary capitalism. Under the existing situation many anticommunists who, in the past, sympathized with the theory of convergence or even participated in its formulation, have begun ever more frequently to voice doubts concerning the practical value of this doctrine. At the same time, even though timidly, the idea of convergence which recognizes the need for "improving" capitalist society is becoming ever more unacceptable to those who want a return to the time of open "cold war."

**65.** **EDITORIAL, "The Unity of Communists' Convictions and Actions,"** **KOMMUNIST, No. 13, September 1971, pp. 10, 11:** The party gives all-round consideration to the specific features of artistic creativity and literary affairs, which, as V. I. Lenin stressed, are susceptible least of all to mechanical leveling and equalization. It resolutely opposes anarchist arbitrariness and subjective capriciousness and advocates exactitude and clarity of ideological position. This is particularly important at this time. In the situation of the acute ideological struggle in the international arena the bourgeois ideologists and their revisionist accomplices are frenziedly attacking the principles of socialist realist art and advancing every possible type of "deideologization" and "deheroization" concepts so as to disorient one or another representative of artistic creativity and channel his efforts into the creation of artistic photographs of the backyard of our revolution, as A. V. Lunacharskiy put it.

. . . . . . . . . . . . . . . . . . . . . . . . . . . . . . . . . . . . . . . . . . . . . . . . . . . . . . . . . . . . . . . . . . . . . .

The special responsibility which the party places on the communists—the workers at the ideological front—for the spiritual life of society and the working people's communist education is perfectly understandable. However, no communist can stand aloof from these problems. Every party member is responsible for the triumph of the party's great ideals and must therefore tirelessly promote and assert them. He must always and in all things occupy positions of militant party-mindedness, and resolutely frustrate attempts to distort the Marxist-Leninist doctrine and besmirch the socialist system. He is called upon to be watchful for ideological subversion by the enemies of socialism.

*66. M. A. SUSLOV, Member of the CC-CPSU Politburo and Secretariat, "The CPSU—the Party of Creative Marxism," KOMMUNIST, No. 14, September 1971, pp. 15-24:* The congress developed, in conformity with the present-day conditions, the Marxist-Leninist tenet on the leading revolutionary reforming role of the working class in all social movements of our time, and shattered attempts to belittle the role of the working class in society. We know that fallacious and capitulatory arguments on the alleged weakening of the revolutionary potential of the working class and the lessening of its importance in the life of society have been widespread abroad in recent years. Unfounded trends to counterpose either the intelligentsia, the peasants, or the students to the working class have been evident. Bourgeois reformism and opportunist ideology and policy are used by imperialism in its attempts to undermine the workers movement from within and "integrate" it into the capitalist system. The 24th CPSU Congress, fully in accordance with Marxist-Leninist doctrine, having scientifically summed-up the modern realistic processes, showed that all the fundamental changes of the age—social, economic, and scientific and technical—have not weakened but strengthened the worldwide historic role of the working class as the gravedigger of capitalism and the creator and organizer of socialism.

The combat vanguard of the working class and its chief and ideological leader are the Marxist-Leninist communist and workers' parties, which have solidly affirmed their position as the most influential and the most organized and active political force of today, standing realistically at the head of mankind's social progress.

The 24th Congress noted that in recent years the working class of the capitalist countries has raised still higher its combat capability as the main and strongest opponent of the power of monopolies. The working class is the center of attraction of all segments of society being exploited and all detachments of the antimonopolistic front. The broadening of the scope of the proletariat's class struggle in the citadels of capitalism and the growth of its popularity and keenness are the forerunners of new and even more forceful battles, which may lead to fundamental social reforms and to the overthrow of the omnipotence of capitalist monopolies and the conquest of power by the working class allied with other toiling strata.

The congress documents provide a scientific substantiation of the growth of the leading role of the working class in strengthening socialism and creating the material and technical base of communism. The growth of the historic mission of the working class is determined by its increased importance in

127

the system of socialist production, its leading role in social relations, and its characteristic features—its revolutionary nature, discipline, organization, and consciousness—since it is precisely the working class which is the standard bearer of the ideas of scientific socialism and which is capable of uniting the broad popular masses round it on the basis of the communist ideal.

*67. EDITORIAL ARTICLE, "The Effectiveness of the Leninist Foreign Policy," KOMMUNIST, No. 14, September 1971, p. 81:* The active nature of the socialist countries' foreign policy is demonstrated in the fact that they wage tireless ideological struggle against any reactionary intrigues. Imperialism's diversionary tactic demagogically named the policy of "bridge-building" is failing. The imperialist doctrine of the "Vietnamization of war," that is, the implementation of American aggression not only through its own forces but also by the hands of hired puppets, has been unmasked in the eyes of the world public.

The provocative role of imperialism, and above all of the United States, in fanning and maintaining the hotbed of aggression in the Near East, in organizing armed conflicts and reactionary coups in a number of "third world" countries, and in supporting regimes of military dictatorship has been unmasked before the entire world. The peoples of the Latin American countries are rejecting the perfidious plans nurtured by American imperialism for "silent intervention."

*68. G. KHROMUSHIN, "Imperialist Reaction Drops Its Mask," KOMMUNIST, No. 14, September 1971, pp. 107-116:* However, toward the end of the '50's, the imperialist politicians and ideologues were forced to acknowledge that the "cold war" and subversive activities conducted in this manner failed to reach their objectives and weaken socialism. Realizing the fatal consequences to imperialism of unleashing military operations against the USSR, they adopted a new tactic in the struggle against socialism, described as the "bridge-building" policy.

The strategic idea of "eliminating" socialism remained the same. It was a question of new methods for its implementation, aimed at promoting in the USSR and other socialist countries a process of "erosion of socialism," of undermining their unity and thus preparing the necessary conditions for the implementation of the so-called "quiet counterrevolution." The period encompassing the decade of the '60's was precisely characterized by the dissemination of the renovated ideological and propaganda schemes; they were based on the former strategic line of the imperialist politicians, a line which, however, was to be pursued not through a frontal attack but through more refined maneuvering.

The ideological struggle has always been the most important realm of the class struggle. However, during the various stages of conflict between the proletariat and the bourgeoisie and socialism and capitalism, its forms and methods have been subjected to considerable changes. In our days, becoming ever sharper and tense, this struggle is acquiring a qualitatively different scale and nature since it has a direct impact on the broadest popular masses and on all social groups and strata of modern society.

A characteristic phenomenon of the contemporary ideological and political situation is the fact that already not only the progressive part of the workers but the broad population masses in capitalist and developing countries see in imperialism the reason for misfortune and the main obstruction to progress. The sharpening of the class struggle in the entire capitalist world and the increased political and social actions launched by the broadest population strata against the reactionary domestic and foreign policy of imperialism force the monopolistic bourgeoisie hastily to seek ways for adapting itself to the new circumstances in the world.

Approximately since the end of the '50's the ideological and propaganda centers of imperialism have been trying somehow to weaken and neutralize the growing influence of Marxist-Leninist ideology. They have raised an entire number of "concepts" aimed at countering the theory of scientific socialism through doctrines with whose help imperialism intended to draw the popular masses away from the class struggle against capitalism. These doctrines were based on the thesis that by itself the scientific and technical revolution would eliminate the old contradictions, changing not only the aspect but, allegedly, the nature of modern capitalism, thus eliminating the need for class struggle and social revolution. Such doctrines were proclaimed as ideological slogans of "popular capitalism," "self disappearance of the proletariat," "post-industrial society," "convergence" of various social systems, "de-ideologization of social life," etc.

. . . . . . . . . . . . . . . . . . . . . . . . . . . . . . . . . . . . . . . . . . . . . . . . . . . . . . . . . . . . . . . . . . . .

On the outside the objectivistic and liberal concept of the "single industrial society" turned out to be not only exceptionally convenient for the apology of imperialism but was used as the methodological foundation for the so-called theory of convergence. This biological term which means a process of the acquisition of resembling features by different species was not in the least accidentally applied to the social sciences. Not so long ago bourgeois ideologues of all trends—from the extreme right to the liberal—were unanimous in their total rejection of socialism as a social system. Today, when the world socialist system has become a force determining the main trend of historical progress, any frontal rejection of socialism would seem, to say the least, stupid. That is why the views of the bourgeois ideologues to the effect that social antagonisms in capitalism will be automatically eliminated once it has reached the stage of the "postindustrial society," were expanded by the new thesis according to which technological progress gradually eliminates class antagonisms and, on an international scale, gradually abolishes the differences between capitalism and socialism.

This idea was the basis of the theory of "convergence," according to which as a result of the evolutionary development and interpenetration of capitalism and socialism a certain single society will arise which would borrow from capitalism its entrepreneurial initiative, profit incentive and bourgeois democracy and, from socialism, the principles of planning and social well-being. "The nature of technology . . . the nature of planning. . ." proclaimed the American economist J. Galbraith, "have their own imperatives. This leads to the convergence of industrial societies."

However, the arguments of the "convergence" supporters are not limited to technology.

Technical research, Galbraith claims, inevitably leads to intellectual emancipation. In the language of the bourgeois theoreticians this presumes a hope for "de-ideologization," of a rejection of the theory of scientific communism, the class struggle and the social revolution. It is precisely here that we clearly see the class nature of the "convergence" theory which, from the very beginning, has had an antisocialist nature, even though concealed behind considerations of the "maturation of similarity characteristics." The "softening" of the ideological foundations of the socialist society, the "de-communization of Marxism," as the *New York Times* wrote, have been considered by the counterrevolutionaries as the principal condition for the "antisocialist evolution," and the gradual "sliding" from socialism to capitalism. In turn, this "erosion" of the socialist countries would be the basis for subversive activities against the CPSU and the Soviet state whose power is universally known.

This most essential aspect of the idea was immediately "seized" by the open apologists of the monopolies and fierce anticommunists such as Z. Brzezinski who, putting his cards on the table, explained that in fact "convergence" means not a rapprochement but the absorption of the system opposing capitalism. That is precisely why the "convergence" theory was the theoretical basis for the specific political course of struggle against world socialism adopted by international imperialism: the policy of "building bridges." During the '60's the monopolistic bourgeoisie and its propaganda made most extensive use of this theory, including it in their anticommunist arsenal.

. . . . . . . . . . . . . . . . . . . . . . . . . . . . . . . . . . . . . . . . . . . . . . . . . . . . . . . . . . . . . . . . . . .

Neither subversive activities and intrigues against world socialism nor out-flanking maneuvers concealed behind pseudo-liberal phraseology stopped the firm advance of the world socialist system. Reality clearly revealed the ground-lessness of the ideological-theoretical foundations of the anticommunist policy of "building bridges."

. . . . . . . . . . . . . . . . . . . . . . . . . . . . . . . . . . . . . . . . . . . . . . . . . . . . . . . . . . . . . . . . . . .

[Sidney] Hook, [Bertram] Wolfe, and other reactionaries reject the "convergence" theory not because they are guided by any kind of theoretical considerations; they fear that its superficially objective nature may change the anti-Soviet climate strongly promoted by the extreme reactionaries in the capitalist world. Furthermore, they are actively using the arguments for-mulated by the "convergence" theoreticians in praise of modern capitalism. However, they call for concentrating all the forces of imperialist propaganda on the support of shameless apologetic concepts of "American civilization" as the only current prototype for the future society! That is precisely the method used by imperialist ideologues such as Brzezinski, who has proclaimed the "diametrical opposition" of this theory of "technetronic era" to the con-cept of the "postindustrial society," even though in reality his theory is a coarse eclectic compilation of various views expressed by Bell, Galbraith and other "post-industrialism" theoreticians. In the "technetronic century" invented by Brzezinski no social explosions or revolutions could occur. "The technetronic revolution," he states, "will create new economic, political and social relations, different from those characterizing the 'industrial society'." Naturally, U.S. imperialism is proclaimed in this case as the "live embodiment of the technetronic era" which, allegedly, gives it the right not only to be considered as an example but to force other countries into accepting the American experience, regardless of their opposition.

. . . . . . . . . . . . . . . . . . . . . . . . . . . . . . . . . . . . . . . . . . . . . . . . . . . . . . . . . . . . . . . . . . .

The liberal wing of the bourgeois ideologues emerged on the arena of big politics with the loud statement to the effect that in the course of the scientific and technical revolution monopolistic capitalism would automatically lose power, which, allegedly, would go to professional specialists and scientists standing above classes and ideologies. This false claim was exposed by the very same monopolistic ideologues who, for the sake of a long-term prop-aganda benefit, refused to flirt with the idea of power. From their viewpoint all the essential parts of the "convergence" theory such as the justification and praise of capitalism, on the one hand, and subversive antisocialist concepts and the distortion of the very idea of the socialist revolution, on the other, were borrowed by the anticommunist arsenal and the liberal-objectivistic views were cynically rejected. The attacks on the part of the extreme reactionaries were a stab in the back of the "convergence" theoreticians. In an atmosphere marked by disorder and disappointment, they hastened to turn from immoderate optimistic hopes to pessimistic utopias and to frank pessimism concerning all social progress.

. . . . . . . . . . . . . . . . . . . . . . . . . . . . . . . . . . . . . . . . . . . . . . . . . . . . . . . . . . . . . . . . . . . .

Therefore, the social pessimism of the bourgeois ideologues is nothing but a screen for antisocialist propaganda; a "new" criticism of socialism and "new arguments" are being brought forth in defense of modern capitalism. However, they obey the old objectives: to remove the problem of the class struggle and the socialist revolution and, at all cost, "deny" to socialism the fact that the future will belong to it.

. . . . . . . . . . . . . . . . . . . . . . . . . . . . . . . . . . . . . . . . . . . . . . . . . . . . . . . . . . . . . . . . . . . .

Discussing the "disappearance" of the proletariat and the establishment of relations of "social harmony" and "partnership" the bourgeois and revisionist propaganda pursues a clearly class related objective: to reduce the intensity of the revolutionary actions of the working class against imperialism, to "prove" to the working people that the socialist revolution is unnecessary and to strike a blow at the Marxist-Leninist doctrine of the historical mission of the proletariat.

This counterrevolutionary objective is in crying contradiction with the objective laws and requirements of historical progress. It also contradicts current social practices which, again and again, confirm the fact that the working class as a whole, regardless of the changes within its structure, remains the leading revolutionary force of our time, the firm foundation for the unification of all working and progressive units within a unified anti-imperialist front.

"The working class alone," said Comrade L. I. Brezhnev at the 1969 International Conference of Communist and Workers' Parties, "can lead this alliance to victory, raise the struggle to a new stage and ensure the total destruction of the power of capitalism and the triumph of socialism."

**69. V. CHEPRAKOV, Doctor of Economic Sciences, "The Monopolies' Advocates," IZVESTIIA, October 23, 1971:** Modern capitalism, in which the basic production relations have not changed, has nevertheless acquired new features which intensify its exploiter essence and which make it particularly aggressive. As a result of the coalescence of private monopolies with the state, state monopoly capitalism has emerged. The monopolies, both private and state, have become the basis of modern capitalism, while the state, having increased its functions of domination and coercion, has become part of the economic base by directly exploiting the workers and interfering in the process of capital reproduction.

As comrade L. I. Brezhnev noted at the 24th CPSU Congress, the features of modern capitalism are to a large extent explained by its attempts to adapt to the new situation in the world, which does not mean, however, its stabilization as a system. Under the conditions of struggle against socialism the bourgeoisie, fearing that class struggle might grow into a mass revolutionary movement, is trying to apply more disguised forms of the exploitation and oppression of the working people and is showing itself ready in a number of cases to make particular reforms in order to keep the masses as far as possible under their ideological and political control.

. . . . . . . . . . . . . . . . . . . . . . . . . . . . . . . . . . . . . . . . . . . . . . . . . . . . . . . . . . . . . . . . . . . . . . . . . . . . .

Revisionism has never been original or self-dependent. It has always shone with reflected light while borrowing and adapting bourgeois theories. In this respect modern revisionism does not differ from its predecessors. However, the new situation is naturally giving rise to certain changes in the content and forms of the revision of Marxism-Leninism and in the way the bearers of revisionism are "touching it up" in attempting to emasculate the revolutionary teaching of the proletariat.

Often slipping into nationalism and anti-Sovietism, the modern revisionists direct attacks against Marxism-Leninism allegedly with a view to "improving Marxism" and "adapting it to the epoch."

. . . . . . . . . . . . . . . . . . . . . . . . . . . . . . . . . . . . . . . . . . . . . . . . . . . . . . . . . . . . . . . . . . . . . . . . . . . . .

The point of departure of such heralds of opportunism as Garaudy, Fischer, Marek, and others like them is the "industrial society" theory created by the ideologists of state monopoly capitalism. From the fact of the increase in the socialization of capitalist production, which had already been revealed by V. I. Lenin, the bourgeois theorists — and in their wake the opportunists we have named — draw a conclusion about "the evolution of capitalist society toward socialism." The growth of state monopoly ownership and also the concentration of private monopoly ownership and the decrease in the proportion of individual ownership in favor of joint-stock or state ownership is claimed by them to be the creation of socialist public ownership. Marek, in his book *The Philosophy of World Revolution,* writes: "In the developed capitalist countries the X-ray of our time enables us to detect the socialist structure."

. . . . . . . . . . . . . . . . . . . . . . . . . . . . . . . . . . . . . . . . . . . . . . . . . . . . . . . . . . . . . . . . . . . . . . . . . . . . .

133

The revisionists deny the need for and the inevitability of the revolutionary changeover from capitalism to socialism as the result of the class struggle. They try to justify their betrayal of the working class by the fact that under the conditions of the scientific and technological revolution the need for social revolution apparently no longer arises. They substitute the concept of the new scientific and technological revolution for the concept of the class struggle as the driving force of the antagonistic society. There is nothing original in these revisionist concepts. They are also hired. Already considerably earlier than they, Raymond Aron, French sociologist and ideologist of monopoly capitalism, wrote: "Social progress is possible without political revolution."

The rejection of socialist revolution naturally means the rejection also of an acknowledgement of the proletariat's historical role as the driving and predominant force of this revolution, allegedly because it has lost its revolutionary potential.

The revisionists maintain that technical progress, having led to changes in the structure of the working class, has at the same time also changed the position of the worker in production, put an end to alienation and created "social symmetry," and that cultural progress, having made the working class better educated, has changed its position in society. The dispersion of property as the result of the issue of small shares and securities has allegedly made the worker the capitalist's "partner," and on the whole, all this is said to have resulted in the working class's integration into "industrial society."

. . . . . . . . . . . . . . . . . . . . . . . . . . . . . . . . . . . . . . . . . . . . . . . . . . . . . . . . . . . . . . . . . . . . . . . . . . . . .

The lot of the modern revisionists, as of all renegades who betray the cause of the working class and the great ideals of communism, is a downward path from ideological capitulation to capitalism to ideological sabotage against socialism. The struggle against revisionism makes it incumbent to strengthen the ideological and organizational cohesion of the communist parties and the whole international communist movement on the basis of Marxism-Leninism. It presupposes also the winning over to the side of the revolutionary proletariat of all those strata, groups, and individuals who are seeking revolutionary paths toward socialism, and the rendering of assistance to them in their attempts to find the correct methods of struggling in alliance with all progressive forces against the omnipotence of the monopolies and for the revolutionary transformation of society based on scientific socialism.

**70. B. N. PONOMAREV, Candidate Member of Politburo and Secretary of the CC-CPSU, "Topical Problems in the Theory of the World Revolutionary Process," KOMMUNIST, No. 15, October 1971, pp. 37-71:** Let us note the following aspect, above all. The influence of world socialism on social life in the non-socialist world is increasing considerably. This is natural since socialism is a qualitatively higher stage of social development. We could say that socialism and capitalism embody, respectively, the ascending and descending lines of social development.

It is also important to emphasize that the antagonism between the two systems is not restricted in the least to strictly determined geographic boundaries or specific social "structures." Since it is a question of two essentially irreconcilable lines of world development all countries, classes, social strata and political currents become in the final account inevitably involved in their struggle, whether directly or indirectly, more or less actively yet.

. . . . . . . . . . . . . . . . . . . . . . . . . . . . . . . . . . . . . . . . . . . . . . . . . . . . . . . . . . . . . . .

However, the fact that the very attempts to adapt to the new circumstances and, above all, to the scientific and technical revolution, are of a limited nature without affecting the exploiting nature of the capitalist socioeconomic system, is of decisive significance. In the final account, these attempts have led not to the strengthening of capitalism but to the further deepening of its basic contradictions and antagonisms. By the turn of the 70's a new sharpening was noted in the overall crisis of capitalism. As L. I. Brezhnev said in his speech at the 8th Congress of the Socialist Unity Party of Germany, the "severe crisis of imperialist policy and the continuous feverish state of its economy, lack of security in the future and a profound crisis in morality is the picture offered by modern capitalism."

. . . . . . . . . . . . . . . . . . . . . . . . . . . . . . . . . . . . . . . . . . . . . . . . . . . . . . . . . . . . . . .

Where the scientific and technical revolution is a powerful ally of socialism, under capitalist conditions its production communization erodes further the foundations of the existing system, creating new forms of antagonism.

. . . . . . . . . . . . . . . . . . . . . . . . . . . . . . . . . . . . . . . . . . . . . . . . . . . . . . . . . . . . . . .

We are faced with new attempts on the part of the ruling class to shift the burden of economic difficulties to the working people. Increased unemployment, higher costs, drops in real wages and an attack against the rights of trade unions have drastically sharpened the class struggle.

. . . . . . . . . . . . . . . . . . . . . . . . . . . . . . . . . . . . . . . . . . . . . . . . . . . . . . . . . . . . . . .

Therefore, we must consider the process of foreign political changes in all its complexity. The socialist comity is proving its capability to impose upon the imperialists a solution of the problems in the interest of peace and peaceful coexistence. However, imperialism is not abandoning its objectives. It is pursuing the tactics of "building bridges" aimed at subverting the world socialist system as well as an open struggle against our line of international detente. The latest example of this is the resurrection of the cold war methods by the British conservatives toward the USSR.

. . . . . . . . . . . . . . . . . . . . . . . . . . . . . . . . . . . . . . . . . . . . . . . . . . . . . . . . . . . . . . . . . . . . .

The ever greater intensification of the ideological struggle is a noteworthy feature of our times. The more restricted became the capitalist possibilities to fight socialism militarily, the greater the tension of the ideological battles in the world.

Relying on the recommendations of special research centers, the huge imperialist propaganda machine is trying to indoctrinate public opinion to the advantage of the monopolistic bourgeoisie. Launching continuous ideological diversions against the socialist countries and the worker and national-liberation movements, our class enemies are making active use of various types of reactionary nationalistic trends. Directly or indirectly they are encouraging revisionists and opportunists from the right and the "left."

However, the imperialist attempts to launch an offensive on the ideological front are not successful. Capitalism does not have the type of spiritual resources which would enable it to be successful in the universal battle for the minds and the hearts of the people. Even many capitalist leaders have admitted that capitalism is rich in commodities but poor in spirit. Not the bourgeois but our own socialist ideology is in a state of historical offensive.

The worldwide political campaign launched by the fraternal communist parties in connection with the centennial of V. I. Lenin's birth represented a major contribution to the ideological struggle with imperialism and the dissemination of the ideas of scientific communism in the world.

The achievements of socialism and of the world revolutionary movement and the deepening crisis of the capitalist system create prerequisites for the even broader ideological offensive against imperialism. The self exposure of the capitalist system and the compromising of its nature in the eyes of the broadest possible masses have assumed unparalleled dimensions. Until recently millions of people indoctrinated by capitalist propaganda assumed that the rulers of the Western world had found some kind of miraculous method for the rejuvenation of capitalism and for restoring its old dynamism. Today these illusions concerning "neo-capitalism" have disappeared. The broad masses are realizing ever more clearly the correctness of the communist views. The understanding to the effect that the vices of the bourgeois society are incurable is growing.

The ideological myths of imperialism are breaking down in the field of social relations as well. The bourgeois ideologues have tried to develop into a capitalist asset a certain increase in the living standards achieved by the working class in a number of countries after adamant class battles and under circumstances governed by the sharp struggle between the two systems. The increased number of people owning automobiles, refrigerators and washing machines was interpreted as the advent of a "consumer society" in which, allegedly, the basic needs of the toiling man are satisfied, for which reason there would be no grounds for social conflicts and for the class struggle.

. . . . . . . . . . . . . . . . . . . . . . . . . . . . . . . . . . . . . . . . . . . . . . . . . . . . . . . . . . . . . .

In turn, the left-wing theoreticians consider any improvement in the material standards of the working people as "bourgeoisification." They combined in their works a nihilistically hostile attitude toward the struggle of the workers for upgrading the living standards, in the capitalist countries, with a gross distortion of the nature of the process underlying the growth of the people's prosperity in the socialist countries. This process as well is interpreted as "bourgeoisification." Revolutionary-mindedness is identified with universal poverty. Petty bourgeois equalization is presented as being just about the highest good from the viewpoint of the interests of the revolution. The struggle against bourgeois and left-wing concepts of a "consumer" society becomes very important. In this struggle our reliable weapon is the practice of real socialism.

. . . . . . . . . . . . . . . . . . . . . . . . . . . . . . . . . . . . . . . . . . . . . . . . . . . . . . . . . . . . . .

However, the question of the origins of the crisis is deliberately ignored. Matters are presented as though the existing crisis of the "industrial civilization" is the inevitable result of scientific and technical progress.

The facts of the capitalist reality expose this ideological mimicry of the bourgeois propagandists. There is a growing understanding of the fact that it is precisely capitalism and its socioeconomic and political system that are the prime cause for the troubles and vices of the "Western world."

In turn, this increases the instability of capitalism. Bourgeois reformism and the policy of social concessions showed themselves unable to stabilize the system. On the contrary, new instability factors have arisen. Financial capitalism has set against itself more strata of the working class, the peasantry, the small entrepreneurs, the white-collar workers, the intelligentsia and the youth. . . .

Should we try to describe briefly the nature of opportunism today we could say that the danger of right-wing opportunism lies in the fact that it tries:

To distort the great doctrine of Marxism-Leninism, proclaiming it obsolete and replacing it with a reformist ideology which rejects the class struggle, the socialist revolution and the dictatorship of the proletariat; to whitewash the main contradictions within the bourgeois society, promoting the idea of

137

the transformation of state monopolistic capitalism into socialism without revolution; to reject the role of the working class as the main revolutionary force.

Furthermore, today the truth is becoming more evident that the front of the anti-imperialist struggle is indivisible and that the defeat of imperialism in one sector weakens its entire system.

The internationalization of the revolutionary struggle is the result of the growing power of world socialism and the dissemination throughout the world of the noble principles of proletarian internationalism which have proved frequently and continue to prove, on a daily basis, their tremendous significance for the successful struggle of the peoples for freedom, independence, and social progress. The policy of the Soviet Union and the other socialist countries, following the path of Leninism, and the internationalist activities of the fraternal communist parties and progressive forces of revolutionary-democratic parties represent a powerful force countering the trends toward nationalistic divisiveness.

*71. P. N. DEMICHEV, Candidate Member of Politburo and Secretary of the CC-CPSU, "The Development of Topical Problems of the Building of Communism in the Resolutions of the 24th CPSU Congress," KOMMUNIST, No. 15, October 1971, pp. 13-36:* The 24th Congress provided a comprehensive analysis of the historical role of the working class under modern conditions. It clearly determined the sociopolitical aspect of the current stage in the building of communism. We know that in recent years revisionist publications have been extensively promoting various types of petty bourgeois ideas propagating the concept of "the new elite," and rejecting the leading role of the working class. The Leninist party congress confirmed the inviolability of the Marxist-Leninist principles on this basic problem. The positions and influence of the working class during the period of expanded building of a communist society increase immeasurably. The working class is the main constructive force of the material and technical foundations of communism, justifiably playing a leading political role.

. . . . . . . . . . . . . . . . . . . . . . . . . . . . . . . . . . . . . . . . . . . . . . . . . . . . . . . . . . . .

The development of socialist democracy is determined by the entire course of the economic, political and spiritual development of our society. Socialist democracy has its own principles and traditions. We consider unacceptable the prescriptions for "improving" democracy, persistently offered by bourgeois ideologues and revisionists.

In the post-war years they organized an entire series of concentrated attacks against the principles of socialist democracy. They are still speculating on the problems related to the consequences of the cult of the personality and subjectivism. The dictatorship of the proletariat is being attacked energetically. Should we try to describe the political and ideological nature of these attacks, we should say that the bourgeois ideologues are doing everything possible to prove that socialism and democracy are incompatible and that the leading and guiding role of the communist party is an obstacle on the path of democratic development in socialist society.

The bourgeois ideologues base their positions on the claim that democracy is some kind of self-satisfying, abstract value, essentially independent of the economic or class structure of society. They actively promote the principles of the so-called "pluralistic" society as the foundations for the existence of democracy in general.

The promotion of "pluralism" as applicable to socialism conflicts with the foundations of the new system. The social nature of the capitalist society is a conglomerate of bourgeois and petty-bourgeois parties and political groups.

The communist parties in bourgeois countries must take into consideration characteristics of the various stages in the struggle and the specific nature of different democratic forces in the struggle for their unification. The victory of the socialist revolution creates objective conditions for the harmonious combination of the interests of the toiling classes and social groups. This provides a basis for the strong and profound political unity among democratic and socialist forces.

. . . . . . . . . . . . . . . . . . . . . . . . . . . . . . . . . . . . . . . . . . . . . . . . . . . . . . . . . . . . . .

Never before have we seen such a flood of books, articles, motion pictures and radio broadcasts in which the bourgeois theoreticians and propagandists are trying to "interpret" in their own fashion the trends governing the development of the economic, political and spiritual life of the socialist countries. This entire propagandist wave is aimed at weakening socialism, eroding its foundations and breaking the unity of our society. However, all the attempts of the bourgeois ideologues and revisionists to split the working class, the peasantry and the intelligentsia, and the generations, nations and nationalities in our country have failed entirely. They have been unable to alienate the artistic intelligentsia and the youth from the communist ideals, and blacken the cause of socialism even though particular and very refined propaganda efforts have been made to this effect.

Naturally, our opponents will not weaken the fight against socialism and communist ideology. The objective historical processes provide ever greater proofs of the correctness of the Marxist-Leninist conclusion to the effect that the development of capitalism at its monopolistic stage will lead to the need for its revolutionary replacement by a new, socialist system. Bourgeois theoretical philosophy is trying to avoid this scientific conclusion by all possible means. We have seen the extensive propaganda of pseudo-scientific ideas to the effect that scientific and technical progress automatically leads to the erosion of the lines separating capitalism and socialism. Pitirim Sorokin, Raymond Aron and other bourgeois theoreticians have promoted the ideas of convergence or, in other words, of the rapprochement between the two systems. They have comprehensively underscored the common technological and organizational aspects of the modern industrial production process in countries with different social systems.

In the ideological struggle anticommunism is trying to pit against scientific communism the ideas of the "general prosperity state," "consumer society," "equal opportunity" society and "industrial" and "postindustrial" society. A number of variations have appeared of the theory of the "mass society" alleging that the 20th century and technical progress create a faceless, damaged man-robot, lacking profound spirtual requirements. All this is periodically used in order to lead the masses away from scientific communism which is becoming evermore attractive.

Many theoreticians have appeared proclaiming themselves "socialist." In fact, however, they bring into the theory of scientific communism an entire number of hostile ideas and prejudices.

. . . . . . . . . . . . . . . . . . . . . . . . . . . . . . . . . . . . . . . . . . . . . . . . . . . . . . . . . . . . . . . . . . . .

The documents and materials of the 24th Party Congress are a powerful blow against anticommunism and against the various manifestations of opportunism and revisionism. Once again the Leninist party proved what scientific communism in action means.

The creative and principled approach adopted by the congress in the solution of the basic theoretical problems defeats the fabrications of bourgeois ideologues and revisionists about an alleged "stagnation" of Marxist-Leninist thinking.

**72.  A. VEBER, "Crisis of the Anti-Workingclass Policy of the Bourgeoisie," PRAVDA, November 3, 1971:** As long as technical progress, rationalization and intensification of labor assured the fast increase in the bulk of profit, monopolists under the pressure of the toilers' demands were able to allow some rise in wages, hoping by this to fill the workers with the illusion of the community of interests of labor and capital.

. . . . . . . . . . . . . . . . . . . . . . . . . . . . . . . . . . . . . . . . . . . . . . . . . . . . . . . . . . . . . . .

At the same time, as the exploitation of the toilers intensified, and their social requirements grew quantitatively and especially qualitatively, the margin for social maneuverability of the monopolies began to narrow on account of the deepening of the general crisis of capitalism and the intensification of international competition.

. . . . . . . . . . . . . . . . . . . . . . . . . . . . . . . . . . . . . . . . . . . . . . . . . . . . . . . . . . . . . . .

The known rise of the living standard of the toilers, achieved by their unyielding struggle, has not resulted in the ideological-psychological "integration" of the working class into capitalist society. . . .

**73.  Lieutenant General A. SHEVCHENKO and Colonel V. ZEV'IALOV,** *"Psychological Warfare in the Plans for Imperialist Expansion,"* **KOMMUNIST VOORUZHENNYKH SIL,** *No. 22, November 1971, pp. 80-86:* By itself, anticommunism is not a new departure either politically or ideologically. It arose as a reaction by the bourgeoisie to the teachings of Marxism-Leninism and the practical work performed by communist parties in their revolutionary transformation of human society. The essence of modern anticommunism is revealed in the CPSU Program: "The principal ideological-political weapon of imperialism is anticommunism, the essence of which is slander against the socialist system and falsification of the policies and goals of communist parties and Marxist-Leninist teachings. Anticommunism reflects the extreme degree of degradation of bourgeois ideology."

Anticommunism appears as a mixture of diverse bourgeois ideas—from extreme rightist to moderately liberal ideas, from which and in the interests of their "psychological warfare" the imperialist ideologists select the most "suitable" for the particular segment of time involved. Thus, as the principal postulates of bourgeois ideology remain constant, the essence of "psychological warfare" operations will appear considerably more active. The accents in their subversive propaganda and the objects of their attacks will change frequently. The evolution of the essence of "psychological warfare" has been particularly noticeable in recent years.

Until recently, the "psychological warfare" ideologists based their calculations on rather primitive evaluations of the socialist system, consoling themselves with the thought that the ideals of communism were not acceptable to the people of the Soviet Union and other socialist countries. Thus the essence, forms and methods of "psychological warfare" were very direct in nature. In particular, great emphasis was placed on making appeals to overthrow the "communist regimes" and "to liberate" the people of socialist countries from socialism.

However the lack of perceptible results forced the imperialist strategists to seriously review the validity of their plans and tactics. In the early 1960s, the American leaders were the first in the West to recognize the failure of the so-called "Doctrine of Liberation."

"The Policy of Liberation proudly proclaimed 8 years ago," stated John Kennedy in 1960, "turned out to be a trap and a mistake. We must now begin to work more slowly and cautiously. We must nurture the seeds of liberty in all cracks in the iron curtain."

John Kennedy thus laid the foundation for a new doctrine of "psychological warfare," which became known as the Doctrine of "Peaceful Penetration." In developing this doctrine, President Johnson advanced the formula concerning the "building of bridges," which was subsequently accepted by a number of other NATO countries.

According to this doctrine, the task of "psychological warfare consists of planting and developing in socialist countries those tendencies which will gradually transform a socialist system into a capitalist one and, in addition, undermine the unity of the socialist bloc. In conformity with these views, the entire "psychological warfare" program was thoroughly reviewed and its methods modified. The ideological saboteurs began to step forward more often as "well-wishers" and "advisers" to those living in socialist countries. They did not appeal to the people to destroy socialism directly, rather they "advised" them to modernize and democratize it. Less frequent appeals were heard requesting that direct attacks be carried out against the communist parties. This was replaced, however, by profuse talk on the need for preventing such parties from playing a leading role in socialist societies, etc.

. . . . . . . . . . . . . . . . . . . . . . . . . . . . . . . . . . . . . . . . . . . . . . . . . . . . . . . . . . . . . . . .

The essence of the "psychological warfare" now began to place great emphasis on the "moral values" inherent in capitalism. The bourgeois propagandists loudly proclaimed the bourgeois "freedoms" and tried in every way to inspire the workers of socialist countries with the thought of a non-class democracy. They appealed for the peaceful coexistence of ideologies, while cherishing a hope for the ideological disarming of socialism.

. . . . . . . . . . . . . . . . . . . . . . . . . . . . . . . . . . . . . . . . . . . . . . . . . . . . . . . . . . . . . . . .

The essence of the "psychological warfare" now began to place great emphasis on the "moral values" inherent in capitalism. The bourgeois propagandists loudly proclaimed the bourgeois "freedoms" and tried in every way to inspire the workers of socialist countries with the thought of a non-class democracy. They appealed for the peaceful coexistence of ideologies, while cherishing a hope for the ideological disarming of socialism.

. . . . . . . . . . . . . . . . . . . . . . . . . . . . . . . . . . . . . . . . . . . . . . . . . . . . . . . . . . . . . . . .

The very heart of present-day imperialist "psychological warfare" is that of undermining the friendship and solidarity existing between socialist bloc countries, particularly between the Warsaw Pact member states. The imperialists wish to drive a wedge between the USSR and other socialist countries.

. . . . . . . . . . . . . . . . . . . . . . . . . . . . . . . . . . . . . . . . . . . . . . . . . . . . . . . . . . . . . . . .

One of the principal goals of the "psychological warfare" being waged by the imperialists against socialist states is that of dulling the class consciousness of workers, thus making it easier to subject the workers to bourgeois ideology. Towards this end the West prepares and disseminates on an extensive scale various "theories" and "concepts," all claiming to have a scientific basis. This includes the clearly bankrupt theory of "convergence" which preaches the transformation of capitalism and socialism into a "single industrial de-ideologized society," the theory of "stages of economic growth" which attempts to prove that communism cannot cope with the "age of mass consumption" since improvements in the standard of living encourage a "consumer psychology" and also the notorious theory of a "post-industrial society" which is viewed as the future of capitalism, one that fully conforms with the new conditions.

The purpose of these and other theories is that of convincing people with regard to the "eternal nature" of capitalism, poisoning the consciousness of workers with petty-bourgeois ideology and dulling their class world outlook.

. . . . . . . . . . . . . . . . . . . . . . . . . . . . . . . . . . . . . . . . . . . . . . . . . . . . . . . . . . . . . . . .

The appeals made by the imperialist apologists for the coexistence of ideologies are in pursuit of just one goal—to intensify bourgeois ideological penetration in socialist countries, to bring about an "erosion" of socialist society, to undermine it from within and to thrust the yoke of capitalist slavery on freedom-loving people.

Now, in the early 1970s, the camp of imperialist reaction is once again examining its "psychological warfare" doctrines and tactics. Having failed in their attempts to achieve an inner demoralization of socialism, the more reactionary ideologists and politicians in the West are once again demanding a return to "cold war" conditions, that the pseudo-liberal ideas be replaced by anticommunist propaganda, that no statements be made regarding socialist achievements and that American imperialism be extolled in every possible way. This program is already being expressed in terms of the imperialist propaganda directed towards discrediting the ideas of the 24th CPSU Congress, particularly those concerned with strengthening international peace.

. . . . . . . . . . . . . . . . . . . . . . . . . . . . . . . . . . . . . . . . . . . . . . . . . . . . . . . . . . . . . .

At the same time and in consideration of the aggravated nature of the ideological struggle taking place in the international arena, it would be a serious mistake to underestimate the danger posed by the imperialist organs of "psychological warfare." The persistent exposure of the overall doctrine of the ideological struggle and "psychological warfare" being waged by the imperialists against socialist countries, the means and methods employed in hostile propaganda operations and the specific subversive actions being carried out by the hirelings of monopolistic bourgeoisie—constitutes an important aspect of the work performed by commanders and political organs, directed towards further strengthening the combat readiness and fighting efficiency of our Soviet Armed Forces.

**74. Professor V. CHEPRAKOV, Doctor of Economic Sciences, "The False Preaching of the Bourgeois 'Theorists,' " SEL'SKAIA ZHIZN', December 17, 1971:** The role of the ideological struggle is growing increasingly in the international arena, as the resolution of the CPSU Central Committee November plenum stresses. The plenum drew attention to the need to defend more actively our country's interests and the interests of socialism and of the entire communist movement in the struggle against imperialist propaganda and the enemies of Marxism-Leninism. The plenum realized that it is essential to continue to wage the struggle against bourgeois ideology, and to educate Soviet people in the spirit of Marxism-Leninism and proletarian internationalism.

. . . . . . . . . . . . . . . . . . . . . . . . . . . . . . . . . . . . . . . . . . . . . . . . . . . . . . . . . . . . . .

In biology there is a concept called "convergence." This means the appearance and development of a resemblance between different organisms which are situated under the same conditions. And so, having borrowed this term, the bourgeois theorists are trying to prove that supposedly "the rapprochement of the two systems and their fusion into a single point" is taking place, as is "their approach to some intermediate point." The supporters of the convergence "theory" are thus trying to resolve two tasks at once. To make it appear as though they have an idea of where contemporary capitalism is going —capitalism which is allegedly developing in a progressive direction—and —this is the main thing—to weaken the increasing influence of the ideas of scientific socialism on the masses.

The convergence "theory" is one of the signs of the intensification of the crisis of bourgeois ideology and of its confusion in the face of the fact of the victorious rule of the revolutionary theory of the proletariat. The very appearance of the theory of the two systems having come together testifies to the indirect "recognition" of the law-governed nature of the socialist system. Indeed, quite recently, when the ideologists of capitalism had immovable faith in it, such a heretical theory—from the exploiters' viewpoint—could not even have arisen.

The deliberate falsity of the convergence "theory" can be seen even from the fact that it erroneously asserts that there are allegedly no fundamental differences between socialism and capitalism and that their movement is progressing along similar lines. Proceeding from realistic assessments of the deep processes in the two opposed systems, Marxism-Leninism establishes a fundamental difference precisely where the convergence theory seeks a resemblance.

. . . . . . . . . . . . . . . . . . . . . . . . . . . . . . . . . . . . . . . . . . . . . . . . . . . . . . . . . . . . . . . .

The programming and compilation of economic growth programs in certain capitalist states and the improvement of planning methods in the socialist countries serve as a special subject for the theoretical speculations of the "convergence theorists." The course of their arguments is more or less as follows: in the economically developed capitalist countries the tendency toward planning and centralized decision-making is being intensified. At the same time the economically developed socialist countries are allegedly abandoning their former centralized planning methods in favor of free market relations. "Deplanning" is taking place, so they say, as a result of which these states are coming to meet the capitalist states.

Reality refutes such a train of argument which is fallacious in its theoretical essence.

The economic growth programs in the capitalist countries do not signify the introduction of a planning system and in no way testify to the fact that their economy is becoming organized. It is only the combination of economic forecasts with direct or indirect measures to regulate the economy by influencing the level and dimensions of monopolies' profit. Such programs are merely of a recommendatory nature and have no binding force at all on private monopolies.

Programming is not in a position to spare the capitalist states from cyclical crises and from various sorts of economic shakeups. Currency crises, the fall in money's purchasing power, and balance of payment and trade deficits are the characteristic picture for the capitalist world. At present, too, a currency crisis has shaken the capitalist countries. No, they will not succeed, with the aid of the state, in creating "crisis-free capitalism" and in achieving plan-governed economic development.

. . . . . . . . . . . . . . . . . . . . . . . . . . . . . . . . . . . . . . . . . . . . . . . . . . . . . . . . . . . . . . . . . . . . .

Turning to the problem of the distribution of the national output in the two different systems, the convergence "theory" tries to prove that an "equalization of incomes" is taking place in the capitalist countries while in the socialist countries inequality is allegedly increasing. Both facts are wrong.

Chronic unemployment is increasing in the capitalist world. The ranks of those thrown out onto the street are being filled by cadre workers whose professional skills have become useless as a result of scientific and technical progress.

. . . . . . . . . . . . . . . . . . . . . . . . . . . . . . . . . . . . . . . . . . . . . . . . . . . . . . . . . . . . . . . . . . . . .

In the Western countries the convergence theory is sowing among sections of society illusions about the possibility of capitalism growing into socialism, and is trying to distract the proletariat and its allies from the struggle for the fundamental rebuilding of the existing system. The supporters of this theory are trying to convince the countries which have liberated themselves from direct colonial dependence and are striving toward social changes of the uselessness of a noncapitalist path of development, under the pretext that, so they say, it makes no difference—the rapprochement of the two systems will occur.

But the main aim of the convergence "theory" in the hands of the anti-communists is the aspiration to build "bridges" into the socialist countries. It is highly indicative that those who deviate from Marxism-Leninism begin from the fact that they operate with ideas and arguments from the arsenal of the convergence theorists.

The enemies of peace are using the convergence "theory" for the struggle against the socialist countries and against the principle of peaceful coexistence between states with different social systems which they are implementing. They try to cast doubt on the sincerity of the communists in the defense of peace, intentionally confusing the question of the socioeconomic rapprochement of the two systems with the question of the peaceful coexistence of states. But the path to real peace in no way lies through convergence which exists only in the writings of imperialist ideologists.

Consistently defending its policy of peace, our party is at the same time waging a decisive struggle against bourgeois ideology and against every sort of bourgeois concept and theory, including the false theory of convergence which is trying to disarm the fighters for socialism and peace.

**75. I. ROZANOV, "Be Vigilant Against the Enemies of Peace and Socialism,"** *PARTIINAIA ZHIZN', No. 24, December 1971, pp.* **52-53:** Indeed, anticommunist "concepts" and "theories" designed for export to the socialist countries have a deliberately subversive inflammatory nature. All the bourgeois propaganda acts against the USSR and other socialist countries are, to one degree or another, in the nature of ideological sabotage.

. . . . . . . . . . . . . . . . . . . . . . . . . . . . . . . . . . . . . . . . . . . . . . . . . . . . . . . . . . . . . . . . .

Having set themselves such tasks, the imperialist special services maneuver, seek out and utilize insidious, refined methods· of ideological and political influence. They are no longer able to deny the enormous achievements of the countries that are building socialism and communism. Therefore the ideological saboteurs have chosen another practice. By using various murky sources, they gather tendentious data about individual aspects of life in the socialist countries. Then the "material absorbed"—according to their own admission—"is distilled until it reaches its most harmful form, after which the final product is channelled back, drop by drop to the targets of the subversion."

According to this recipe, new, so-called "liberal" forms of anticommunism are, as a rule, constructed and are based on reformism and revisionism. Anticommunists of this trend talk not about the destruction of communism, but "only" its "improvement." The "liberal" anticommunists are not averse to passing themselves off as "well-wishers, friends and advisers." However, they are pursuing far-reaching objectives—to gradually prepare conditions for the activization of struggle against the socialist system. The Czechoslovak events of 1968 are a graphic confirmation of this system.

To undermine the moral-political potential of the socialist system and to weaken the influence of Marxist ideology, the apologists of imperialism are prepared to form an alliance with any political current and use any concepts merely on the condition that anti-Sovietism exists in them. In this respect, bourgeois nationalists and antisocialist elements of every stripe, and any revisionist and reformist manifestations which have, in the final analysis, an anti-Soviet orientation are "the most convenient" for them.

In the depths of the imperialist special centers, a multitude of "works" are fabricated in which sovietologists strive to prove that inherent in modern socialism are such sociopolitical tendencies whose development must inevitably lead to an undermining of the foundations of the socialist community, to the "erosion" of socialist society and to the "softening" of its foundations. One of the "fashionable" methods of modern anticommunists is setting socialist democracy against the socialist state. "Theories" of this kind all have an identical purpose—to engender a lack of confidence in the success of building communism among some portion of the population of the socialist countries, to win wavering persons over to their side, to stimulate the hostile activities of antisocialist elements, and to promote their grouping on the basis of revisionist views. All this is done not only to undermine the positions of socialism, but also to divert public opinion away from "weak spots" in the domestic and foreign policy of their own, that is the capitalist, countries.

*76. Colonel V. KHALIPOV, Candidate of Philosophical Sciences, "The Main Front of the Class Confrontation," KRASNAIA ZVEZDA, January 6, 1972:* The past few decades have been marked by great social and political changes and by sharp confrontation between the forces of progress and reaction, socialism and imperialism. The modern world is witnessing the development of mighty revolutionary processes and the opening up of new prospects for social progress. Two gigantic revolutions—the world socialist revolution and the scientific and technical revolution, which have coincided in time in a law-governed manner—are bearing mankind aloft through stages of historical progress like two mighty wings. These revolutions prove that preconditions are ripe for a general radical renewal of life on the planet.

Capitalism has been forced to retreat. In defending its lost frontiers it is putting up frenzied resistance, maneuvering and adapting to the new situation. We are witnessing the translation into reality of the prediction made by V. I. Lenin, who wrote that the transition from capitalism to socialism constitutes an entire historical epoch and that, until it ends, "the exploiters will inevitably preserve hopes of a restoration, and these hopes will become attempts at restoration" (*Complete Collected Works,* Vol. 37, p. 264).

. . . . . . . . . . . . . . . . . . . . . . . . . . . . . . . . . . . . . . . . . . . . . . . . . . . . . . . . . . . .

The three main revolutionary forces of the present—the world socialist system, the international workers' movement and the people's national-liberation struggle—are united in the anti-imperialist struggle. As the 24th CPSU Congress noted, this great alliance is continuing to grow stronger and deeper. It possesses great revolutionary potential, a complex internal structure, and diverse ties between all its component detachments.

. . . . . . . . . . . . . . . . . . . . . . . . . . . . . . . . . . . . . . . . . . . . . . . . . . . . . . . . . . . .

The working class in the bourgeois countries is striking powerful blows against capitalism. Its outbursts are growing in all the continents. The strike movement has become extremely broad in scale. Whereas in 1965 36 million people came out on strike in the capitalist countries (the United States, Western Europe, Japan and other countries), the number of strikers amounted to approximately 60 million people in 1969 and exceeded 63 million in 1970.

A characteristic feature of these outbursts is that the workers are presenting political demands along with their economic demands. The onslaught not only on individual groups of capitalists but also on the entire system of state monopoly domination is intensifying in capitalist countries with developed traditions of class struggle and the strongest communist parties.

Imperialism is being dealt an ever greater rebuff by the national liberation forces, primarily the new and independent anti-imperialistically inclined states. The main point here is that the struggle for national liberation has in fact begun to evolve into a struggle against exploiter relations—both feudal and capitalist.

The international communist movement is marching in the vanguard of the anti-imperialist forces of the age. The cohesion of its multimillion-strong ranks is growing ever stronger.

The strengthening unity and growing might of the forces of progress is causing fear in the imperialist camp. The ruling circles of the capitalist countries are now more afraid than ever that the present-day class struggle will evolve into a mass revolutionary movement. They are changing their tactics, maneuvering, attempting to utilize more veiled forms of exploitation and oppression of the working people, and stating their readiness in the number of instances to agree to partial reforms and a few concessions to keep the masses under their ideological and political control as far as they can.

. . . . . . . . . . . . . . . . . . . . . . . . . . . . . . . . . . . . . . . . . . . . . . . . . . . . . . . . . . . . . . . . . . .

The center of gravity in the economic confrontation between the two systems is now shifting into the sphere of scientific and technical progress. A considerable struggle lies ahead here. But here too the future belongs to socialism. Even today it is already in leading positions in a number of branches of scientific and technical progress. The Soviet Union has made an enormous contribution to solving the cardinal problems of the age—our country initiated the era of man's entry into space and has blazed trails in the peaceful utilization of nuclear power. Soviet scientists have also been responsible for many other discoveries, including in the spheres of mathematics, radio-electronics, aerodynamics, theoretical physics, the theory of solids, and so forth.

The socialist countries have a powerful scientific and technical potential. More than 1 million scientific workers (almost one-third of the world's scientists) and approximately 2.5 million engineering and technical workers are actively employed in these countries.

Such, in brief, are the prospects of the economic competition between the two systems, prospects which testify to the continuous consolidation of world socialism's positions.

. . . . . . . . . . . . . . . . . . . . . . . . . . . . . . . . . . . . . . . . . . . . . . . . . . . . . . . . . . . . . . . . . . .

The fraternal communist and workers' parties deal a resolute rebuff to any intrigues by their ideological enemies. Life itself supports our socialist reality and does so at every step. In the face of actual reality the imperialist ideologists' myths like the notorious "convergence" theory and the theory of the "society of universal affluence," revisionist slogans of "improved" and "human" socialism, and so forth are collapsing one after another under the powerful influence of Marxist-Leninist ideas. A great deal of purposeful work is being done in the socialist countries to expose such fabrications, educate people politically, and augment their ideological maturity and tempering. All this activity is built on the unshakable foundation of Marxist-Leninist doctrine. Marxism-Leninism is winning over the minds of increasing millions of new people and has become a powerful weapon in the struggle for the revolutionary transformation of life on earth.

In the struggle against socialism, imperialism has abandoned neither its "from a position of strength" policy nor its attempts to resolve the fundamental contradiction of the age by force of arms. During the past 5 years, imperialist foreign policy has provided further proof of the unchanged nature of its reactionary and aggressive policy. The most sinister offspring of this policy has been the unprecedented growth of militarism.

. . . . . . . . . . . . . . . . . . . . . . . . . . . . . . . . . . . . . . . . . . . . . . . . . . . . . . . . . . . . . . . . . . .

The socialist world is on a resolute offensive. It has given to the communist and workers' movement experience of enormous and truly historic significance. This experience testifies that, in the confrontation with capitalism, the socialist system has convincingly demonstrated its viability. The world socialist system is a powerful accelerator of the historical progress initiated by Great October, acts as a decisive force in the anti-imperialist struggle and is making an enormous contribution to averting a world war. The fraternal countries' revolutionary experience is arming the struggling peoples with a correct understanding of the general and specifically national characteristics of social development and with a knowledge of the main general law-governed patterns of socialist building. This experience and the growing might of the socialist system are a guarantee of new victories in the struggle for the complete triumph of the new system and for the peoples' ultimate social and national liberation.

**77.  V. BOL'SHAKOV, "The Subversive Strategy of 'the War of the Minds,' "**
**PRAVDA, January 13, 1972:** The times have passed when our enemies openly threatened to submerge socialism in an atomic fire. The power of our socialist Motherland, of the entire socialist camp, has grown to a tremendous level.

The doctrines of "balancing on the edge of war" and "the liberation of Eastern Europe from communism" are completely bankrupt.

Imperialism, however, despite the change in the correlation of forces in the world arena which is taking place, although not to its benefits, has not renounced its basic objectives which are dictated by its economic nature, its social-political essence. The methods of acting by imperialism, the forms of struggle, are changing, but the class essence of the historical conflict between capitalism and socialism remains unchanged. The struggle between the capitalist and socialist systems manifests itself in all spheres: military, economic, political and ideological.

"We live in the conditions of an unceasing ideological war," said L. I. Brezhnev in the Accountability Report of the Central Committee to the 24th Party Congress, "which is carried on against our country, against the world of socialism by imperialist propaganda, utilizing the most refined methods and powerful technical means. All instruments for influencing minds available in the hands of the bourgeoisie, the press, the cinema, the radio, are mobilized for leading people into confusion, for instilling in them the representation of the almost-Paradise-like life under capitalism, for slandering socialism. The ether is literally filled with all kinds of contrivances about the life of our country, of the brotherly countries of socialism."

Having announced about the transition from confrontation with the socialist countries to negotiation with them, imperialism has not rejected finally either armed actions against them as the aggression of the USA against the DRV demonstrates, or from ideological aggression. Imperialism has not retreated from its main strategic objective about which, in their time, the known American theoreticians of anti-communism R. Strausz-Hupe, W. R. Kintner, and S. T. Possony, wrote very frankly in their book: *The Contemporary Strategy of America.* "The opinion which is widely disseminated that supposedly it is possible to improve basically the relations between the communists and free world is mistaken," orated this trio. "How the current situation of the cold war is called coexistence or long-term conflict has no significant meaning. The conflict began in 1917 and it remains unchanged up to the present."

Of course, the contemporary slander of imperialist propaganda against socialism differs in form from the previous anti-communist roars of the dinosaurs of "the cold war." But it is the same in content and in direction.

The Jesuits of bourgeois propaganda frequently appear in our days under the mask of "concern" about the fate of socialism, declaim about its "democratization," "liberalization," and "modernization." What the recommendations of these "well-wishers" mean in practice is known from the experience of the actions of the counterrevolutionary forces in Czechoslovakia in 1968. These events were an attempt to implement the new tactics of the struggle of imperialism against socialism, against the socialist commonwealth that is known under the label of the policy of "building bridges."

Officially, this tactic was announced on February 25, 1964 by the former State Secretary of the USA, Dean Rusk. Simultaneously was worked out the so-called "doctrine of rewards" directed toward planting and encouraging nationalism, anti-Sovietism there, where, in the opinion of American intelligence, for this there could be found suitable soil. "In accordance with this doctrine," Bernard Gwertzman wrote in May, 1968, in the newspaper, *Washington Evening Star*, "the USA, by all means, strove to support friendly relations with those communist countries which encouraged liberalism within their country or operated independently of the Soviet Union, or, preferably, pursued both of these courses."

Bourgeois propaganda is counting on arousing nationalist feelings in these or those socialist countries. In 1970, C. Sulzberger wrote in *The New York Times:* "In such hostile areas as the Soviet Union and its bloc, the organization of the Warsaw Treaty, we enthusiastically support nationalism."

The purpose of this "encouragement" according to Sulzberger is to "revive hostility between the Russians and their Allies." Nationalist intoxication led at the end of last year to the counterrevolutionary statements and disorders in Croatia (SFRY), the traces of the instigators of which lead to the West. The poisoned weapons of bourgeois nationalism are actively utilized also by the Zionists, who operate together with the subversive imperialist services for "building bridges" on the anti-socialist, anti-Soviet front.

As the theoretical foundation of the "bridges" is utilized to the present day, the frankly anticommunist "theory of convergence," the authorship for which is vied by the American Walt Whitman Rostow; the Frenchman, Raymond Aron; the Dutchman, Jan Tinbergen; and a native of Russia, Pitirim Sorokin. As these Cassandras of anticommunism dream, "capitalism and socialism in the process of development, in the final analysis, will meet each other and will combine." As a result, they say, will arise some "new society." What kind of society?

In 1967, the "think tank" Hudson Institute, in the person of its director, Herman Kahn, and a colleague, Anthony J. Wiener, published a collection of "scenarios" under the title, *The Year 2,000.* In the collection were examined the possible variants both of military conflict and of the "evolution" of the socialist system. Thus in Chapter 5, entitled "International Politics in the Standard World," Kahn and Wiener make an attempt to present objectively the process taking place of the development of socialist democracy in the USSR and in other socialist countries as some kind of "liberalization," "softening" of the regime, and predict presenting the desired as reality: "Gradually this softening, if it continues, evidently will lead to other important political changes including the legalization of tolerance of some kind of organized political opposition. Communism evidently will become even more divided and will lose to a large extent its traditional unity of purpose, both internally and in the international plane."

Such was one of the "scenarios" worked out in the bowels of the Hudson Institute for the Soviet Union. Special "scenarios" were worked out for Poland, Czechoslovakia, Bulgaria, Hungary, GDR, Rumania, Yugoslavia, etc.

One can judge what the authors of these "scenarios" attempted to achieve, particularly by the chapter "Czechoslovakia: To One-Party Pluralism?" by the Associate Professor of Political Science of the University of California, the Sovietologist, Morton Schwartz, published in 1967 in the American journal, *Problems of Communism.*

In the concluding part of the article, Schwartz in the following manner formulated the essence of this "single-party pluralism": "Any such mechanism which within the framework of a single-party system is capable of assuring the possibility of the expression of various views—that is, of a definite form of pluralism—leans at least one step forward in the direction of finally building a consultative system, which is necessary for filling the gap between the communist political system and the complex industrial society." (i.e., capitalism-V.B.)

Schwartz and those like him purposefully ignore the principle of democratic centralism which is the basic organizational principle of the activity of the communist parties. What does Schwartz have to do with socialist democracy which is receiving further development in the USSR and in other countries of socialism which assures genuine freedom for the expression of various views in the interests of moving forward the affairs of the toilers. It is not about this freedom that Mr. Schwartz stewed, painting a warped picture of the situation in the socialist world. He is interested up to this very day only in one form of "freedom"—freedom for the activity of counterrevolutionary forces which they, naturally, will never receive under socialism.

The slogans "single-party pluralism," "socialism with a human face," (in itself the formulation is a confusion of words since socialism is the highest manifestation of genuine revolutionary humanism) remain in the arsenal of the imperialist strategists of the "war of minds."

The strategists of anticommunism now count on the so-called "dissidents" in socialist society (in a literal sense, disagreement with the generally accepted views, with the ideology supported by the majority of the members of society). To the "dissidents" our class enemies refer in the first instance the ideologically unstable, those torn from the people, from creative and scientific workers in these or those socialist countries. The statements by the West encouraging "the dissident" must, in the view of the ideological diversionist, pass under the slogan of "concern" about socialism, about "improvement of the system." Bourgeois propaganda already does not hide that under these "improvements" is subsumed "the quiet" restoration of capitalism.

The strategists of anticommunism, having analyzed the reasons for the failure of their counterrevolutionary plans, are attempting to remake in a new form the bankrupt doctrine "of the liberation" of the socialist countries of Eastern Europe.

As is known, the authors of this doctrine, headed by the former State Secretary of the USA, Dulles, counted not only on an internal counterrevolution, but also on direct interference in the affairs of the socialist countries threatening them with armed aggression. Now the ideologists of the type of Brzezinski are depending on ideological aggression. Writing in the pages of the journal, *Newsweek*, Brzezinski writes that: "Long-term reconciliation between the West and East cannot be based on the status quo of the East European countries remaining frozen." In Brzezinski's opinion, the West must agree on peaceful coexistence only under the conditions "of the transformation of the Eastern regimes into something close to social democracy." Not more and not less! Brzezinski directly calls for subversive work against the socialist countries. "We have technological means," he wrote, "for directly addressing the peoples of the communist countries (through 'the Voice of America,' the radio stations 'Liberty' and 'Free Europe')." Isn't this the reason for the recent decision of the Congress of the USA to support openly the latter two subversive radio stations previously supported by the CIA?

For the purposes of the most rapid realization in life of his anticommunist dreams, Brzezinski recommends in a most active manner the utilization of all forms of contacts and cooperation between capitalist and socialist countries, and believing that with the assistance of "building bridges" it will be possible to achieve together with the exportation of industrial goods also counterrevolution. But this is an unrealizable dream of all counterrevolutionaries.

The idea of "convergence" as a result of the drawing together of capitalism in the form in which the renegade Kautsky wanted to see it—that is, "democratic capitalism," with "democratic socialism" in the form in which it is represented by the contemporary renegades like Schick, Label, Garaudy, Fischer, etc.—attracted not only the leading circles of the USA but the right elements of social democracy. They are attempting to impose upon the countries of socialism the long-rejected renegade "theory" about the necessity of the liquidation of the leading role of the working class which, according to their estimates, must lead to the realization of the recommendation of that same Brzezinski to the restoration of capitalism in "a social-democrat variant."

The cohorts of anticommunism in their ideological "crusade" objectively join not only the right renegades but also the Peking leaders. The thought of utilizing Maoism for the purpose of struggle with communism wasn't born today. The presently published documents speak about the fact that American diplomats and intelligence officers having contact with Mao Tse-tung during the war fervently recommended to Washington the utilization of him for their purposes, characterizing Mao as no other manner than "an apostate," and "a margarine Communist."

These recommendations, as witnessed by C. Sulzberger, were remembered in the early '50's at the State Department which was working out a policy for relations with the Chinese People's Republic. Knowing the anti-Soviet feelings of Mao, at that time very carefully hidden by him, the American strategists of "the cold war" considered that the Maoists "will be as unfriendly to Russia as to the USA."

Their hopes were realized during the course of the notorious "cultural revolution." With its beginning underscores the newspaper, *Christian Science Monitor,* Washington reviewed its "working theory" according to which, up to 1966, the socialist countries were regarded as a single whole. The new "theory" provides for an individual approach to each socialist country. One counted on the breaking up of the socialist commonwealth because of propaganda and "the encouragement" of anti-Sovietism.

Profuse talk about the necessity of "independence" from the USSR, with equal will, is utilized in the propaganda both from Peking and the information agency of the USA (USIA), not to say anything about the subversive radio stations of the type of "Free Europe." In the secret memorandum of the USIA of February 1967, published by the Ceylon weekly, *Tribune,* all workers of the foreign section of the agency were instructed to "utilize all possibilities for strengthening the position of the partisans of Mao." Since the United States desires that "Mao and his group remain at present in power," inasmuch as their activity is directed against the CPSU and other communist parties. Judging by how actively USIA utilized the recent propaganda materials of Peking, misrepresenting the position of India and the USSR in the Indo-Pakistani conflict, and the anti-Soviet speeches of the representatives of the Chinese People's Republic in the UN, it is possible to assert that this memorandum is in force to this very day.

The anti-Sovietism of the Peking leaders naturally brought them to the anti-communist mud just as the partisans of "human socialism." Such is the logic of the class struggle which is incompatible with the position of detached on-lookers with various types of agreements with imperialism at the expense of betraying the interests of the working class of all toilers.

We are convinced of this by the fate of the "dissidents" and the "liberals," who began with the revision of Marxism and ended with the transfer of support to the anticommunists, to the enemies of the working class. We are convinced of this also by the current position of the Peking leadership, which is forming an alliance with USA imperialism both in the struggle against the national-liberation movement and in the ideological war against the USSR, other socialist countries, and against the international communist and workers' movement.

There cannot be a cease-fire on the ideological front. The struggle of ideas, the struggle of the two systems, continues. The ideas of communism will achieve victory in this struggle. In support of them is the truth of life, and truth is unbeatable.

78. *M. A. SUSLOV, Member of the CC-CPSU Politburo and Secretariat, "The Social Sciences are the Party's Combat Weapon in the Building of Communism,"* KOMMUNIST, *No. 1, January 1972, pp. 19-20, 26:* We have every reason to say that in the field of the social sciences and in the development of all the component parts of Marxism-Leninism—philosophy, political economy, and scientific communism—we have definite successes. The problems of scientific research have become more urgent, and the level of scientific research has been raised and its connection with the practice of communist building intensified. The struggle against bourgeois ideology, anticommunism, and revisionism is being waged more actively. The works of Soviet philosophers, economists, historians, and legal experts are receiving ever wider recognition from the foreign scholarly public.

However, the party believes that there is still great work to be done in the field of the further development of revolutionary theory.

Many vitally important problems have only been outlined and await a fundamental theoretical elaboration. Taking this into account, the 24th party congress pointed to the need to raise considerably the level of work of the scientific and educational institutions, to consolidate the social sciences' ties with the practice of party and state work, and to intensify the ideological activity of all party organizations. The main thing toward which the 24th CPSU Congress directs our social scientists is the theoretical elaboration of the fundamental problems of the developed socialist society and the scientific substantiation of the ways and means of its gradual development into communism.

Whatever sphere of social life and activity we take, it contains many problems whose creative elaboration from the positions of Marxism-Leninism must constantly be at the center of the Soviet scholars' attention.

. . . . . . . . . . . . . . . . . . . . . . . . . . . . . . . . . . . . . . . . . . . . . . . . . . . . . . . . . . . . . . . .

In our era of the antagonism between the two world systems—socialism and capitalism—the ideological struggle, which extends into all fields of social life, including science, is inevitably exacerbated. In recent years our scholars have waged the struggle against bourgeois ideology, anticommunism and revisionism more skillfully and profoundly. However it is still lagging behind the demands made on it by the party. As we noted at the 24th party congress, "the convincing nature of the criticism of bourgeois and revisionist attacks on our theory and practice is intensified to an immense degree when it relies on the active and creative development of social sciences and Marxist-Leninist theory." The creative development of Marxist-Leninist theory as a basis for intensifying the struggle against bourgeois ideology in all its manifestations is one of the most important tasks for our social sciences.

*79. Academician P. FEDOSEYEV, "The 24th Congress of the CPSU and the Fundamental Directions of Investigation in the Sphere of the Social Sciences,"* **KOMMUNIST, No. 1, January 1972, p. 61:** The apologists of the capitalist system do not abandon the attempts to argue that the scientific-technological revolution perpetuates capitalism, refutes Marxist-Leninist theory, makes socialist revolution unnecessary. Numerous technocratic theories, which have appeared in the West in the last 10-15 years, serve this aim. Their authors, H. Kahn, Z. Brzezinski, J. Galbraith, D. Bell, R. Aron and others, acknowledging the acuity of the problems which contemporary capitalism is experiencing, nevertheless believe that they can be resolved on the basis of the scientific-technological revolution, by means of the perfection of bourgeois society.

*80. EDITORIAL, "Program of Peace in Action,"* **KOMMUNIST, No. 1, January 1972, p. 17:** We must vigilantly and constantly keep in our field of vision and expose to keen party analysis various types of bourgeois, reformist "theories," called upon in any case to substantiate or justify a foreign-policy course directed against world socialism, the revolutionary liberation movement, and the peace and security of the peoples. This first of all has to do with those ideas which have gotten wide circulation in bourgeois "science," propaganda, and practical politics: military blackmail, "convergence," "the two superpowers," nationalism and anti-Sovietism. It is necessary to unmask resolutely the attempts to activate the policy of "building bridges," for it is directly connected by certain circles of the West with the "possibilities," which show up, from their point of view, in the new conditions on the European continent. This demands from the foreign policy, ideological, and propaganda organs a rise in the level and effectiveness of their activity.

**81. INSTITUTE OF MARXISM-LENINISM OF THE CC-CPSU,** *"The Falsifiers of the Theory of Scientific Communism and Their Bankruptcy,"* **KOMMUNIST, No. 3, February 1972, pp.** *107-108:* The revisionists decline to determine the nature of the revolution in the contemporary world. Their "works" mention neither the socialist revolution with its anticapitalist and antiexploitation nature nor the national-liberation revolutions which, in our time, are assuming an ever deeper social content; these works speak of "revolution" in general. It is not always clear what problems would such "revolution" pose and resolve, what class or classes are its motive force, what production relations it eliminates, and what would be the nature of the system which would develop as a result of its victory. The natural process of the replacement of capitalism with socialism is replaced by abstract considerations of "evolution," "reform," and "renovation."

Of late the revisionists are leaning even further toward the technocratic interpretation of revolutionary processes in the spirit of open bourgeois apology. They do not base the need for the reorganization of society on the social contradictions within capitalism, considering it as the automatic consequence of the scientific and technical changes.

**82. S. TSVIGUN,** *"Ideological Diversion–A Tool of Imperialist Reaction,"* **KOMMUNIST, No. 5, March 1972, pp.** *109-118:* The failure of the imperialist plans to alienate Czechoslovakia from the socialist comity dealt a tangible blow at the anticommunist tactic—the policy of "building bridges." Yet, even though the very concept of "building bridges" disappeared as a result of this from the official appeals, the special imperialist services and centers of ideological diversion undertook the expansion of their subversive activities against the socialist states on an even broader scale. Several essentially new aspects appeared in the tactics of modern anticommunism.

Directing their efforts on "shattering" world socialism as a system and on the "erosion" of the individual socialist countries, the imperialists tried to pit one or another socialist country against the Soviet Union and achieve an "internal evolution" of the socialist countries as well as their political and ideological "softening." Here they are relying to an ever greater extent not only on the remnants of the defeated exploiting classes but on revisionist and opportunistic elements.

The facts show that imperialist ideologues have developed their next roundabout maneuver to achieve the basic objective of the anticommunist strategy. Initially, analyzing the circumstances in the socialist countries, it is planned to seek out and inflate contradictions among them. Then, the plans call for a frontal subversion of the international solidarity of the socialist countries. According to the plans of imperialist ideologues, the victory of the forces of nationalism and petty-bourgeois individualism must mark the completion of such subversive activities.

**83. EDITORIAL, "The Philosophical Bequest of V. I. Lenin and the Contemporary Period," VOPROSY FILOSOFII, No. 3, March 1972, pp. 6-7:** The Leninist idea about the need to realize in this or that form a "union" with the progressive elements of the bourgeoisie, of the representatives of bourgeois culture remains extremely urgent also in our day. . . . The absence of any clear historical perspective, the senseless waste of human effort in contemporary capitalist society push many of the best representatives of the intellectuals, scientists and philosophers toward Marxism. . . . When progressive scientists of the bourgeois world in search of truth try to approach Marxism, it is our responsibility as Marxist philosophers to assist them in understanding the complex collisions in the contemporary world . . . and to carry on with them a dialogue which attracts them to the side of fighters against imperialism.

**84. S. A. KHAVINA, Doctor of Economic Sciences, "Criticism of Bourgeois Economic Theories of Socialism," VESTNIK AKADEMII NAUK SSSR, No. 5, May 1971, p. 134:** Representatives of contemporary bourgeois political economy and sociology attempt to propose their alternative to scientific socialism and its real embodiment — socialism in the USSR and other countries of the world socialist system of economy — in order to refute the revolutionary replacement of capitalism by socialism. They strive to derive laws of social development directly from the general trends in the development of technology and engineering, rejecting production relations. The theories of the "industrial" and "postindustrial" societies represent a variety of bourgeois reformism in political economy and sociology. In them is indirectly reflected a recognition of the inevitability of giving up the annihilation of socialism by force, on which the most aggressive and shameless ideologists of imperialism base their hopes.

One of the varieties of the theory of the "industrial society" — "technocratic models of socialism — was critically examined in the reports of F. Ia. Polianskiy and S. A. Khavina and the statements of S. P. Peregudov and others. The real processes of the scientific and technical revolution and the establishment of a mature socialist economy on that basis are treated by the proponents of those models as a shift of economic and political power into the hands of a technocratic elite (engineers, technicians, and also scientists, specialists and organizers of production). In "technocratic" models there is distortion of the essence of state (national) ownership of the means of production, which is depicted as an inevitable source of the bureaucratization of the economy. However, tendencies toward bureaucratization do not at all flow from the essence of that form of ownership of the means of production. On the contrary, the development of the relations of state (national) ownership requires wide economic and political democracy and creates the conditions for all possible improvement of democratic centralism and the attraction of the masses of the people into the control of the economy.

An analysis of the theory of "convergence" and its bourgeois and social-democratic variants was contained in the statements of G. B. Khromushin, V. N. Mineyev, A. I. Kredisov, and others. Starting from the thesis of the decisive role of ownership in determining the socio-economic structure and economic mechanism of a society, the theoreticians of "convergence" draw the conclusion that the existing differences in the forms of ownership (social socialistic and private capitalistic) are not an obstacle to the drawing together of the two economic systems — capitalism and socialism — to their merger into some sort of "mixed system of the economy."

The ideological and political meaning of the theory of "convergence" consists in an attempt to extend the principle of peaceful coexistence to the area of ideology. Marxist-Leninist criticism of that theory is based on the fact that the general tendencies of the development of technology and engineering in countries with different socio-economic systems cannot erase radical qualitative difference in the economic, social and political structures of society.

**85.  L. I. BREZHNEV, speech in Moscow at dinner for Fidel Castro, PRAVDA, June 28, 1972:** We soberly and realistically evaluate the current situation. Despite the successes in relaxing international tension, a hard struggle against the enemies of peace, national and social liberation faces us. Marxist-Leninists do not entertain any illusions in relation to the anti-peoples essence of imperialism and its aggressive aspirations. . . .

Striving for the confirmation of the principle of peaceful coexistence, we recognize that successes in this important matter in no way signify the possibility of weakening the ideological struggle. On the contrary it is necessary to be prepared that this struggle will intensify, will become a still sharper form of the antagonism between the two social systems. And we do not have any doubts about the outcome of this struggle, for the truth of history, the objective laws of social development are on our side!

**86.  "The Leninist Course of the Foreign Policy of the CPSU," KOMMUNIST, No. 9, June 1972, p. 79:** The ideological struggle retains all of its sharpness and acquires even greater significance. Furthermore, under conditions of the wider acceptance of the principles of peaceful coexistence, imperialism deploys the most refined activities with the aim of ideological penetration into the socialist countries. In the West they have not given up, for example, attempts to prove that international detente is impossible supposedly without the "convergence" of the two systems. It is impossible not to see the ill intents and lies of this assertion, which is being portrayed as "a sign of the times" and obviously aimed at naive, politically unsophisticated people. No, communists will never give up their ideas and principles, they have always struggled and in the future will energetically struggle for their worldwide triumph. They vigilantly watch imperialist maneuvers, understanding that also in the present international-political situation, which is new in its character, there is no place for placidity, complacency, and ideological demobilization. It cannot be otherwise, for the nature of imperialism has not changed.

We recall the words of V. I. Lenin: ". . . .The form of the struggle may change according to various, relatively special and temporary causes, but the *essence* of the struggle, its class *content* as such *cannot* change, while classes exist" (*Collected Works,* Vol. 27, p. 372).

87.  *Colonel D. VOLKOGONOV, Doctor of Philosophical Sciences, "A Patriot, an Internationalist,"* **KRASNAIA ZVEZDA, *July 4, 1972:*** The most frightening thing for the class enemies of socialism is our international unity. It is therefore no accident that in the ideological struggle imperialism is particularly gambling on nationalism and national differences, and not on the common faith that unites people. On the other hand, the ideological pirates deny the idea of patriotism from the viewpoints of cosmopolitanism. The essence of the latter is the demand for "broader contacts" for "fusion" with Western culture and morality, and a frank aspiration to replace the class conception of internationalism in the abstract schemes about "a citizen of the world" and to impose peaceful coexistence in ideology.

88.  *EDITORIAL, "Pressing Tasks of Ideological Work,"* **PRAVDA, *July 8, 1972:*** The peaceful coexistence of states with different social systems, the possibilities for which are extending thanks to the party's purposeful, energetic and flexible foreign activities, does not mean the cessation of the class struggle between the two systems but only a renunciation of the use of military methods in this struggle. Any kind of reconciliation with reactionary bourgeois ideology is inadmissible; in the field of ideology there is not and cannot be peaceful coexistence between socialism and capitalism.

Our society's mighty ideological-political unity dooms to defeat any attempts by imperialism to influence the Soviet people. However, it would be erroneous not to see that individual politically immature people still fall under the influence of bourgeois propaganda and are provoked to antisocial acts. We must resolutely expose bourgeois slander against communism and the Soviet Union, and suppress any ideological diversion by imperialism.

**89. Lieutenant General A. SHEVCHENKO, "An Insidious Weapon,"** **KRASNAIA ZVEZDA,** *August 18, 1972:* The psychological warfare strategists palm off on us the petty ideas of "pan-human spiritual convergence" and pontificate about bourgeois "freedoms," "classless" democracy, "supra" class, "panhuman" interests, "evolutionary changes," a "new approach," and a "regrouping of forces" in socialist society. The imperialist bourgeoisie discourses, through the psychological warfare troubadours, on some kind of "erosion" and "peaceful absorption" of socialism and "class neutrality" and philosophizes on the "de-ideologization" of present society and the "peaceful coexistence" of various ideologies calculated to ideologically disarm socialism.

At the same time, they falsify and belittle in every way the successes of the Soviet Union and the socialist countries, distort the essence and nature of their community, primarily the Warsaw Pact countries, stir up nationalism, and support revisionist, anti-Marxist, and nationalist elements and trends. A graphic example of this were the attacks by the forces of imperialism and internal counterrevolution on the socialist achievements in Czechoslovakia in 1968. As experience shows, the main attention of the psychological warfare organs is concentrated on the creative intelligentsia, youth, and servicemen. They seek out and support in every way individual politically immature people and, even resorting to outright falsification, laud to the skies "works" and their authors ideologically alien to us, invariably representing themselves in this respect as zealots and defenders, as they put it, of "humane" socialism.

. . . . . . . . . . . . . . . . . . . . . . . . . . . . . . . . . . . . . . . . . . . . . . . . . . . . . . . . . . . . . . . . . .

In striving for affirmation of the principle of peaceful coexistence we realize that the successes in this important matter by no means signify a relaxation of the ideological struggle. On the contrary, as L. I. Brezhnev stressed in his speech in honor of F. Castro in the Kremlin, we must be prepared for an intensification of this struggle and for its becoming an increasingly acute form of the struggle of the two social systems.

And we have no doubt as to the outcome of this struggle, since the truth of history and the objective laws of social development are on our side.

**90. M. K. IGITKHANIAN, Candidate of Philosophical Sciences, "The Revolutionary Ideology of the Working Class and Its Revisionist Falsifiers,"** *RADIO MOSCOW, August 2, 1972:* The concept of "deideologization" has nothing in common with science, for it fundamentally contradicts objective and natural tendencies in social life and class relations. Calls to "deideologize" public life, politics, social sciences, culture, morals and so on are of a plainly demagogic nature. Those who support them merely profess to reject any ideology. In fact their criticism is spearheaded against one particular ideology—Marxism-Leninism, socialism.

. . . . . . . . . . . . . . . . . . . . . . . . . . . . . . . . . . . . . . . . . . . . . . . . . . . . . . . . . . . . . . . . . .

Thus at the foundation of the revisionist theory of "deideologization" are to be found the same principles which open anticommunists use to distort the essence of Marxism-Leninism and to undermine scientific ideology. Following in the footsteps of bourgeois philosophers and ideologists, revisionists assert that the objective basis for the withering away of ideology is to be found in the modern scientific and technological revolution. In their opinion this revolution leads to the so-called convergence of opposing social systems and the erasure under capitalism of the differences between the bourgeoisie and the working class.

*91. V. V. ZAGLADIN, editor,* **THE INTERNATIONAL COMMUNIST MOVEMENT: SKETCH OF STRATEGY AND TACTICS,** *2nd edition, Moscow, Politizdat, 1972, translated in JPRS, No. 57044-2, p. 326:* Anticommunism has been and remains the basis of bourgeois ideology in the struggle against the revolutionary movement. It has now acquired new and more refined forms. Imperialist propaganda skillfully varnishes the reality of the contemporary capitalist world. In striving to disorient the working class and toilers, it instils the thought that allegedly the scientific-technological revolution leads to creation of a "society of mass consumption" and the elimination of class antagonisms in capitalist society. With the aim of discrediting socialism, bourgeois ideologists propagandize the idea of a certain nonclass "humanistic socialism," which is set in opposition to the allegedly existing "nonhumanistic" society in countries of socialism. The theory of "convergence" of capitalism and socialism and other such ideas are also widely disseminated.

Ideologists of the bourgeoisie direct their greatest efforts at weakening the influence of ideas of Marxism-Leninism and hindering their further dissemination in the world. Having suffered failures in open attacks on the ideology of Marxism-Leninism, ideological defenders of capitalism seek ways to bypass the struggle against it. They support and encourage any ideological tendencies, organizations, and groups of people who are for "renovation" and "improvement" of Marxism-Leninism, which in fact signifies an emasculation of its essence and a deviation from its basic principles.

The bourgeoisie is attempting to corrupt the communist and entire revolutionary movement from within. Imperialists are relying on differences in this movement and on nationalism. They count on disuniting the communist

163

movement, setting revolutionary detachments against each other, and hindering the unification of toilers of different countries.

**92. L. MOSKVICHYOV, *"Anti-Communism Under the Guise of 'De-Ideologisation,' "* INTERNATIONAL AFFAIRS *(Moscow), No. 10, October 1972, pp. 41-47:* The "decline of ideology" theory ranks among the neo-liberal hypotheses that have been propounded chiefly in the United States. It hooks up closely with the "growth stages," "unified industrial society," "new industrial society," "technotronic society" and "convergence" theories, whose elaboration proceeded with contributions from many bourgeois authors including the creators of the "end of ideology" doctrine.

All these theories are inter-related and are founded on essentially similar ideological and, to a large extent, political premises. In fact, they supplement each other. Their authors consider the various aspects of reality, from an essentially identical viewpoint. They portray the 1950s and the 1960s as the end of the epoch of "traditional capitalism" and "traditional socialism," of the epoch of the class struggle, social revolutions and so on in the developed countries of Europe and America. Present-day state-monopoly capitalism is characterized as the highest stage of civilization, as an "industrial," "post-industrial" and "new industrial" society, which, they claim, differs essentially from the capitalism of the 19th and even of the first decades of the 20th century. S. Lipset goes so far as to call it a "good society" in order to stress that there is a fundamental distinction between modern capitalism and the capitalism of the 19th century.

The point of departure of all these theories is thus an apology of state-monopoly capitalism founded on a theory of its "progressive" development.

. . . . . . . . . . . . . . . . . . . . . . . . . . . . . . . . . . . . . . . . . . . . . . . . . . . . . . . . . . . . . . . . . .

On the political level, the doctrine of "the decline of the era of ideology" proved to be a convenient means of reorienting anticommunism at the close of the 1950s and during the 1960s, for it made it possible to go over from crude frontal attacks on communism, the socialist countries and the international working-class and communist movement, to more flexible and mobile tactics that allow using the slogans of development, science, progress, the defence of liberty and democracy from "ideological totalitarianism," and so on.

. . . . . . . . . . . . . . . . . . . . . . . . . . . . . . . . . . . . . . . . . . . . . . . . . . . . . . . . . . . . . . . . . .

The ideological struggle is currently acquiring an unprecedented scale and depth. It involves huge masses of the population, political parties and governments in all parts of the world. The growing economic and political antago-nisms rending modern capitalism are generating processes that inevitably develop into ideological conflicts not only between the bourgeoisie and the working class, but also between various groups of the monopoly bourgeoisie itself, between the monopoly and non-monopoly bourgeoisie, and so on.

. . . . . . . . . . . . . . . . . . . . . . . . . . . . . . . . . . . . . . . . . . . . . . . . . . . . . . . . . . . . . . . . . . . . .

The bourgeois slogans of "de-ideologisation" and "re-ideologisation" are evidence of the ultimate doom of bourgeois ideology, of modern capitalism's inability to advance ideas conforming to society's requirements and the basic interests of the people, and of bourgeois ideology's helplessness against the life-asserting ideas of Marxism-Leninism.

# Index

168